BUSINESS SKILLS FOR YOUR CAREER
RETAIL

VIC ASHLEY

SHEILA ASHLEY

GILL MORRIS

City&
Guilds

About City & Guilds

City & Guilds is the UK's leading provider of vocational qualifications, offering over 500 awards across a wide range of industries, and progressing from entry level to the highest levels of professional achievement. With over 8500 centres in 100 countries, City & Guilds is recognised by employers worldwide for providing qualifications that offer proof of the skills they need to get the job done.

Equal opportunities

City & Guilds fully supports the principle of equal opportunities and we are committed to satisfying this principle in all our activities and published material. A copy of our equal opportunities policy statement is available on the City & Guilds website.

First edition 2012

ISBN 978 0 85193 238 5

Publisher Louise Le Bas
Cover design by Select Typesetters Ltd
Typeset by Cenveo Publisher Services
Printed in the UK by CLOC

Publications

For information about or to order City & Guilds support materials, contact 0844 534 0000 or centresupport@cityandguilds.com. You can find more information about the materials we have available at www.cityandguilds.com/publications.

Every effort has been made to ensure that the information contained in this publication is true and correct at the time of going to press. However, City & Guilds' products and services are subject to continuous development and improvement and the right is reserved to change products and services from time to time. City & Guilds cannot accept liability for loss or damage arising from the use of information in this publication.

City & Guilds
1 Giltspur Street
London EC1A 9DD

T 0844 543 0033
www.cityandguilds.com
publishingfeedback@cityandguilds.com

Picture credits

Every effort has been made to acknowledge all copyright holders as below and the publishers will, if notified, correct any errors in future editions.

City & Guilds/Andover College: p311; **HM Revenue and Customs:** p306; **iStock:** p51, p279; **Shutterstock:** p15, p60, p61, p62, p123, p124, p125, p153, p155, p169, p189, p203, p204, p225, p235, p245, p265, p281, p296, p309, p313.

CONTENTS

ABOUT THE AUTHORS

Vic and Sheila Ashley are experienced authors in the business and education fields. They have published Business and Administration Student Handbooks at Levels 1, 2 and 3 through the Council for Administration (CfA), online resources for Retail and Business and Administration for the City & Guilds SmartScreen website (www.SmartScreen.co.uk) and workbooks supplying the knowledge and understanding for a range of qualifications available through www.aspect-training.com.

Vic has extensive retail experience, mainly with the Debenhams Group, and has spent 25 years working with Awarding Organisations including City & Guilds in a number of roles including consultant, lead verifier, regional verifier and external verifier. He is also the Chair of Examiners for the 14–19 Diploma in Retail Business for AQA – City & Guilds.

Sheila has operated a successful catering business and acted as Centre Co-ordinator for her own training provider delivering Assessor and Verifier Awards, PTTLS, CTTLS and DTTLS.

Gill Morris has been involved in vocational education and employment issues for 30 years. She is a member of the Education & Employers Taskforce and her passion is supporting S.M.E.s across all fields of vocational business. Gill's main area of interest is coaching young vocational entrepreneurs in the importance of business skills and realizing that being a great technician is not enough to guarantee business success.

Gill is a Chartered Marketer, Fellow of the RSA, a Professional Speaker and a director of GMT Business Training. In her early career she worked in equipment research and development, product development and general marketing, she has lectured extensively nationally and internationally and judges various vocational business awards. Gill is an author of text books, distance learning workbooks, industry articles, a member of education and employer advisory committees and a sought after M.C. and speaker on business issues.

INTRODUCTION

This book will be a valuable guide to those of you already working in the retail industry and planning your future career, those looking to improve the retail business they are already operating and, primarily, people looking to start and run their own retail business.

If you are looking to set up a business of any kind, you will quickly realise that it will take up a large part of your time. When deciding what type of business to start, you will find that owning a retail business is exciting, rewarding and can be very profitable. In the early stages, you may well find yourself working seven days a week; even on the days your shop is not open, you will be buying stock, planning or doing the books. It is important, however, that as quickly as you can, you reach the point where the business can operate in your absence so that you can at least have a day off – and even, possibly, holidays!

To run a retail business – particularly a small one – successfully, you will need belief in the products you are selling. If you cannot be enthusiastic about your products, you will find it very difficult to persuade the public to buy them from you. You will also need to like dealing with people. Customers can be difficult, demanding and sometimes even downright rude, but you have to deal with these characteristics and still want the people to come into your shop. Keep in mind that the great majority of people will be friendly and responsive. If you are running a convenience store, for instance, for some of your customers you may be the only human contact they have in their day. It is part of your role to be cheerful and helpful.

THE RETAIL SECTOR IN THE UK

In 2011 the total retail sales in the UK were over £303 billion; in fact, more than a third of consumer spending goes through shops. There was a total of 284,490 retail outlets in the UK, of which 187,390 were VAT registered, making up 9 per cent of all VAT-registered businesses. These figures show that approximately 34 per cent of retail businesses have a turnover below the VAT registration threshold of £73,000 per year, while the average turnover of a retail business is slightly over £1 million per year. The retail sector employed approximately 3 million people, or one in 10 of people employed. In addition, there are 150,000 online retail businesses responsible for 17 per cent of the total UK retail market and providing 600,000 jobs either directly or in a support role.

You will have seen the newspaper stories about high street chains closing stores because of the downturn in the economy, but every cloud has a silver lining. As these premises become vacant, there is pressure on the level of rents that can be asked for, so there will be deals to be done when looking to open a new retail business. When Woolworths collapsed in December 2008, 807 stores became empty, mostly in good high street locations. In July 2009 70 per cent of the stores were still empty, in August 2010 this had reduced to 40 per cent and by January 2012 87 per cent of the stores had re-opened as other retail businesses; 29 per cent have re-opened as discount stores and 17 per cent as supermarkets. These figures demonstrate that the retail sector, while coming under pressure from the general economic situation, is resilient and will recover by adapting to meet the demands of the ever-changing conditions.

TRENDS

Anyone thinking of starting a retail business will need to understand the commercial world in which retail operates at the moment. Attempting to meet the demands that customers had five years ago rather than those they have now is a recipe for disaster. The retail sector has traditionally been built on the foundations of product, service, price and customer. Each of these is going through changes as retailers evolve to compete in the future.

PRODUCT

Multi-channel retailing plus greater availability of products from around the world have allowed retailers to greatly extend their range of products. The risks involved in this strategy include the difficulties involved in moving the products through the supply chain and the possibility of losing the strength of your brand. An example of how this trend is being led is the way that Tesco now seems to sell everything imaginable, from financial services to online shopping with free delivery. The way this could be translated into a small retail operation is, for example, a bookshop that gives over some of its space to sell giftware or even to open a coffee shop.

SERVICE

Retailers have claimed for years that their offer is based on 'excellent customer service', but experience tells us that in many cases this concept is paid lip-service to while the customer is treated as an inconvenience who disturbs the staff from carrying out their roles. In the future, the idea that 'the customer is king' will need to be adopted and carried out by all retail staff. or customers will simply go elsewhere or resort to carrying out all their transactions online. If your customer service is no better than your competitors', your only differential will be price, meaning that you will have to sell your products at a lower margin in order to achieve sales.

PRICE

In the current economic climate, the successful retailers have been those selling luxury brands and top-end products, and those selling staple products at discount or value prices. While the customers who are unaffected by the economy are still willing and able to pay top price for top quality, the remaining customers are comparing prices very carefully and buying those goods that represent good value. This does not necessarily mean they buy the cheapest option, but they do need persuading that the more expensive choice represents better value. For example, in the past, customers would buy branded tuna at twice the price of own-brand; now they will still buy the branded product, but will expect it to be much nearer the own-brand price.

CUSTOMER

Customer demographics are changing as the population becomes increasingly multi-cultural and the traditional socio-economic groups are no longer clearly defined. While it has always been important for retailers to recognise who their customers are, this becomes increasingly vital for retailers who are going to thrive in the future. Retailers will need to maintain high levels of customer engagement and an ability to respond quickly to change.

Let's look at where retail is now and what the hot products of the near future are predicted to be. The attitudes of customers have changed. People are growing their own vegetables, baking bread and cakes, and printing their own photographs from their digital cameras. To combat this, greengrocers may diversify into selling seeds and compost, bakers into selling flour, icing kits and cake decorations, and shops that previously concentrated on developing films now provide services transferring film to CD, photo editing services and printing large-size posters and canvases from customers' digital photos, as well as selling photographic equipment, photographic paper, frames and albums.

Another shift in customers' attitudes is a move away from purely environmental concerns towards economic concerns. Sales of organic products have fallen sharply as customers are unwilling to pay extra for products that benefit the environment if those products cost considerably more. At the same time there is a move towards buying local products, as customers perceive this as a way of protecting the local economy. Also, customers are moving away from buying products that are multi-functional but so complex that the customer cannot make full use of the features.

A third move that customers are making is towards the attitude that buying products at low prices is now acceptable. Where until recently customers would boast to their friends how expensive something they had bought – such as the latest mobile phone – was, now they are more likely to be proud of finding a really good bargain. In the supermarket sub-sector, customers are trading down between segments. Customers who previously bought premium products are now buying everyday brands, while previous purchasers of everyday brands are now buying value brands. Second-hand shops, car boot sales and online auctions are becoming more popular and, even when buying new, customers are becoming more prepared to haggle over prices. Vintage items and clothing swaps are also thriving as customers take care of their possessions rather than throwing them away and replacing them.

In order to keep up with the trends, existing retail businesses and new entrants to the sector are constantly looking for the next big thing. While all predictions must be viewed as only educated guesswork, the products forecast to be big sellers in the near future include items popular with people reaching retirement age such as fitness items, health-related products and leisure activities.

Another growth area is in products to entertain people who are, increasingly, staying in rather than going out to theatres, cinemas, pubs and restaurants. People are spending money on gaming consoles, games and accessories, and consumer electronics, but increasingly looking for these to reduce in price. Pet products are also growing in demand as people turn to pets for company.

The third area of growth is predicted to be in products for babies and children, from pushchairs and cots to toys and games. Economic downturns traditionally are followed by increases in the birth rate and, as with the previous category, parents are spending money on amusing their children at home rather than taking them to theme parks.

While these are the predictions of some retail experts, all retailers will be watching closely to see whether something completely unexpected takes the market by storm. Remember, there is always room for a completely new idea if it is properly marketed and correctly priced.

DIFFERENT TYPES OF RETAIL BUSINESS

The retail sector is divided into retail sub-sectors and retail channels. Sub-sectors include:

- Automotive
- Books and newspapers

- Clothing
- DIY
- Electrical goods
- Footwear
- Homewares
- Music and video
- Non-specialised stores
- Personal care
- Second-hand goods
- Food and grocery, which is sub-divided into:
  - Fruit and vegetables
  - Meat and meat products
  - Fish, crustaceans and molluscs
  - Bread and cakes
  - Alcoholic and other beverages
  - Specialised food stores.

Retail channels include:
- Shops
- Department stores
- Chain stores
- Superstores
- Showrooms
- Market stalls
- Catalogues
- Online retailing
- Home shopping
- Mobile technology.

One of the growing business models within retail is franchising. This is seen as a secure way to start a business, as the business is locally owned and run by the small business owner while enjoying the branding, economies of scale and support from a wider network.

The largest area by volume of sales is new goods sold in specialised stores. These make up most of the shops and stores found on the high street, in shopping centres or in retail parks. They include the many independent clothing shops, shoe shops, jewellers, music shops, hardware and DIY stores, timber yards and builders merchants; in fact, everything except food shops.

The second largest area is non-specialised stores, which are generally the largest stores – supermarkets, chain stores and department stores selling everything from food to clothes to financial products.

In third position are specialised stores selling food, beverages and tobacco; often independent bakers, butchers, greengrocers, grocers, fishmongers, newsagents and convenience stores. These shops are usually found on high streets or in secondary retail locations.

The group with the smallest sales by volume of new goods comprises pharmaceutical, medical, cosmetic and toilet articles. These are sold in small independent shops such as opticians and chemists, and health and beauty retailers, which are often national chains.

Second-hand goods, including those sold in charity shops, auction houses and pawnbrokers, make up approximately 2 per cent of retail sales in the UK and, as mentioned above, are an increasing market.

The fastest growing area of retailing is online or 'e-tailing'. There are two distinct areas within online retailing. There are online-only and catalogue retailers who have no bricks-and-mortar shops and there are multi-channel retailers who offer both traditional shopping and home shopping. During December 2011 in the UK £7.9 billion was spent online, an increase of 16.5 per cent on the previous December. In 2011 overall £68 billion was spent online, an increase of 16 per cent on 2010. The forecast for 2012 is a further 13 per cent increase to £77 billion. Within these figures there is a trend towards online-only retailers growing faster than online sales of multi-channel retailers.

The 10 largest increases in online sales comparing December 2011 with December 2010 were in:

Health and beauty	63%
Accessories (handbags, gloves, hats, purses, etc)	46%
Home and garden	45%
Lingerie	35%
Footwear and accessories (shoe laces, shoe polish, suede brushes, etc)	21%
Beers, wines and spirits	18%
Gifts	13%
Clothing	12%
Electricals	11%
Travel	4%

If the current economic climate is making you have second thoughts about starting a retail business, consider the story of Nadir Lalani and his family, who started the 99p Stores business in 2001 with a bank loan of £10,000 and one shop and now have a business with 150 outlets, sales of £231 million and a business valued at £60 million. This is an example of a business where a viable idea, backed by hard work and understanding their customers, have combined to create a remarkable success story.

GETTING STARTED IN RETAIL

So, you have decided that you are interested in starting a retail business. If you already have experience working in the industry, you may well be ready to take the step into self-employment, but if you have no experience it is probably a good idea to try working in the sector for a while, both to make sure that this is really the life for you and to give you the opportunity to learn from people who have made a success of it.

Depending on your age and previous experience, you may want to enter retailing through a Saturday job or part-time employment, but to gain a wide range of experience entry as a trainee manager will give you access to the different areas of a retail organisation. Many of the larger retailers recruit their managers by promoting from within, so entering at trainee manager level will give you the opportunity to progress relatively rapidly. To enter at trainee manager level, you will need:

- To be competent in maths and IT – Most functions in retail require the use of a computer, whether that is operating a till or ordering online. An ability to handle figures mentally is needed to deal with customers' queries on volume discounts or the cost of buying a number of items.
- Communication skills – Retailing is about people, so you will need to be able to communicate with customers, colleagues, suppliers, delivery drivers and senior management.
- People skills – Dealing with people requires the ability to recognise that they are all different and that each individual has good days and bad days and will need handling differently.
- Planning and organisational skills – Retail managers need to plan ahead but also be flexible enough to deal with the constantly changing situation.
- Ability to work under pressure – After all the planning and organising, you are still dealing with one uncontrollable variable – customers. Statistics may show that Thursday afternoon is always quiet, so you plan to have a minimum level of staff, but customers don't know that and you may well have a rush to deal with.
- Ability to work to deadlines – If your January sale is starting on Boxing Day and you need to keep your Christmas displays on until closing time on Christmas Eve, you have very little time to re-stock the shop floor and change over the promotional material.

- A focus on customer service – Without customers, there is no business.
- Self-confidence – You will need self-confidence to deal with your colleagues in your team leading role and to deal with customers who will make demands that you are unable to meet.
- Commitment – Retailing requires long hours, often on your feet. If you lack commitment, your team and your customers will soon realise it.
- Enthusiasm – There will be times when you need to motivate your team to make a special effort to meet targets; if you cannot be enthusiastic, you cannot expect enthusiasm from others.
- Ability to make decisions and solve problems – You will need to be able to think on your feet to deal with unexpected issues as they arise; if a key member of staff fails to arrive for work, their tasks will need to be reallocated promptly, for instance.
- Good business sense – Many of the decisions that you make will be based on good business sense; should you move the umbrellas to the front of the store when it starts to rain?
- An understanding of figures – Management depends on analysing data presented; whether sales figures or staff availability, you need to be able to look at the figures and use them to make decisions.

Many trainee managers will start as a team leader while training. During training they may cover many different areas of retailing, including sales, customer service, cash handling, administration, cash office operations, human resources, staff training, buying, merchandising, visual merchandising, stock handling, warehousing and distribution, the supply chain, stock management, security, and health and safety.

Promotion to store management may be available in as little as one year. In larger organisations, experience and willingness can lead fairly quickly to progression to area or regional management. This experience will stand you in good stead for opening your own business. Use your time wisely to absorb what is going on around you; you may not get direct experience of visual merchandising, for instance, but you will be able to learn from watching the experts and put this to good use in your own business.

RETAIL SUPPORT ORGANISATIONS

There are a number of organisations whose purpose is to support retailers. These include:

- Skillsmart Retail, the Sector Skills Council for Retail. A not-for-profit organisation established in 2002, its mission is to raise skills levels in retail through improving training and qualifications in the sector. Skillsmart Retail is led by retailers for the benefit of retailers who employ people in the UK. Using authoritative labour market intelligence, the organisation develops qualifications including apprenticeships and foundation degrees, and can be contacted on www.skillsmartretail.com.
- British Retail Consortium, which describes itself as 'the authoritative voice of retail, recognised for its powerful campaigning and influence within government and as a provider of excellent information'. Its mission is to make life easier for its members by:
  - Campaigning to promote and defend retailers' interests.
  - Advising retailers of threats and opportunities to their business.
  - Improving the perceptions of retailing in the UK.
  - Offering members a range of services and products which add value to their business.
  - The organisation can be contacted on www.brc.org.uk.
- British Independent Retailers Association, which brings independent retailers together nationally to represent and lobby on behalf of its members, influencing legislators, local councils and suppliers. Established for over 100 years, they 'fight for all that makes independent retailing an integral part of British society' and can be contacted on www.bira.co.uk.
- Interactive Media in Retail Group (IMRG), a membership community set up to 'develop and share the latest best practice advice to enable retailers to succeed in the world's most competitive online market'. IMRG has supported and promoted online shopping and digital commerce since 1990 and can be contacted on www.imrg.org.

In addition, there are associations of retailers in different sub-sectors, for instance:

- Toy Retailers Association, which can be contacted on www.toyretailersassociation.co.uk.
- Retra (for electrical retailers), which can be contacted on www.retra.co.uk.
- National Childrenswear Association, which can be contacted on www.ncwa.co.uk.
- Association of Convenience Stores, which can be contacted on www.acs.org.uk.

All of these organisations both help existing retailers and are happy to advise prospective retailers.

CHAPTER 1
UNDERSTANDING YOUR BUSINESS

INTRODUCTION

Being good at what you do is no guarantee of retail business success. There are plenty of brilliant people whose businesses have failed – you probably know one or two. This section gives you an overview of the key questions to answer, and activities to carry out to increase the likelihood of your business succeeding.

It doesn't matter at this stage whether you are already in business or are planning to start one now or in the future – the information and activities in this chapter will help you get a clear picture of where your business is, where you want it to be and how you might get it there. It will give you the opportunity to explore what you want from your ideal business.

By the end of this chapter you should have a realistic picture of the retail business you want to be running and what will make it stand out from the competition.

WHO ARE YOUR CUSTOMERS?

Understanding who your customers are is vital to your business. This understanding impacts on:

- what you offer
- how you offer it
- when and where you offer it
- the skills and training you need to offer it
- who else you may employ to offer it and how they are trained
- how much you charge.

If you don't know who your customers are and what they want, how can you hope to satisfy their needs? Many people start out in retail business thinking: 'What is it I want to do? What do I want to offer? What am I good at? What am I passionate about?' These are important, of course, but you also need to add 'What do my potential customers want now and in the future?'

OVER TO YOU

Think about the business you want to be running and the customers you would like – who are they? Give yourself 10 minutes to write down as much as you can about them. What do they want to buy from you? How often? What do you think matters to them most?

UNDERSTANDING YOUR CUSTOMERS

There are three key questions to keep in mind when analysing your customer base:

1   Who are you targeting?
2   What are customers buying from you?
3   What's different about your **offering?**

Who are you targeting?

You will have many different kinds of customers, but you can sort them into broad groups of similar-minded people. Doing this will help you tailor your offering – the different groups may want different things from you.

The starting point is to understand which groups of customers are the most profitable for your business. These are the ones you need more of – not the ones who make just a little for your business, allow you to break even or perhaps make a loss. This doesn't mean you shouldn't have any customers who make you little money, but you need to ensure that you have a lot more of the profitable ones. This idea is covered in more detail in later chapters. The key points to establish here are how to identify your different customer types, and how to work out which you need more of.

Think what you need to know about your customers. This might include factors such as:

- Lifestyle characteristics
- **demographics**
- financial stability
- disposable income.

Customer profiling will help you build up a picture of your ideal customers and identify your primary or main customers – the ones who make you the most profit. These are the customers you want to concentrate on. The information you will need to gather includes:

- which customer types spend the most
- how regularly different customers shop
- which products different customers buy
- how far customers travel to shop.

? JARGON BUSTER

Demographics are statistics that show the characteristics of a population. They can be used to identify market needs. For example, if there are a lot of teenagers in a certain area, a computer games store may do better than in an area where the population is older.

YOUR TYPICAL CUSTOMER PROFILES

	Primary Profile		Secondary Profile
Gender:		Gender:	
Age:		Age:	
Lifestyle:		Lifestyle:	
Products/Services/ Equipment They Buy:		Products/Services/ Equipment They Buy	
Postcode:		Postcode:	
Frequency of Purchase:		Frequency of Purchase:	
Average Purchase Amount:		Average Purchase Amount:	

Two typical customer profile forms for your retail business

OVER TO YOU

What would the customer profile form look like for your business? Have a go at identifying your top two groups of customers and filling this information in about them.

? JARGON BUSTER

Customer profiling is about dividing your customers into different groups and gathering information on each group. It's used to identify your ideal customers and help you work out how to attract them.

What are customers buying from you?

Take the phone off the hook, switch off your mobile, turn off the computer, lock the office door, stand back from your business and look at what you offer through the eyes of your customers. What are you giving them? What are they coming to you for? What it comes down to is that they are buying a solution to a problem. This solution is an answer to a need or a want that they can't, or don't want to, provide for themselves. It might be a major-cost item or a small service.

If you understand what your customers' key 'problems' are, you're well on your way to working out what you should offer them. This may be as simple as identifying your best-selling product, or it may be understanding that good customer service is more important than low prices. When you understand what is most important to your customers, you can shape your retail business to deliver that and market it to get the message across.

Knowing what your customers want to buy from you is very important, but you also need to identify the most profitable product or service that you provide. To do this you need to know what every offering costs you to deliver – this is covered later in the chapter.

When you know how profitable all your offerings are, divide them into four groups:

1 most profitable
2 averagely profitable
3 least profitable
4 no profit – costs you to deliver.

When you undertake this analysis, be prepared to discover that the most profitable offering is not what you expected. Just because you sell a lot of something does not necessarily make it the most profitable item, nor does the most expensive offering always turn out to be the most profitable.

You can use this information to work out which offering you want to sell to which type of customer. Later chapters focus on how to use this information to target your marketing.

What's different about your offering?

You can only identify what is unique about your offering when you compare it to what your competitors are delivering. You need to strip back your business and look at everything that impacts on your customers. Ask yourself how you can improve the way you deal with your customers and how you can add value to their experience.

List all the points of contact customers have with your retail business, from the moment they first get in touch with you to the point when your service, equipment or product is in use.

When you have all the information, you can then decide how to make your customers' experience the best it can be. There are no right or wrong answers and much will depend on your competitors. You can gain an edge in many ways: the quality of your equipment and products; competitive pricing and promotions; payment options, low cancellation fees and better-than-usual service guarantees; extended opening hours; employing staff with additional qualifications, skills and experience; even how you answer the phone, how quickly you respond to emails or the warmth of your welcome.

 CASE
STUDY 1

Alex Dale was a master baker in charge of a production line making sliced bread for sale to supermarkets for 22 years.

When the bakery went out of business, Alex was made redundant and decided to invest his redundancy payment in opening a specialist bakery shop.

Alex carried out market research into several small to medium-sized market towns as possible sites for the new business. He settled on Chesterton, in the Cotswolds, as his research revealed that Chesterton has a population within the High Street's catchment area that met the characteristics which Alex had identified as most desirable for his new business:

- mostly in socio-economic groups A, B and C1
- high level of interest in the 'green' agenda
- high level of interest in healthy eating and organic produce
- purchasing decisions based on quality rather than price or convenience.

Research also indicated that Chesterton would give him access to local producers of the different types of flour needed to produce specialist breads, cakes and pastries, and other ingredients such as eggs, butter, cheese and herbs produced organically.

Continued

Chesterton also provided available premises suitable for conversion to a bakery together with space for a retail shop in which the produce could be sold.

Alex realised that the bakery shop would need to be manned from 4am each day, when the preparation would need to start, until 5.30pm when the shop closed. There would also be the need to visit the local suppliers in order to buy produce. He decided that the best format for the business would be a partnership with a former colleague of his who had similar bakery experience, so he approached Cheryl Conran, who agreed to go into partnership with him.

As neither Alex nor Cheryl had any retail experience, they decided to employ an experienced shop assistant, who would provide the expertise in customer service and cash handling.

Alex and Cheryl take turns doing the early morning baking and the visiting of suppliers. They work alongside the shop assistant to gain experience and to talk to the customers to get feedback on the products they sell, and listen to suggestions for new products or services.

They hold regular meetings to discuss the sales of different products and the feedback they have had from customers and from the shop assistant.

After 12 months' trading, they decided to offer celebration cakes made to order, sandwiches and filled rolls to meet lunchtime demand and a small café area within the shop. They have also decided to employ an apprentice baker and Saturday staff in the shop.

As a result of the careful market research Alex carried out before opening the business and the partners' willingness to listen to feedback and react, the business is thriving.

ASSESSING HOW YOUR RETAIL BUSINESS IS DOING

As this chapter so far has shown, you can't think about your business in isolation. This section looks at some of the tools that will help you understand how your business is doing in comparison to others and respond to changes in the market.

There are three Cs to keep in mind:

- your **customers**
- your **competitors**
- your **company** (and all its associated suppliers).

The three Cs are all part of your retail business environment and impact on each other. For example, a change in a competitor's opening hours could mean that your business will lose customers who prefer to be able to shop later in the evening. In turn, this will impact on your company's suppliers as a result of your smaller orders.

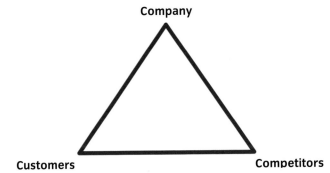

The 3 Cs (your customers, competitors and company) are interdependent

Being aware of the three Cs will help you to fully understand your business and how you can improve it. There are many tools to help you get a picture of how your business is doing. They are straightforward to create and use, and the resulting information is easy to read, evaluate and adapt over time. The two most common are covered here: SWOT and PEST analyses.

SWOT — STRENGTHS, WEAKNESSES, OPPORTUNITIES AND THREATS

Carrying out a SWOT analysis of your business will very quickly help you see what is good, what could be better, and what is available that you could take advantage of. It will also identify things you need to keep an eye on.

- **Strengths** – These are things that make you better than your competition. They may include how you deal with customers, the qualifications or experience of your team and their ongoing continuing professional development. It may also include the quality of your products and equipment, the range or depth of your offering, opening hours, parking availability and so on.
- **Weaknesses** – These are areas that are not as good as they could be and where you may be worse than your competitors. These will vary but may include a poorly qualified or inexperienced team, cramped conditions, noisy environment and so on.
- **Opportunities** – These are any external factors that could directly help your business or be of benefit in some other way. For example, a new housing estate nearby may be full of potential customers, or a competitor might be closing down. In the longer term, perhaps a new college or training provider is opening locally that offers training in your trade, allowing you to offer work experience placements or apprenticeships, leading ultimately to better-trained job applicants and employees.
- **Threats** – These are the issues that are out of your control but could harm the success of your business. For example, a change in legislation that affects your line of work or a competitor moving into the area. Although you may not be able to change these things, it is important to be aware that they are happening – the earlier you know, the earlier you can plan how to limit the damage to your business. If there is a health and safety issue, for instance, your local area Environmental Health Officer may be able to give you guidance on how to comply with any changes. If it's a competitor issue, carry out an investigation into what they offer – make sure what you offer is better and that all your customers know it.

You'll find it helpful to record your SWOT analysis on a form. This will provide a clear snapshot of the current state of your business. On a piece of paper, create a list of the strengths of your business and another of the weaknesses or areas where you could make improvements. Ask others (including any staff you may employ) for their opinions, too – but only if you know they'll tell the truth, otherwise there is no point. Revise the list a few times until you have a set of succinct bullet points, then add them to the chart. Create similar lists for opportunities and threats, mull them over for a few days, then add these bullet points to the chart too. The strengths will form the basis of your marketing – they're something to shout about. You'll need to address the weaknesses with training, or whatever is applicable.

SWOT ANALYSIS

1. STRENGTHS	2. WEAKNESSES	3. OPPORTUNITIES	4. THREATS

For example, you might include:

- **Strengths:** stable team, good range of skills, no skill gaps, established and well-known company, quality products, latest equipment, late-night opening, training programme in place, good margins, loyal clientele, local press coverage
- **Weaknesses:** not enough payment points, old/cold building, no staff room, concerns over rent review, not enough new customers, owner too busy with customers to work on the business, lack of team communication, sales, older team members struggle with IT
- **Opportunities:** new housing estate, new school, new business park, free 'Q&A' column in local paper, can offer new products and services
- **Threats:** pedestrianisation of the area, car park being closed, poor street lighting, local competition opening, supplier introducing 'minimum order' requirement

 OVER TO YOU

Fill in your own SWOT analysis form to create a snapshot of your business. You will need to make sure that you regularly review and update it.

Business strengths and weaknesses need to be analysed frequently – at least seasonally. The issues raised are dynamic and businesses need to change to meet the needs of the environment. Recognition of strengths and weaknesses is only the first step – action and change need to follow. Decide what the most important and urgent issues are for your business and prioritise them. Plan how to make changes to your business in order to convert a weakness into a strength. A SWOT analysis ensures that you consider the wider environment in which your business operates and that you are prepared for any changes that need making.

PEST — POLITICAL, ECONOMIC, SOCIAL/ CULTURAL, TECHNOLOGICAL

PEST analysis is a means of classifying data into categories that makes it easier to review and manage. In this case, you are looking at aspects that affect the wider environment within which you operate. These are generally not factors that you can control or influence, but if you are aware of them, you can plan how your business will respond.

- **Political** – These are the political and legal issues that you have to comply with. Legislation can affect you, your business, your team, your customers or your suppliers. Examples that impact directly on your business include health and safety legislation, employment law, the Sale and Supply of Goods and Services Act, and discriminatory practices on the basis of age, race, gender or disability. Ignorance is no defence, so an awareness of the legal issues and any changes that may affect you is vital.
- **Economic** – These are factors in the external environment that affect the money your customers have available to spend. Economic recession and growth affect everybody in some way and dictate the amount of money customers feel 'safe' spending. Being aware of economic trends means that you can make plans to minimise their detrimental effects.
- **Social/cultural** – These factors affect the environment in which your customers and potential customers live. Social issues such as housing, education and employment play an important part in the lives of your customers and affect their decision-making. To avoid embarrassing customers or even seriously offending them, you should make it a priority to become aware of cultural differences and how they may affect what you offer and how.
- **Technological** – New technologies and innovations change how customers access products and services. Keeping up to date with this area is almost a full-time job; you'll need to judge its relevance to your particular business. For example, it may now be easy for your

customers to access a product or service online, which historically only you could provide. If you don't respond to technological changes by adapting the way you work or your marketing message, you might be left behind.

OVER TO YOU

Record the findings of your PEST analysis in a form and regularly review and update it.

PEST ANALYSIS

POLITICAL	ECONOMIC	SOCIAL/CULTURAL	TECHNOLOGICAL

For example, you might include:

- **Political:** Environmental Health Inspectors, disabled access, use of plastic bags
- **Economic:** local big company making redundancies, rates going up, petrol costing more, bus services being cut, local small business going bust, wholesalers selling retail and competing with us
- **Social/cultural:** clients buying items on eBay, clients sharing info about products on social networking sites
- **Technological:** internet shopping

KEY TO SUCCESS

If you have a partner or employ staff, involve them in the PEST analysis; give them something to research so they feel involved and gain an understanding of the wider environment.

Mystery shoppers visit your competitors' businesses to find out more about them and report their findings back to you. They are normally family members or friends whom you trust to tell you the truth.

GATHERING THE INFORMATION YOU NEED

For SWOT and PEST analyses to be most useful, you need to make sure you're gathering real information about your retail business, your customers and your competitors. Don't just rely on what you think your strengths and weaknesses are – view them through the eyes of your customers. You can do this via formal research (for example questionnaires) and informal research (for example chatting with customers). These types of research and data are good indicators of what your business is perceived to be good at and not so good at from the customers' viewpoint.

Benchmarking can be used to compare what you offer against other businesses whose offering is the same or similar. Ideally you should study a business more successful than yours, to give you something to aim for. In addition, industry or trade surveys from websites, magazines, sector skills councils, standard setting bodies and trade associations can provide vital pieces of data to benchmark against.

Mystery shoppers (in person or on the phone) are useful for gathering information about your competitors. Provide your mystery shopper with a checklist of questions to ask or things to look out for, and get them to rate each aspect on a scale of 1–10. They will also need to mark your business against the same criteria, which will help you to see the areas where you are stronger or weaker than your competitors.

When you have listed all the ways in which your business compares to the competition, and which is better, you need to put the information into a format that can be easily read – a graph, pie chart or another type of chart.

COMPETITOR SUCCESS SUMMARY

	Price	Offering	Customer service	Specialist areas	Suppliers	Payment methods accepted	Team capabilities	TOTAL
COMPETITOR 1								Score /10
COMPETITOR 2								Score /10
COMPETITOR 3								Score /10
YOUR BUSINESS								Score /10

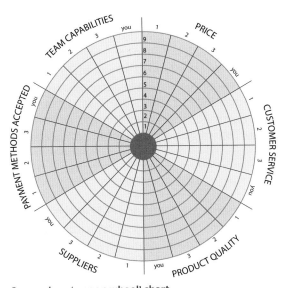

Comparison 'wagon wheel' chart

Shown here is a 'wagon wheel' or 'spider web' chart, which is more unusual. This type of chart can be altered but the example shown allows you to measure your business against three other businesses on a scale of 1–9 across six areas. Let's say competitor number 1 scores 4 out of 9 on staff expertise; colour in cells 1–4. Competitor number 2 scores 6, so cells 1–6 need to be coloured in. Competitor 3 scores 7, so colour in cells 1–7. Your wonderful business scores 9, so all your cells would be coloured in and it can easily be seen to be better than the rest.

You can create this kind of chart in Excel, and it can be used for any comparison purposes; you can design it to have more or fewer than the six sections shown, and more or fewer than the nine circles to increase or decrease the number of scores you can give. It is a tool to be used and adapted – the main thing is that whatever it's measuring can be seen easily.

You can also watch your competitors' premises to see how many customers go in and out, and whether they come out with one or more bags. You can also visit their websites, follow them (anonymously) on Facebook and Twitter and read their promotional literature. You may even get unintentional feedback and information from suppliers you share.

Write a research plan detailing what questions you want answered, how you can find this information, who will do the research and in what timeframe, which competitors you want to compare your business to, who will assess and mark your business, when you'll collate the data and what you will do with it.

KEY TO SUCCESS

If you would like to create more complex charts and diagrams there are numerous websites to assist you. Try www.smartdraw. com and www. shapesource.com.

KEY TO SUCCESS

You work in a competitive marketplace, so make sure you know what your competitors offer and how they deliver it.

If you have a team, why not give each member a local geographical area to research? Suggest that they do this by reading the local paper, listening to local radio, and watching competitors and new entrants into the market to gain any information relevant to your SWOT or PEST analysis. Collect the data gained in a folder or online file and discuss it at monthly staff meetings. Use the data to evaluate opportunities and how they can be exploited to maximum benefit, and to recognise any threats and how their negative impact might be managed.

⤵ OVER TO YOU

Look at the issues that your SWOT and PEST analysis and mystery shopper comparisons have flagged up. Which ones are you going to tackle and in which order? Put dates in your business calendar (see page 47) to review the SWOT/PEST analyses and update your action plans.

SETTING UP A RETAIL BUSINESS

By this stage, you should have tools to enable you to understand some of the key points about your business – who your customers are and how you can serve them competitively. These are important considerations, whether the business you are running is your own or one that you are managing. This section of the chapter looks at some of the key aspects of setting up a business yourself.

NAMING AND BRANDING

There are a number of considerations when naming your business. Some are legal requirements (which you must adhere to) and others are subjective. A subjective view is a person's individual opinion – some people will like the name and others won't, but this doesn't make the name right or wrong.

Choosing and registering
Think about your business name. Do you want it to:

- say what you do? For example, 'ABC Books', 'Beauty Box', 'Floristry 4 U' or 'George's Greengrocers'.
- not say what you do, so it could be anything? For example, 'Aspire'. A name that means nothing can by definition mean anything, and you can make it your own. It will also allow you to change direction without having to change your business name.
- have your name in it? For example, 'Joe Brown Butchers', Alison's Nails', 'Kim's Antiques'.
- be witty and amusing? Be careful, though – what is witty and amusing to one person might be offensive to another; your customers might not 'get' it.

- be short so it fits on a standard business card, a carrier bag or the side of a van?
- be unique to you? There is no point publicising someone else's business!

If you choose to have a limited company you will need to have 'Limited' or 'Ltd' in the business name, and likewise if you have a Public Limited Company (PLC). See pages 32–36 for more information about the different types of company.

The Business Link website (www.businesslink.gov.uk) has a very useful section on naming your business. The website www.startups.co.uk also has useful information and links.

To check whether someone else already has a business with the name you want, visit the Companies House website: www.companieshouse.gov.uk.

Your business name is part of your **branding**. Branding is what you want to say to your customers and potential customers about your values – who you are, what you do, how you do it, what you stand for and what they can expect in terms of service and quality. If you call yourself Speedy Grocers and have a Formula 1-type logo but you turn up in a very old, rusty three-wheeler van, the van doesn't match the rest of your business image and the power of your brand is lost. Everything needs to say the same thing, to communicate the values of your brand. (And a clapped-out van is probably saying the wrong thing to your customers!)

? JARGON BUSTER

Branding is a process that uses advertising, distinctive design and a unique business name to ensure that people associate a specific offering with a specific business. Its aim is to attract and retain customers by being different.

⤷ OVER TO YOU

List six brand values you want people to associate with you and your business. For example, trustworthy, up to date, reliable, honest, value for money, professional. Alongside each value, list how you can communicate it to customers and potential customers.

Where you will operate from

As an extension of branding, consider where you intend to carry out your business. Think about the following options and what they will say to customers. Do you want to:
- be mobile, working from a vehicle? What impression does your van give of you/your business? Does it match your brand values?
- be static, but work within a 'host' or another business? For example, a shop-in-a-shop. Does the fact that customers may have to walk through the other business to get to yours 'say' the right thing?

- work from your own business premises – either rented, leased or purchased? Does this say you're successful, or does it mean you're charging too much? Similarly, an expensive vehicle might say you're good at what you do to some customers; to others it can say you're expensive and only in it for money.
- have a franchise? A franchise is not a legal structure but a business model that can operate under one of the legal structures laid out below. There are various types of franchise you might consider:
  - single-unit franchises, where you own a single outlet. Start-up costs are low and the franchise can be managed by you personally.
  - multi-unit franchises, where you open a number of outlets in an area. This increases your turnover and, hopefully, your profit but needs the employment of managers to operate the individual units.
  - taking over an existing franchise, which means you will already have a customer base but you need to investigate the reason the franchise is for sale; if it is failing under the previous owner, you need to be sure that you can turn it round.

Information on franchising is available from the British Franchise Organisation (www.thebfa.org/) and the websites www.whichfranchise.com and www.franchiseinfo.co.uk.

For retailers, location is the key to success. There are many different types of retail location available if you are thinking of operating a public-facing retail unit. Think about where you live; there are probably long-established shopping areas, newly opened retail centres and individual shops on street corners in residential areas. The business rates and rent that you pay will also be driven by the location. The choice of a cheaper unit in a relatively low-profile location will impact on your marketing spend – you may have to spend more money advertising to attract customers instead of relying on passing trade.

Each type of location will have advantages and disadvantages, depending on the type of stock you are planning to sell, the type of customer you are targeting and the size of business you are operating:
- An **individual shop** in a low-profile location will usually have no restrictions imposed by the landlord on what may be sold, and will probably have parking available and a reasonable rent. On the downside, there may be fewer reasons for customers to pass the shop than there will be in locations where several shops are situated together.
- A **shop in a local shopping centre** consisting of maybe half a dozen shops and often services such as a doctor's surgery, sub-post office or a bank. There will probably be parking; rents will be considerably higher than for individual shops but each shop will benefit from passing trade from the others. There may also be high management fees for shopping centres over and above the rent and rates.

- A **high street shop** will also usually have no restrictions but may have parking issues and will definitely have a higher rent. There will, however, be more passing trade from customers visiting neighbouring shops. There may be a supermarket or department store nearby to attract higher numbers of customers. Shops situated on streets running off the high street, known as secondary position, will benefit from some of the additional footfall, although less than those on the high street, but will sometimes have substantially lower rents.
- **Market stalls** are a relatively cheap form of town centre trading with good passing trade. The disadvantages are that you are working outside in all weathers, and the stock and perhaps the stall has to be packed up at the end of the day. Often markets are only open one day a week and you have to move to a different town each day.
- **Covered shopping centres** or 'malls', which may be in towns, such as the Bullring in Birmingham, or out of town, such as Brent Cross or Meadowhall. These will have two or more anchor stores, which are large national department stores, chain stores or supermarkets and dozens of smaller shops. These centres are designed to contain shops of all sizes, right down to kiosks and shopping carts, which are placed in the walkways between the shops. This allows specialist retailers to have a presence in these large centres. Parking is plentiful and usually free, and footfall is much higher than in other locations, but rents will be very high and there will be restrictions on the way you trade and the hours that the centre is open.
- **Retail parks** are usually open-air and situated out of town. Shops in these locations are usually large and occupied by national chains selling electrical goods, DIY, furniture and homewares, etc. There is free parking but little opportunity for smaller or specialist retailers.

There are also ways of operating retail businesses without a 'bricks and mortar' shop. For example, you could operate a party plan business. This is where you host a social event, either in your home or in a customer's home, and demonstrate stock available and take orders. During the event you will also be recruiting customers who are willing to host an event in their home. You may think this is restricted to plastic kitchenware and is old-fashioned. However, www.findaparty.co.uk lists over 80 party plan companies. The advantages of party plan are that you don't need premises and you need only enough stock to act as samples; the disadvantage is that you need a continuously changing group of people to attend the events.

KEY TO SUCCESS

Where you work from communicates a message to your customers and potential customers. Make sure you're portraying your business and what it offers in the right way.

You could also operate a retail business entirely online from home but you will need storage space for your stock and an online presence with an appropriate website that will generate enough custom, which can be expensive to set up and operate. Marketing and advertising can also be prohibitively expensive for a start-up online business.

In deciding on the best location for your retail business, you will need to consider the rent that will be charged. In a slow economic climate, there will be deals to be done on rents as landlords attempt to fill vacant properties, so it is worth haggling over prices. You will also have to pay business rates. There are sometimes reliefs available for small businesses, so investigate these with your local authority. More information on business rates can be found in Chapter 9. Useful information on deciding whether to rent or buy premises can be found on www.businesslink.gov.uk.

CHOOSING THE RIGHT LEGAL STRUCTURE

One of the key decisions when setting up a business is which legal structure is the most appropriate for the type of work you are doing and the lifestyle you want.

Do you want to be a sole trader, a partnership or a private company? Even if you are managing an existing business and do not have control over the structure, it is important that you understand the differences. The format that is best for your business depends on a number of factors and should be discussed with your accountant and financial advisor. Wherever you work, the legal structure you choose for your business must be suitable. The legal structure is not based on where you operate from, but on how you wish to operate.

Chapter 7 takes a detailed look at the paperwork and forms you will need to set up and run a business. However, the key points of each main legal structure are covered here.

Sole trader

Being a sole trader is the most common way to operate, and is the simplest way to start and run a business. The benefits are that you don't have to pay any registration fees, the record-keeping and accounts are straightforward and you get to keep all the profits. The only real downside is that you are personally responsible for all aspects of your business, including raising the start-up capital and paying off any debts that may occur. The liability issue can also make banks and other investors nervous, particularly if the business carries a lot of perceived risk.

The main features of operating as a sole trader are:

- Set-up – You need to visit the Her Majesty's Revenue and Customs (HMRC) website, www.hmrc.gov.uk, to register as self-employed when you are about to start.
- Managing and money – You have ultimate authority, and responsibility, for how your business is managed. You will need to raise all the money required for your business; this can come out of your own savings and/or from loans from family, friends, banks and other lenders.
- Records and accounts – You must keep accurate and clear records or 'books', which show your business income and expenses. You (or your accountant on your behalf) must complete and send the annual Self Assessment tax return to HMRC.
- Profits – All profits are yours and can go into your bank account, but they have to be declared and tax paid on them following Self Assessment.
- Summary of tax and National Insurance Contributions (NICs):
  - profits are yours and are classified as income so you will be taxed on them
  - you'll pay fixed-rate Class 2 NICs
  - you'll pay Class 4 NICs on profits.

For more information on NICs visit: www.litrg.org.uk.

As a sole trader you are personally liable (responsible) for any debts run up by your business. At worst, this means that your home and other things you own may be at risk in the last instance if you are unable to pay your debts.

For more information on working as a sole trader, visit www.hmrc.gov. uk, www.directadvice.co.uk or www.smallbusiness.co.uk.

Partnership

Setting up as a partnership is the next most common way to start a business – this is a relatively straightforward way for two or more people to own and run a business together. Most often in small businesses it involves two people who have worked together in the past, who share common goals and who can both achieve more by working together than they can individually. Having someone else to share the problems of running a business with is also a consideration. Alternatively, you may go into partnership with someone who provides the money (this might be a member of your family), while you provide the knowhow.

 **KEY POINT**

Both Class 2 and Class 4 NICs are for the self-employed. For Class 2 contributions, the amount paid is currently £2.65 a week for 2012–13 and is the same regardless of your profits. Class 4 contributions are based on profits and are collected with your income tax.

The main features of operating in a partnership are:

- Set-up – You need to visit www.hmrc.gov.uk to register as a partnership as soon as you are about to start. Note that a partner doesn't have to be a person; it can be another business.
- Managment and money – Management of the business is normally carried out by the partners (usually with the help of an accountant) but certain aspects can be delegated to employees. Money for the business is from the partners' own possessions, property, or through loans. If your partner leaves the partnership, you may be liable for all the debts of the partnership, which includes those of your partner(s).
- Records and accounts – You must keep records showing business income and expenses. One of the partners is designated as responsible for sending a partnership return to HMRC. Partners are still self-employed, must register as such with HMRC and must complete the annual Self Assessment tax return.
- A partnership agreement is highly recommended for partnerships. This is an agreement that sets out the conduct of the partnership, including the division of earnings, procedures for dividing up assets if the partnership is dissolved, and steps to be followed when a partner becomes disabled or dies. An accountant and solicitor can normally advise on the content of this.
- Profits – Normally the profits are divided equally between each partner; if this is to be different it needs to be stated in the partnership agreement.
- Tax and NICs – The profits are yours and your partners' and are classified as income, so you will be taxed on them. Income tax and National Insurance payments are deducted from each partner's share of the profits. You will pay Class 4 NICs on the profits.
- Liability – The partners, including **sleeping partners**, are equally and personally liable (responsible) for any debts run up by the business, regardless of which partner caused them. At worst, this means that your home and other things you own may be at risk if you are unable to settle any debts in the first instance.

A Limited Liability Partnership (LLP) is a partnership where one of the partners is said to be 'limited'. This means that the amount the limited partner is liable for is set (limited) to the amount of money they have put into the business themselves, or any personal guarantees they have given to raise money. This type of partnership gives some protection to partners if the business runs into trouble. For more information on partnerships, visit www.hmrc.gov.uk and www. settingupyourbusiness.co.uk.

The main features of operating as a limited partnership are:

- Set-up – You need to visit www.companieshouse.gov.uk to register the company as soon as you are about to start.
- Managing and money – The directors make the decisions. Finance comes from shareholders (who may also be directors), or from loans and profits from the business.
- Records and accounts – There are more requirements from HMRC for this type of business, such as Pay As You Earn (PAYE) for employers, and VAT.
- Profits – Money from the profits which is required to run the business (known as working capital) is kept in the business. The remaining profit is divided between the shareholders in the form of regular payments called dividends.
- Tax and NICs – The company pays Corporation Tax on profits. Directors pay tax and NICs via PAYE. There are specific rules in respect of NICs for directors; for more details visit: www.hmrc.gov.uk.

Private Limited Company

A private company is a more involved and complex way to run a business than as a partnership or sole trader. There is a lot of detail involved in setting it up and running it; consequently this is not an option for most start-ups. There are two types of private company: a private unlimited company or a private limited company. A Private Limited Company is very similar to an unlimited one in terms of set-up and running apart from one vital point – that your liability is limited. Unlimited companies are very rare in the UK, as the main reason people choose a private company is to have limited liability. How the company is limited varies, but briefly, a company is either 'limited by guarantee' or 'limited by shares':

- Limited by guarantee means that your liability is limited to the amount you have guaranteed to contribute to the company in the event of it being wound up.
- Limited by shares means your liability is limited to the amount unpaid on your shares and any guarantees you have given to raise money, such as a bank loan.

The limited company is a separate legal entity, which means that its finances are separate from yours; this offers the most protection from liability. However, if as a director you have agreed to be personally liable for your business debts in the event that the company goes under still owing money, you will be liable for those debts. You could lose your house if you have put that up as a guarantee.

For more information on Private Limited Companies, visit www.hmrc.gov.uk.

	Sole trader	Partnership	Private Limited Company
Ownership	One owner	Partners	Shareholders
Size	Small	Fairly small	Generally fairly small, but some are large
Liability	Unlimited	Most unlimited	Limited
Who takes profit?	Owner	Partners	Shareholders
Advantages	Sole charge	Someone to share responsibility and decision-making	Limited liability
Disadvantages	Hard work	Partner disagreements	Accountable to shareholders

Quick comparison of business structures

CASE STUDY 2

Chloe and Louise have been best friends since school and share an interest in antiques and collectables. Two years ago Chloe was made redundant from her job as a human resources manager and persuaded Louise to leave her job and go into partnership in an antiques shop in the high street.

They saw the benefits of working in partnership as sharing the costs, sharing the responsibilities and sharing the risks while using their complementary skills and giving each other support and motivation.

They agreed they would put an equal amount of money into the business as capital. Chloe would use her redundancy money and Louise would use money saved by her and her husband. They also agreed they would work an equal number of hours and split their profits 50:50.

For the first 18 months the partnership has worked well – sales have steadily increased and they have managed to produce a small profit. Louise has recently told Chloe that she is expecting her first child. Chloe is pleased for her friend, but Louise has started taking increasing amounts of time off for medical appointments, which puts pressure on Chloe to carry on the business. Chloe is concerned that when the child is born Louise will need even more time off to look after it.

Continued

CASE STUDY 2 (CONTINUED)

The partners did not include in their partnership agreement how they would deal with a situation when one partner was not able to contribute an equal amount to the partnership. They are now in a situation where one is contributing more than the other while the profits are still being divided equally. They will need to discuss how they can take the business forward before the business fails as a result of their falling out over the situation. They are at risk of losing not only the business, but their friendship. As John D. Rockefeller said, 'A friendship founded on business is a good deal better than a business founded on friendship'.

SUCCESSFULLY RUNNING A BUSINESS

Having analysed your business environment, including what you need to offer, how it needs to be different from your competitors, who your most profitable customers are, naming and branding issues and the various legal structures, you will now have a clearer idea of the business you want. Armed with this information, it's now time to pull it all together, analyse the risks, understand your costs and plan your business success. If you fail to plan then you plan to fail!

KEY TO SUCCESS

It's no use being the best at what you do if you go out of business!

This section will guide you through the planning process. By the end of it you will have prepared a business plan to guide you and your business.

IS RUNNING YOUR OWN BUSINESS RIGHT FOR YOU?

You should not go into business without assessing its viability in terms of the financial rewards and management of risk. You must take into account the risks involved; however, this should not necessarily deter you from following your dream if the data you have collected suggests it will work. Life is full of risks and it's more a case of being aware of them and then managing them than trying to avoid them completely.

You will need to assess a business's impact on your work/life balance; use the following chart to help you. Although by no means a definitive list of the issues, it will give you food for thought. Having your own business can be the making of you both personally and financially – but you could also lose everything.

For	Against
Be your own boss	Working on your own can be lonely
All profit is yours	Uncertain income
Work when you want to	Long hours
Choose suppliers	Emotional stress
Choose customers	

Reasons for and against having your own business

How entrepreneurial are you?

In order to decide whether running your own business is for you, you may want to carry out a self-audit. The attributes needed by an entrepreneur include:

- Innovation – Can you see a gap in the market and find a way to fill it?
- Commitment – Will you be able to cope with the long hours and the sheer hard work of providing a retail service to customers?
- Perseverance – Can you cope with disappointments and pick yourself up, brush yourself off and start again?
- Risk taking – Are you able to recognise calculated risks, as opposed to making rash decisions?
- Being driven by results – Are you motivated by making tomorrow's sales higher than today's?

Be honest with yourself – do you have all of these attributes? What other skills will you need? If you identify a skills gap, can you create an action plan to gain the missing skills? There is a lot of information in this book which will help you.

If you have a partner or family, it's also worth considering the pressure that you having your own business will put on them. Will they worry about irregular income? How will they react to the amount of hours you need to put in? How supportive will they be when they hardly see you? You need to consider how much time you're prepared to put into the business. Your time needs to be spent not just working *in* the business but also working *on* the business – this includes keeping neat and ordered records of all transactions, working on the marketing of your offering, carrying out research into competitors and customer trends, and watching and evaluating everything that might impact on your business (including updating your SWOT and PEST analyses).

When you get it right, being your own boss, expanding your business and improving your lifestyle is exhilarating and immensely rewarding – but it is *not* an easy option.

Sit down and write a list of the advantages and disadvantages of setting up your dream business, based on and adding to the issues shown previously. Be realistic and think about which factors carry the most weight with you. If you have a partner or family who will be affected, show the list to them and get their input.

WRITING YOUR RETAIL BUSINESS PLAN

A business plan does the following: it describes your business's aims and objectives (pulling together all of the aspects we've looked at so far); it sets out the strategies and tactics by which you'll achieve them; it studies the market you're operating in, including the competition; and it provides the financial forecasts. On a less formal level, it also acts as a guiding light or map for your business journey, keeping you focused and stopping you getting sidetracked. You need to think about this, otherwise you'll be the busy fool – terribly busy but in actual fact not making any money, just going round in circles with no direction.

You may need to borrow money to set up your business or improve it. Any bank or other potential backer will want to see your business plan so they understand where and how their money will be used and, in particular, when they might see a return on their investment (referred to as ROI). It is their window into your business; a badly prepared business plan will give the impression that you are a badly prepared person and therefore a high risk, in which case you are unlikely to get the investment you need.

KEY TO SUCCESS

No-one invests out of the goodness of their heart. All investors want a good ROI and to have their money working for them.

When putting your business plan together, write it as though the person reading it knows nothing about your business; in other words, include everything and assume nothing. The process of writing it is not quick; it needs to be detailed and well researched. It should focus your mind on everything you want to achieve, what has to be done to achieve it and at what cost. This must be laid out in a clear, logical and precise way, as it is the blueprint for the future of the business, and others may need to read it – the bank manager or other potential investors, for instance.

The research you undertake for your business plan will help you assess the viability of your business; you must be receptive to information. Remove your rose-tinted spectacles and be open to alternative views, whether you agree with them or not. Be aware that one of the greatest barriers to listening is that we only hear opinions that coincide with ours.

There are many types of business plan and, depending on where your business is in its journey, the plan will reflect this. For example, a small business start-up plan will be different from an existing business development plan.

Start-up business plan

The plan should cover where the business will be based, where you are going to find your first customer(s), what it will cost to set up and run, and how much you plan to make in turnover and profit. The structure below works well:

- Title page – Title of your plan, your name and date.
- Contents page – A well-spaced list of all the contents, as listed below, with page numbers.
- Introduction page – Purpose of the plan.
- Executive summary – This is key, as it summarises the whole plan in no more than one page and includes conclusions, recommendations, actions to be taken, financial returns on investment and so on. It should be clearly readable in a few minutes.
- Body of the plan:
  - A succinct description of the business
  - Stock: the value of the stockholding
  - Marketing and sales strategy: who your customers are going to be, routes to market, price strategy, how you are going to promote the business
  - Information on your management team: who they are, their background and remuneration
  - Information on your operations, including business premises, IT and management information systems
  - Costs and financial forecasts: how much money you need to start the business, where you are going to get it from, fixed costs, how much you think the business is going to make, profit margins and what salary you plan to take.

- Appendices – Additional detailed reference material. This can include trade and/or consumer information, trends, examples, statistics and so on. This is for reference only and supports your case but is not a part of the main presentation. A good selection of appendices demonstrates the breadth and depth of your research data.

You should also write separate, more focused, plans for each of the areas in your business. The most important of these would be marketing (how and what you are going to communicate to your customers) and sales (how much are you going to sell, at what cost, at what profit margin, where are you going to buy, terms and so on). These smaller plans are often referred to as 'business unit plans' and set out how the separate parts of the business will contribute towards achieving the aims and objectives of the whole. Each will have its own set of aims, objectives and budgets.

Business units can include:
- sales
- marketing
- finance
- human resources
- production
- research and development
- new product development.

Business development plan

This type of plan would be produced by a business already in existence but wanting to expand. It will involve more detail, as the current performance and background of the business needs to be explained. A typical structure might include:
- Title page
- Contents page
- Introduction page
- Executive summary
- Body of the plan:
  - Your current market and business to date
  - Brief quantification of the potential new market(s): include size, how you plan to segment and an overview of the research data
  - Detailed research data regarding potential market(s): include competitor analysis, industry trends and **business drivers**, sales plan, PEST analysis and **Ansoff matrix**
  - Potential customer analysis including research data and projected buying behaviour

Boston matrix is a marketing planning tool, relating to market share and market growth, used to assess your current and potential offering across four categories:

- Question marks – Low market share but with the potential for high market growth; unsure how to proceed with opportunities as will need investment.
- Stars – High market share with high market growth; doing well with great opportunities.
- Cash cows – High market share with low market growth; doing well but with limited opportunities.
- Dogs – Low market share with low market growth; weak and difficult to make a profit.

- **Boston matrix**, means of differentiation and competitive advantage
- Routes to market
- Any specific research data such as external case studies, for example UK Trade and Investment (UKTI) or other evidence which will add weight and gravitas to your plan
- Competitor analysis, including benchmarking and SWOT comparisons of each of your potential competitors
- Sales plan
- Marketing plan.
- Costs in detail across all business functions.
- Acknowledgments – if you have taken data from other sources they can be listed here, but this is normally only necessary for very large, detailed plans.
- Appendices – additional detailed reference material, such as trade and/or consumer information, trends, examples, statistics, spreadsheets and so on. This is for reference only and supports your case but is not a part of the main presentation. A good selection of appendices demonstrates the breadth and depth of your research data.

Business is dynamic and your business plan should reflect any changes made by you or influenced by external factors; it is not a document that is written once and left to gather dust. There will be new and ongoing issues, both internal and external to your business, that will have an effect on it. These issues need to be recognised and the plan adapted to address their impact – positive or negative – as they occur. Generic updates should be carried out at least once a year as a matter of course, but also when applying for any investment; investors (your bank or your partners and family) will want to see that you have up-to-date and relevant information.

For more information on writing business plans (and other business support) try these sources:
- most banks offer business start-up advice and support, which includes the writing of a business plan
- Business Link: www.businesslink.gov.uk (type 'business plan' in the search box)
- www.startups.co.uk (type 'business plan' in the search box)
- Nesta (formerly the National Endowment for Science, Technology and the Arts) offers non-financial support, including mentoring and management support, events and sponsorship: www.nesta.org.uk
- Shell LiveWIRE provides a range of online support and information for new businesses, as well as networking opportunities: www.shell-livewire.org.

Depending on whether you are already in business or are planning to be, list the headings for either a set-up or a development plan. Write a short paragraph under each heading saying what you need to put in that section, where and how you will find the information required, what information each source will give you and what it is relevant to. Then create your business plan with a view to asking the bank manager for a loan. Present it to the friends and family you used in the previous presentation activity (see page 40).

UNDERSTANDING COSTS AND REVENUES

For your retail business to be successful you need to have more money coming in than going out; how much more depends on many factors, and this is covered in depth in Chapter 8. However, it's vital to understand from early on the relationship between your costs and your sales income: without this, you won't be able to assess your business's viability or construct a business plan. Below is an overview of the key terms and concepts:

- **Turnover** is the money that comes into your business in a set period of time.
- **Profit** is the money that is left in the business, in the same period of time, after all costs including your **drawings** have been paid or accounted for (put to one side for when they are due).

Profit is key for any business. In order for you to work out your profitability you need to know what your exact costs are for every aspect of the business – right down to toilet rolls and tea bags.

Costs should be broken down into three areas:

- **Fixed costs** – Those that you have to pay to operate the business, including bills for heating, lighting and telephone line rental, insurance, rent, rates, accountancy fees, bank charges and wages. These costs have to be paid regardless of whether you are working or not (for example, when you are on holiday or snowed in, you will still incur these costs).
- **Variable costs** – Those that are incurred only when providing an offering. Typically, but not exclusively, these will be costs associated with suppliers: stock, consumables and so on. They can also include additional staff for busy periods or to cover illness, and need to include the delivery and marketing costs associated with selling the offering. These costs vary depending on how much you are selling. For example, the major variable cost for a bookshop will be the cost of buying the books that it sells.
- **Total costs** – The sum of the fixed and variable costs.

? JARGON BUSTER

Drawings is the term for the money a self-employed person takes out of their business to live on, like a salary.

Apportioning costs

When you know how much it really costs you to operate the business, you need to work out how much profit you want/need to make. If you had no competition you could charge what you wanted within reason; however, it's unlikely that you are in that position so you must be competitive. Being competitive doesn't mean being the cheapest – being the cheapest and not making any money is a sure way to lose your business! Price, apart from bringing the money in, is also a marketing tool. It is an indicator to your customers and potential customers of the likely quality of your offering. If your offering is cheaper than your competitors', customers may decide you are not as good as those charging more. You may only attract customers wanting the cheapest option, and they are never loyal – they will always go with the cheapest option, and next time that may not be you.

Your pricing strategy and the sales profit margin you want to achieve must be worked out at the beginning. Making a profit on an offering is not a good enough measure – that profit must be enough to cover the costs apportioned to it. Working out the profit margin gives you a percentage profit figure, based on costs and sales revenue, which all of your offering should be priced to meet.

Sales profit margin

This is a percentage figure that allows you to compare the profitability of each part of your offering to ensure nothing is delivered at a lower sales profit margin than is needed to meet your financial requirements.

To find out the sales profit margin for an individual range of products, divide the profit (the price the customer pays minus the cost) by the sales figure, and multiply by 100:

price the customer pays (sales revenue) – cost = profit

profit ÷ sales revenue × 100 = profit margin

Profit margins can also be used to assess the business as a whole and can be given as net or gross:

- **Net profit margin** is calculated by dividing net profit (the money earned after costs, expenses, salaries, taxes and so on have been deducted) by revenue and then multiplying by 100.
  For example, net profit of £12,000 ÷ sales of £120,000 x 100 = net profit margin of 10 per cent.

- **Gross profit margin** is calculated by dividing gross profit (the money earned before costs, expenses, taxes and so on have been deducted) by revenue and then multiplying by 100. For a quick online gross profit calculator, visit www.online-calculators.co.uk.

Profit margin figures vary from sector to sector, but higher profit margins equal higher profitability. There is no ideal profit margin; you will use your profit margin from one year to measure and compare with profit margins from previous years to see if you are losing, gaining or staying the same in terms of profitability. You can also compare yours with similar businesses (if their accounts are published) to see how you are performing in relation to them.

YOUR RETAIL BUSINESS CALENDAR

It is important that you adhere to the legal requirements of running a business as laid down by the government, and in particular HMRC. There are key dates by which you must complete certain activities (tax returns, for instance) but when running your business day to day, things can easily get overlooked. As there are legal ramifications if you don't comply within the set timescales, it is good business practice to create a business planner or calendar to which you can add all the important dates, starting with the HMRC deadlines (see below). It is also good practice to include other key dates, deadlines and information. These could include:

- accountancy/bookkeeping fees
- bank charges
- utility and phone bills
- expenses
- holidays/staff out for training
- insurance – public liability, sickness, building and contents, etc
- pension (if applicable)
- petrol account
- rates
- rent
- salary
- suppliers accounts due
- suppliers on holiday/shutdown
- web hosting renewal.

The planner/calendar should be on show in the office and easy to see, otherwise its value is lost. It might be a shop-bought annual wall planner or a spreadsheet you have created yourself – use whatever you feel comfortable with, the main thing is that you use it!

**OVER
TO YOU**

Start putting together a business calendar for your business. Include all the key dates that you know about, and make a note of those you need to look up. Include dates and seasons that may be important for the type of product you sell, too – for example, Christmas, Easter, Mother's day. Think about the key times of year for your business – when are your busiest periods? Mark these on the calendar and see whether they clash with any planned team event, holiday or supplier shutdown. Start planning how you will get around any clashes.

The Business Link website (www.businesslink.gov.uk) provides a useful email alert service for key tax dates. You will need to enter information about your business online and it will then create a calendar of key tax deadlines for the next 12 months. You can also sign up to receive regular email alerts as each date approaches.

Add sample dates of bank holidays, team holidays (spread out over main holiday times), supplier shutdowns, peak customer demand periods such as Christmas, Easter and seasonal periods specific to your business. Input them onto the calendar on page 47.

HMRC DEADLINES FOR SENDING IN YOUR TAX RETURN

Paper returns must reach HMRC by or on 31 October. Online tax returns must be completed on the HMRC website by midnight on 31 January the following year.

There are penalties for late return – for advice on this and what to do if you have missed a deadline, visit www.hmrc.gov.uk.

DEADLINES FOR RECEIPT OF TAX

Payment must be received by 31 January after the end of the previous tax year (which always ends on 5 April). So, you would pay tax by or on 31 January 2013 for the tax year ending 5 April 2012. 31 January is the deadline whether you file paper or online returns.

On/by this date you'll be paying one or both of the following:
- tax owed for the previous tax year
- the first of two payments on account. This payment is for half the tax liability and is paid in advance; the remaining half is payable the following July.

	M	T	W	T	F	S	S	M	T	W	T	F	S	S	M	T	W	T	F	S	S
January						1	2	3	4	5	6	7	8	9	10	11	12	13	14	15	16
	17	18	19	20	21	22	23	24	25	26	27	28	29	30	31						
February		1	2	3	4	5	6	7	8	9	10	11	12	13	14	15	16	17	18	19	20
	21	22	23	24	25	26	27	28													
March		1	2	3	4	5	6	7	8	9	10	11	12	13	14	15	16	17	18	19	20
	21	22	23	24	25	26	27	28	29	30	31										
April					1	2	3	4	5	6	7	8	9	10	11	12	13	14	15	16	17
	18	19	20	21	22	23	24	25	26	27	28	29	30								
May							1	2	3	4	5	6	7	8	9	10	11	12	13	14	15
	16	17	18	19	20	21	22	23	24	25	26	27	28	29	30	31					
June			1	2	3	4	5	6	7	8	9	10	11	12	13	14	15	16	17	18	19
	20	21	22	23	24	25	26	27	28	29	30										
July					1	2	3	4	5	6	7	8	9	10	11	12	13	14	15	16	17
	18	19	20	21	22	23	24	25	26	27	28	29	30	31							
August	1	2	3	4	5	6	7	8	9	10	11	12	13	14	15	16	17	18	19	20	21
	22	23	24	25	26	27	28	29	30	31											
September				1	2	3	4	5	6	7	8	9	10	11	12	13	14	15	16	17	18
	19	20	21	22	23	24	25	26	27	28	29	30									
October						1	2	3	4	5	6	7	8	9	10	11	12	13	14	15	16
	17	18	19	20	21	22	23	24	25	26	27	28	29	30	31						
November		1	2	3	4	5	6	7	8	9	10	11	12	13	14	15	16	17	18	19	20
	21	22	23	24	25	26	27	28	29	30											
December				1	2	3	4	5	6	7	8	9	10	11	12	13	14	15	16	17	18
	19	20	21	22	23	24	25	26	27	28	29	30	31								

Calendar for planning your business year

You will normally receive a Self Assessment Statement from HMRC that tells you what you owe. However, if you don't get this, you or your accountant will need to work out what tax you owe. This is straightforward to do online. Use the following link to HMRC Online Services and use the 'Register' button if it's the first time you've done this, or 'Log in' if you've previously registered: www.hmrc.gov.uk.

31 July is when you have to pay the second half of your tax liability. So, on 31 July 2012, you'd be paying the second payment for the 2011–12 tax year.

VAT RETURN AND VAT PAYMENT DEADLINES

Unlike tax return dates, which are set, the date when your VAT return and VAT payment are due is one* calendar month after the end of your VAT period. Your VAT period begins from the date you registered for VAT.

* If you use the annual accounting scheme your return and payment is due two calendar months after the end of your VAT period; your accountant will advise which is best for your business.

By the end of April 2012 you will only be able to send your VAT return and make payments through the HMRC website.

Further information on VAT is available on the HMRC website (www.hmrc.gov.uk) and from Business Link (www.businesslink.gov.uk).

CORPORATION TAX DEADLINES

The payment deadline date for Corporation Tax is nine months after the end of your Corporation Tax accounting period. So, if your business accounting period ends on 31 May, your Corporation Tax payment is due on or before 1 March the following year. This date is referred to as the 'normal due date' by HMRC. However, the deadline can vary depending on how much taxable profit your company makes, so you'll need to ask your accountant or contact HMRC (www.hmrc.gov.uk).

CLASS 2 NATIONAL INSURANCE CONTRIBUTIONS (NICS) DEADLINES

See www.hmrc.gov.uk.

There are a variety of ways in which you can pay your Class 2 NICs (after April 2011). If you're self-employed, you can pay:
- monthly by Direct Debit
- six-monthly by Direct Debit

- in October and April when asked by HMRC
- you can also make one-off payments for any arrears.

The following table shows the dates for payment of Class 2 NICs and the timescales they covered in 2011–12.

Payment requested	Period covered by payment	Number of contribution weeks	Date payment is due
October 2011	10 April 2011 to 8 October 2011	26	31 January 2012
April 2012	9 October 2011 to 7 April 2012	26	31 July 2012

Table for payment of Class 2 NICs

If you are late paying your Class 2 NICs you may be charged extra and it might affect your benefit entitlements. For further details, visit www. hmrc.gov.uk.

PAYE DEADLINES

If you employ staff, you will need to operate a payroll and deduct tax from their earnings using the PAYE scheme. The main deadlines are set out below. A key requirement, if you are an employer, is to file your Employer Annual Return (forms P35 and P14). This can only be done online, so you'll need to register. Registration can take seven working days so allow plenty of time – there are financial penalties if you file your return late. For details visit www.hmrc.gov.uk.

These are the latest dates for receipt of information or payment to an HMRC Accounts Office or bank account:
- 19 April – PAYE tax and Class 1 NICs (if paid by post)
- 22 April – PAYE tax and Class 1 NICs (if paid and cleared electronically)
- 19 May – File your Employer Annual Return (P35 and P14) and paper returns
- 31 May – Give form P60 to each of your relevant employees
- 6 July – File annual return for expenses and benefits (forms P11D, P9D and P11D(b)); give copy to employees if relevant
- 19 July – Class 1A NICs (if paid by post)
- 22 July – Class 1A NICs (if paid and cleared electronically)

WHERE TO GO FOR MORE INFORMATION

You do need to spend significant time on your business where finance is concerned. You need to know your figures: what money you need to make, what you are making and what you are spending. However, there are people with expertise in this area, so don't be afraid to seek help and advice:

- HMRC (www.hmrc.gov.uk) – The HMRC website is a great source of information and your accountant will be able to guide you through it.
- Your accountant and/or financial advisor – If you don't have an accountant it is advisable to get one. Their costs are normally worth it and your bank should be able to recommend one suitable for your needs.
- Your bank – Banks are a good source of help and advice about running a business, including sales and marketing as well as financial aspects. They often run networking events so you can meet others in your shoes.
- Business Link (www.businesslink.gov.uk) – This is an incredibly useful and wide-ranging website which covers virtually everything you need to know, from setting up a business to closing it down and most of the issues in between.

Business training should be important to you as your business grows and your knowledge develops. The Institute of Leadership and Management (www.i-l-m.com) offers courses in all aspects of leadership, management and related business skills through approved centres. A good source of information on other training courses is govknow.com/training-home.html.

CONCLUSION

KEY TO SUCCESS

It takes time to work on your business, so ensure you plan time to do this.

You should now have an understanding of your business environment; what you need to offer to compete and make money; your costs; accountancy and legal obligations; and the ability to pull it all together to create a business plan that will keep you on track and provide investors with the necessary information should you need additional funds.

As stated at the beginning of this chapter, being good at what you do is no guarantee of business success. You should now appreciate that you need to update your business plan as soon as anything affecting your business arises, and that regardless of this it needs to be reviewed at least once a year.

CHAPTER 2
UNDERSTANDING YOUR KEY CONTACTS

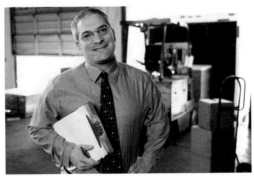

INTRODUCTION

In this chapter you'll learn more about understanding the people who are key to your retail business: why they are important, the effect they might have on your business and how you can measure that effect. Your business relies on your team (covered in detail in Chapter 5), your customers and your suppliers. As you should now be aware, you also need to understand your competitors and how their behaviour might affect you.

These three key groups of contacts – customers, suppliers and competitors – are the focus of this chapter. Understanding key contacts helps you ensure that your offering is wanted and needed by the right customers – at the time they want it, at a price they can afford and better than your competitors can deliver. As a business, you are also a customer of your suppliers. You need to ensure that you are dealing with the right suppliers, that you get what you want from them at the time when you need it, and at a price that gives you a decent profit. Their support will help you service your customers better than your competitors can.

YOUR CUSTOMERS

You cannot improve on the service you give your customers or increase your customer base unless you understand who they are and what they want. As mentioned in Chapter 1, this involves identifying your key customers and finding out more information about their wants and needs and what influences their choices. The way to do this is by using market research techniques, which are looked at in detail in this section. Market research is a thread that weaves throughout this book. In all successful businesses there is a continual need to examine all aspects of the wider business environment through research. This section also looks at how to target your research for the best return on your investment of time and money.

USING MARKET RESEARCH TECHNIQUES

There are two ways of carrying out market research:

- Primary, or field, research – This is specific to you, your needs and requirements. It is the more expensive form of research but is the most accurate and up to date. It can be carried out by you, by members of your team or by a research agency (an expensive option, but one that will produce good results). A good place to start looking for research agencies is the Market Research Society (www.mrs.org.uk).
- Secondary, or desk, research – People normally start with secondary research, which involves accessing research that has already been carried out. This might be research you've done in the past or findings someone else has published. This type of research data is already available – either published in a trade magazine or online – and will cost you little or nothing to obtain. Government statistics are a good example of secondary research; the Office of National Statistics (www.statistics.gov.uk) is a mine of information.

The research process for small start-ups normally begins with secondary data gained from sources such as local or regional government, specific interest groups, trade associations and membership groups, relevant articles, search engines and so on.

 OVER TO YOU

Create a list of secondary research sources where you might be able to find information that would benefit your business.

Whether you are looking at primary or secondary **data**, it will most likely contain two types of **information**: **quantitative** and **qualitative**.

Quantitative research gives you data that can be analysed, is generally dependable and, most importantly, can be measured. Examples of data that you could gain through quantitative research:

- Average customer spend has decreased from £55 to £52.35.
- Average number of customers per day has increased from 35 to 40.

This type of research is most often gained by looking at your business records – the data is there, it just needs to be presented in a format where the information can be measured and compared and trends noted. For example:

'In June 2010 we supplied 50 customers, and in June 2011 we supplied 60 – an increase of 20 per cent.'

'Sales of toys account for 45 per cent of our turnover but 67 per cent of our profit.'

Visual formats such as graphs, pie charts, tables and spreadsheets are often used so the information can be understood at a glance.

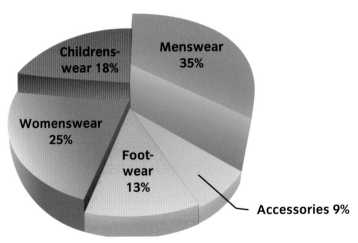

Sales income can be presented in a range of formats such as pie charts

Menswear 35%
Childrenswear 18%
Womenswear 25%
Footwear 13%
Accessories 9%

Qualitative research gives you data based on quality, or the customer experience – specifically, how people feel about your offering or any other issue. This data is often gathered through one-to-one questioning and interviews (either face-to-face or on the phone), as it's about feelings and emotions. Formats such as questionnaires, which give people the option of ticking boxes relating to feelings, can be useful when you want to gather information from a lot of people. Qualitative information can be an indicator of future customer behaviour, while quantitative data is invariably based on past performance (though you can use it to plot trends). Bear in mind that questioner bias (where questions are 'loaded' or leading and affect the response given) can be an issue with face-to-face questioning, and some customers may not want to cause offence and will tell you what they think you want to hear rather than the truth.

Examples of qualitative questioning would be:

- How would you feel if we were open late nights Monday to Thursday?
- If we moved out of the city centre, how would that impact on your journey to us?

Good data needs to include the findings of quantitative and qualitative research to give the full picture – quantitative to give you the facts, and qualitative to help you understand the issues behind the facts. You also need to question a reasonable number of customers. The **sample size** of your research must be large enough to reflect the views of the majority. If you have 800 customers, a sample of 10 will not be enough; you should aim for 80 (10 per cent) at least. However, if you have given your customers a questionnaire that they fill in and hand in when they leave, you could expect a sample size of 320–400 (40–50 per cent). In contrast, cold calling-type questionnaires that are completed away from your premises have a much lower return rate – generally about 5–8 per cent.

IDENTIFYING YOUR CUSTOMER BASE

So who are you going to carry out the research on? There are two main groups: existing customers and potential customers.

Existing customers

With existing customers you have the option of using formal or informal research techniques. Formal techniques include questionnaires, focus groups and interviews; informal techniques are those that occur naturally – for example chatting with a customer, either face-to-face or on the phone.

The process of creating questionnaires is covered here in detail – you can apply the same principles to the other techniques. Your starting point, when thinking about questions to ask, should be the end result – what information do you want to have gathered? When that is clear in your mind you can develop the questions. Try to word the questions so all the answer formats can be the same – circling a number or ticking a box, for instance. This is quicker for the customer, looks neater and makes it easier to collate the results. The questions need to be clear, to the point and not open to interpretation. Aim for 10 to 12 questions.

There is standard data you need to collect from customers to give you information across all areas of your business. This data can be obtained by asking questions that are mainly to do with rating customer service, your team, opening hours, parking facilities, decor, phone manner, ambience, environment, complaints procedure, communications, promotions, your website and how likely they'd be to recommend you to others. These factors could be rated in a number of ways: a scale of 1–10, 'very unlikely' to 'very likely', or even a range of smiley faces ☺ ... ☹.

You also need data from narrower fields relating to specific areas of your offering. The questions here are targeted to that single area and the data can become even more specific if you divide this group of customers, for example by age, gender and spend. Questions might be about how well you have met customers' expectations, whether they are happy with the cost, their awareness of competitors in that area or prompting feedback on you, your team or a recent promotion.

It is worth testing the questions on family and friends before you start the process with customers, to ensure that the person reading the question has the same understanding of it as you. You may need to ask the same question in different ways to clarify answers to important points, for example 'How do you feel about us opening on a Sunday?' and 'Would you come to us on a Sunday?'

Data from anonymous questionnaires can be of most value. To avoid upsetting you, customers may tell you what they think you want to know if they can be identified. However, if the questionnaire is anonymous, you are more likely to get the truth, which of course is what you want. After all, you don't need to know which customer thinks your phone manner is dreadful – it's enough that any customer thinks it is. It is quicker for customers to complete your questionnaire (and they know they won't be identified by their handwriting) when you give them a range of answers from bad to good and they can circle a number or tick a box to indicate their opinion.

KEY TO SUCCESS

If you are constructing a multiple-choice questionnaire, you need to decide whether to offer an odd or an even number of answer options. If there is an odd number, some people will always go for the middle one, meaning average or satisfactory. If you offer an even number you are forcing your customers to decide whether you are better than average or worse than average. There is no right or wrong here, it just depends how brave you are!

Below is an example of a customer satisfaction survey. It includes standard questions that you will want to know the answer to every time you run the survey, and ad hoc questions, which you can use to gain useful feedback about seasonal or of-the-moment issues important to your planning.

CUSTOMER SATISFACTION QUESTIONNAIRE

STANDARD QUESTIONS	Poor			Excellent
Efficient staff handling of your booking	1	2	3	4
Friendly and knowledgeable staff	1	2	3	4
Look and feel of the store/business	1	2	3	4
Quality and range of products	1	2	3	4
Value for money	1	2	3	4
How likely are you to recommend this business to a friend or colleague?	1	2	3	4
Opening hours meet your needs	1	2	3	4
OTHER QUESTIONS	**Poor**			**Excellent**
	1	2	3	4
	1	2	3	4
	1	2	3	4
	1	2	3	4

OVER TO YOU

Quickly write a list of the top 15–20 issues for which you need customer feedback. These issues might be to do with new offerings or proposed changes to existing ones. Leave the list for a day while you think about it, then review it and condense the list to no more than eight key issues that require information. Now create 10–12 questions designed to deliver the information you need.

The drawback of using tick-boxes and ratings on a questionnaire is there is no opportunity for customers to add their individual thoughts. To counter this, consider adding some open-ended questions: 'How can we make our service better?', 'In what ways can we improve?', 'Is there anything different you'd like us to offer?' There are disadvantages to this type of question, though. First, they take longer to answer, which can be annoying for the customer. Secondly, if customers think you might recognise their handwriting, they may not respond honestly. Open-ended questions are often best left for informal research.

Potential customers

Your potential customer base will be a much larger group of people, and can be thought about in the following way:
- Where your business is.
- How far you would travel to deliver to customers or how far they would travel to shop with you.

Ask yourself:
- Of all the population in that area, how many are in the age group you supply?
- How many of those people potentially want/need what you offer?
- How many of those people can potentially afford what you offer?

For example:
- The average distance customers travel to your business is 3.6 miles.
- Your customer age range is 16–75. This includes some men, but the core of your business is women aged 25–60, of which there are 12,000 in that area.
- You have 800 customers, which represents 6.7 per cent of the potential market.
- Research is required to find out how many of the remaining 93.3 percent of your potential market (11,200 potential customers) want/need what you offer and have the time and money to spend with you.

Your potential customers are everybody in the geographical area you identified. They are the people who could be using your business but aren't at the moment. You want to find out as much as you can about why they are not coming to you, to turn them from potential customers into existing, repeat customers.

If you have, or intend to have, an internet presence with online sales, your area for potential customers will be much greater. You would define your potential online customers in a similar way to your locally based ones. However, there is a difference in how you gain access to them – IT will play a major part. For instance, you may be able to link in with other websites that share a similar target audience but provide a non-competing product. For example, if you were selling flat-roof sealant you might link in with a home insurance company or a DIY site.

Think about what you want to find out from your potential customers and how that information is going to help you market your business to them. Just as for existing customers, you need to be very clear about what information you require, and design both the questions and answering mechanisms to deliver this information.

Open-ended questions are possible, but you need to be aware of the potential customers' time constraints – they are certainly not going to write you an essay! You are likely to want to know some or all of the following about your potential customers:

- Have they heard of your business?
    - If yes: what is their perception of your business?
- Do they currently use a competing business?
    - If yes: which is the first part of that business's postcode (LE10, for example)?
    - How often do they buy from that business?
    - How much do they spend per visit?
    - What products or services do they buy?
    - If no: why don't they currently use this type of business?
    - What factors might interest them enough for them to start using it?
- What age range are they in (20–34, 35–49, 50–64, 65+)?
- Are they male or female?

Their responses to these questions will tell you:

- How well your marketing is working, both for potential customers who use your type of business and for those who don't. Is your message getting out there? Is their perception of your business as you would like?
- What types of offering existing customers of other businesses are interested in (which tells you if you're missing out on anything); how far they are prepared to travel (so you can target specific geographical areas); how valuable they could be to your business (how much you are losing by not having them as customers, which may dictate how much you spend on marketing to gain them).

- What reasons people have for not visiting your type of business (any fears or apprehensions can then be addressed in your marketing communications) and what might make them come (such as a product or service you don't offer or one that you do but seems to be a well-kept secret).
- Enough to build a basic profile of a typical potential customer and where they live (so you can target specific geographical areas).

Once you've identified exactly what you want to find out, you need to plan how you are going to reach your target audience – these people are not yet your customers, so you don't have an easy method of contacting them. There are a number of ways you can do this:

- employ a market research agency
- stand on busy street corners with a clipboard and carry out your own research
- knock on doors in the postcode areas most likely to have customers who want/need your offering
- use existing customers.

How can existing customers help you? Formal feedback can be gathered from existing customers using questionnaires and from customer contacts to gain information from their friends, colleagues, neighbours and family, who are not customers.

You may wish to include a money-off voucher with the questionnaires that you use to gain formal feedback to thank them for participating in the research plus an incentive for existing customers to give out the questionnaires. What you really want from this research is to understand why people are not coming to businesses in your sector in general or to your business in particular. You can use this information to plan your marketing campaigns, so it is extremely valuable. Do make sure that once you get it, you use it – otherwise it is wasted and you will play into the hands of your competitors.

↳ OVER TO YOU

Write a list of the top 15–20 issues for which you need feedback from your potential customers. Although there may be some overlap with the issues affecting your existing customers, it is likely that many will be different – and so will the information you need. List what you need to know and then create the questions to deliver that information.

Once you have information from your potential customers, you need to analyse it – and be aware that there are different ways of looking at the same piece of information to come up with a different answer. In Chapter 1 you were encouraged to present your ideas to family and friends and receive their honest feedback, rather than relying on a view through rose-tinted spectacles to judge your ideas.

Think about this: would you describe the glass as half full or half empty?

A half full/half empty glass

If you are in a negative frame of mind you may well say that the glass is half empty; if in a positive frame of mind you may say that it is half full. When you receive information, the way in which you analyse it will be coloured by your negativity or positivity at the time, as well as your general views, judgements, past experiences, values and upbringing. Taking this into consideration, you can see how invaluable feedback is from truthful friends and family.

 CASE STUDY 1

This is a very old story illustrating the difference between positive thinking and negative thinking.

Many years ago two salesmen were sent by a British shoe manufacturer to Africa to investigate and report back on market potential. The first salesman reported back, 'There is no potential here – nobody wears shoes.' The second salesman reported back, 'There is massive potential here – nobody wears shoes.'

This provides a great example of how a single situation can be viewed either negatively or positively. Which are you, negative or positive? Do your friends and family agree?

MARKET SEGMENTATION

The previous section looked at profiling your customers based on profitability; this section looks at the benefits of **segmenting** your customer base. Targeting segments and delivering specific messages to them can help to give you a competitive advantage and a greater return on your time, effort and money.

Your customer base can be split into segments

Your customer segments can be based on a number of factors. No two markets are segmented in the same way, but the overriding issue regardless of sector is: 'Is the segment profitable?' To help you see the segments, here is an example from the car sales market. The total market (the whole orange, if you like) is all car drivers aged 17–80. The customers could be segmented based on:

- gender
- driver age
- driver location
- age of car
- cost of car
- engine size
- model type
- insurance group
- transmission type
- commercial or personal use
- frequency of purchase.

Once you have identified these segments, you can use them to your advantage. For example, you might decide to target drivers under the age of 21, particularly women, who may be less confident and experienced. You might aim to differentiate yourself from your competitors by offering extra help when these customers come to view your cars, giving guidance about guarantees and insurance, advising on the best type of car to meet their needs and so on. Once you become known in your area for helping young drivers, offering an unbeaten level of support and customer care, this will foster trust among your young customers, who will then come back to you for their next car.

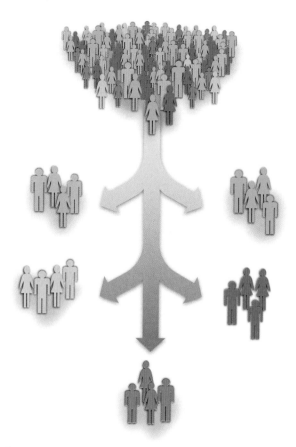

Segmenting your customers means that you can target specific segments

Segmentation is a tool for you to use, not a solution in its own right. So you need to be clear what your segments are, what it is you want from the different segments, how you plan to communicate with each segment and what you hope to achieve from each segment.

For you to market profitably to a segment – which means getting a good return on your investment of time, effort and money – people in the segment must be:

- homogenous – they must all act in a similar manner
- measurable – you can count them
- accessible – you can get to them
- profitable – there are enough of them to make you money
- attractive and relevant – they want what you offer.

Each one of these five criteria is vital: having four out of five isn't good enough, as the case study demonstrates.

A few years ago Mr and Mrs Smith were desperate to go and live in Spain, having holidayed there for many years and got to know lots of people. They didn't have enough money to retire, however, and needed to set up a business to support themselves. They decided that delivering English newspapers to the expat community (English people living abroad) would be a good idea. Until then the expats had had to get up and drive to the shops to get their papers, but the couple knew that people wanted to have their papers delivered as they used to in Britain.

They carried out some research and found the following:

- All expats behaved in the same way – they wanted their papers delivered to their homes by 9.00am every day and were fed up with having to drive to get them.
- They were able to find out how many expats there were by contacting the equivalent of the local council.
- They could promote their services via the various expat social and sport clubs, as well as churches, pubs and restaurants where the expats congregated.
- Potential customers at these places said they thought it was a great idea and that yes, they'd pay for the service.
- The business was viable if 45 per cent of the expats took up their offering. Their research told them 68 per cent would sign up for the service.

Mr and Mrs Smith were very happy with their research and duly moved out to Spain and started their newspaper delivery business.

Within three months it was bust. The one thing they had not taken account of was that although they could communicate with lots of potential customers in one area via social settings, they had to deliver to each customer's home. This was the stumbling block, as they lived in a thinly populated and almost mountainous area. It took them too long to deliver to all their customers, who eventually got fed up with the papers being late and went back to driving down to the shop. What Mr and Mrs Smith failed to realise was that they couldn't service their customers in the right timeframe. It was also too expensive in terms of fuel use; they hadn't budgeted for the size and complexity of the area, so the business wasn't profitable.

How many segments are there in your customer base (your orange)? Create a list of all your segments, ensuring that each one meets the five criteria described. Write one objective for the next 12 months against each of the segments you listed. Then write a plan for how you are going to achieve the objective for your biggest sector.

MAKING AND MAINTAINING GOOD RELATIONSHIPS

KEY TO SUCCESS

You do not have a right to your customers' patronage; it has to be earned each time.

There is a well-known saying – 'It costs five times as much to gain a new customer as it does to keep an existing one' – and there are some who say it costs seven times as much. What are you doing to ensure your existing customers are looked after and that they continue to use you? Beware of taking existing customers for granted: they are the lifeblood of your business as far as income and recommendations are concerned. Always remember that customers have a choice of where to go, that you need them more than they need you and that without them you have no business. Plus, they pay your wages!

Customer journey

Read through the passage below and remember its message.

Remember me?

I am the potential customer who goes into a business, and patiently waits for the staff to do everything but acknowledge my existence.

I am the existing customer who goes into a business and stands quietly, being ignored, while the team members finish their little chat.

I am the regular customer who never complains when stock locations are moved frequently for no apparent reason.

You might say I am the good customer, but do you know what else I am…? I am the customer who never comes back.

All you had to do was give me a little service and show me a little courtesy.

The customer satisfaction surveys described earlier in this chapter are an important part of maintaining good relationships with your customers – they give you a platform for communication – but they are not the only method. Every time you answer the phone, greet someone in person, reply to a letter or email, deliver your offering or give advice, you are communicating your views of the customers. Do you see your customers simply as pound signs, as a means of making money? If so, they will pick up on this. Instead, see them for what they are: people who require your skill and expertise, who deserve to be treated with the highest standards of customer care and who will be loyal if, and only if, you treat them correctly and aim to exceed their expectations.

OVER TO YOU

Make a list of how and where in your customers' journeys you can go the extra mile. How well do you explain what you are going to do, why you are going to do it and what the result will be?

KEY TO SUCCESS

Never assume that customers know: explain everything, think as they do and remember what it's like not to know.

Gap analysis

During your customer research (surveys and conversations), have any gaps been flagged up between what you think you are delivering and what your customers actually receive? It is worthwhile carrying out **gap analysis**, which will help you to see such gaps.

Gap analysis can be used in a variety of situations and is a useful tool when analysing data. It gives you a simple visual indication of the information you have uncovered regarding any gap, difference or deviation from what you want to achieve. This tool can be used to indicate both internal issues – such as what you want your team to do and what they are actually doing – and external issues. You can plot your actual customer service experience rating (gained from your customer satisfaction survey, see page 56) on the vertical axis against what you believe you are offering on the horizontal axis, to make a graph.

? JARGON BUSTER

Gap analysis visually highlights the gap, difference or deviation between what you think is happening and what actually is.

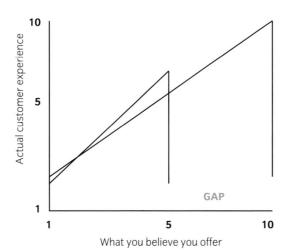

Gap analysis of customer experience/your perceived offering

For more information and examples of gap analysis, visit www.enotes.com.

CUSTOMER RETENTION

So you've got your customers, and you've uncovered what they think about you, your team and your offering. Now you need to do something with the information. You should put procedures in place to ensure that you keep the customers you have – it costs a lot more to get them back than it does to keep them, and if you don't hang on to them you are giving them to your competitors.

Retention is therefore critical to your business – otherwise it will be like trying to hold onto grains of sand, with all your efforts going into putting customers into your business but nothing stopping them from 'slipping through your fingers'.

It is important to retain your customers, so they don't slip through your hands like grains of sand

The best way to keep customers is to keep giving them what they want, when they want it, at a price they can afford and better than anyone else. Customers do like to feel valued and there are ways to do this that needn't cut into your profit margin. One such idea is loyalty schemes. The most common type of scheme offers points, such as the Nectar card (usable in a range of shops) or specific company loyalty cards operated by stores such as Boots, Argos, Costa and Tesco, all of which give you either money off, a free product or special promotions.

Financial incentives are also used to maintain loyalty by tying customers in – for example 'Buy five cups of coffee and get the sixth free'. You should find out what loyalty schemes or retention programmes your competitors offer and ensure yours are competitive; it's rare for a customer to leave you because of a better loyalty scheme on offer elsewhere, but they may leave if they feel undervalued. For further information on loyalty schemes visit the Business Link website: www.businesslink.gov.uk.

Do you know how many customers slip through your fingers every year? Do you know why you lose them? Do you contact them to find out why they left? People are often reluctant to call a lapsed customer but you need to know if they have moved away, been made redundant, died, or are unhappy with your service... and if it's the last of these, you need to put it right. Always start the conversation by saying you are carrying out a survey with lapsed customers to see if there is anything you can do to make your business better; don't put them under any pressure to come back. Stress that the call is just about getting their views, listening to their comments, thanking them for their time and acting on their comments when you return to work. Chapter 4 looks in depth at listening skills and dealing with complaints.

If the reason your customers have left is external, for instance they have lost their jobs or are feeling less affluent as result of the global recession, it is important that you understand the resulting changes that are taking place in the retail environment, in order that you can react to them.

A recent survey shows that shoppers are making fewer shopping trips, travelling beyond local shops to larger shopping centres or out-of-town retail parks but spending more per trip than before. Where road access is improved, and increased parking (especially free parking) or improved public transport is available, shopper numbers will increase.

The survey also showed a large increase in the number of shoppers who will do their comparison shopping online but prefer to make their purchases in 'real' shops where they can feel and touch the goods, and perhaps (for clothes and shoes) try them on. The experience of online shopping with its wait for delivery and need to return goods that don't fit or don't work is driving customers back to shops, as long as the in-store experience and the level of customer service is positive.

The challenge is to ensure that these shoppers are able to find your offer online and that your offer is more attractive than your competitors'. Make sure you have a presence on social networking sites and that you update it regularly, for example with special offers. Ensure that the offers you are showing in-store and in your shop windows are the same as those shown online.

When faced with major external changes that you are unable to influence, the critical thing is to be flexible to deal with them. If, for instance, your business is dependent on a group of customers whose employers then go out of business, you need to make every effort to retain their custom or attract new customers. However, your only way of surviving may be to reduce your own costs to reflect the reduced sales you will be able to make and ride out the recession. As long as you can stay in business, you will be in a position to take advantage of the upturn when it comes.

↳ OVER
→ TO YOU

What does it cost you to lose customers? Look at your records and list how many of your customers have not dealt with you for a significant period of time. If you know the average value of your customers' annual spend you will be able to see what this is costing you in lost income. Twenty lost customers with a £500 average annual spend adds up to £10,000 lost per year.

'People buy people', so in response to your customer satisfaction surveys discuss with your team how you can do more for your customers: how you can go the extra mile, how you can surprise them by being better than they thought you could be. This is covered in greater detail in Chapter 4, but start giving it some thought now and think like the customer. For example, if a customer were leaving your premises and had just turned to say something to you before leaving, would he find you waving him off with a smile, would he find you laughing and joking with a fellow team member or would you already be dealing with your next customer? A lot is written about the need to make a good first impression, but there is an equal need to make a good final impression. Final impressions are about more than just leaving. If the customer is in his car and the carrier bag you have provided breaks, spilling goods and making a mess, his frustration will be directed towards you and your business. Remember, everything about your business that customers come into contact with needs to meet their expectations, or preferably exceed them.

YOUR SUPPLIERS

Suppliers include anyone who provides you with goods or services that you use to carry out your business. You may not realise it, but suppliers hold considerable power over your business. Think about the effect there would be on your customers and business if your main supplier suddenly stopped supplying you for eight weeks because of a problem outside your, or their, control.

Do you have all your eggs in one supplier basket? You need to evaluate each supplier in terms of the value for money that they offer you, the power they hold over you and therefore the risk you take in dealing with them. Use the charts below to present and analyse this information.

Make a list of everyone who supplies you (with products, consumables, stationery, health and safety items, and so on) and then rate them in terms of price and quality by placing them in the relevant boxes in the form below. This will allow you to see where you are getting the best value for money. Then rate each of them again in terms of the power they have over your business (and therefore the risk they represent) using the chart on page 56.

SUPPLIER VALUE FOR MONEY

	PRICE		
LOW	The ideal! Great quality but at a low price	Medium quality but cheap	Cheap rubbish
MEDIUM	High quality but with a high price bracket	Medium quality but at a high price	Poor quality at a relatively high price
HIGH	Still high quality but at a high cost	Medium quality but at a high price	Poor quality at a very high price
	HIGH	**MEDIUM**	**LOW**	*QUALITY*
TOTALS	SUPPLIER 1 _____	SUPPLIER 2 _____	SUPPLIER 3 _____	

For example, a genuine designer handbag purchased from the designer would be in the 'Still high quality but at a high cost' box, while a high street copy purchased direct from the manufacturer in the Far East would be in the 'Cheap rubbish' box.

	High power	Medium power	Low power	
	X			**High risk**
		X		**Medium risk**
			X	**Low risk**

Supplier power/risk chart

Look at the chart above:

- High power/high risk suppliers – These provide something essential to your business that you can't get elsewhere.
- Medium power/medium risk suppliers – These provide something important to your business; you could get it elsewhere, though it may be more expensive.
- Low power/low risk suppliers – These provide something you don't really need and can get elsewhere easily and at low cost.

For example, Bang and Olufsen will supply only retailers of their choice, so your business would be at risk if they chose to stop supplying you.

Having analysed your suppliers in this way, you will be able to see which are bad value for money and quality and those that represent a high risk. You will need to look urgently at alternative suppliers for those highlighted – but what do you do if a supplier is good value for money and quality and this is why it holds a lot of power over you? Often in business you will have to weigh up the pros and cons of any situation before you make a decision. Isn't great service at a great price what you are trying to provide to your customers? The supplier is doing nothing wrong or hurtful to your business, but nevertheless you will need to do your homework. You should create a contingency plan that lists other suppliers of similar quality, pricing structure, delivery times, payment terms and so on, and be prepared to swap to them if you need to. However, do remember that suppliers need you as much as you need them – as long as the relationship is mutually beneficial, the risk is minimised.

OVER TO YOU

Rate your current suppliers using the value for money and risk matrices. Are you getting what you need from your current set of suppliers?

MAKING AND MAINTAINING GOOD RELATIONSHIPS

When you have evaluated your suppliers you will appreciate the vital role they play in your business. This is not one-sided: you are their customer and they need you too, just as you need your customers. The relationship between you should be like any good relationship – win:win. They provide you with the goods and support you need to carry out your business and you give them income, feedback and recommendations. Each party is dependent on the other and shares the same goal – for you both to be more successful.

Finding good suppliers

Your first port of call should be friends and business contacts who, unless they are in direct competition with you, will be happy to tell you their experience with suppliers – good or bad. If you are a member of organisations such as the local Chamber of Commerce, Business Link, or have access to a local Enterprise Agency, they may be able to give you advice. Advisors will often have been in your position themselves, so will know the sort of help you need.

If you are looking for new stock or new products or services to sell, exhibitions or trade fairs are a good source of information and contacts. In Chapter 3 there is information on networking – the ways in which you can meet potential customers and suppliers and people who can recommend you and your business. Directories such as the *Yellow Pages* or *Thomson Local* list potential suppliers, and trade magazines will carry advertisements for suppliers. Trade magazines will be available from your local library.

Some retailers may find cash-and-carry depots or wholesale warehouses a good source of stock at reasonable prices. The advantage of cash-and-carry is that you only buy what you need; there is no minimum order level. The disadvantages are that you have to collect the stock and pay for it on collection; there is normally no credit period.

Information on providers of utilities such as electricity, gas, telephone and broadband, as well as business insurance, can be found on comparison websites. These enable you to compare prices from large numbers of suppliers by entering your requirements just once.

Comparison websites include:
- www.moneysupermarket.com
- www.comparethemarket.com
- www.uswitch.com
- www.confused.com
- www.gocompare.com.

Making the relationship work for you

Don't rush in when choosing suppliers; be very clear about what you want from each potential supplier and, based on that, create a set of criteria against which you will measure them. Don't make decisions based on the fact that you like the salesman or that the company had an impressive stand at a trade show; look at price, delivery time and cost, minimum order size, payment terms, technical support, guarantees, stock availability, opening times, training, whether there are dedicated representatives and so on.

When you have a shortlist of suppliers, ask yourself more emotionally based questions such as 'Can I work with them?' or 'Do they understand my business?' Don't be afraid to ask for references, but only contact those who are not your direct competitors otherwise you may not get truthful answers.

Communication is the single biggest issue in any relationship, and your relationship with suppliers is no exception. Make sure you follow up phone or face-to-face conversations with written confirmation to ensure that you both have the same understanding of any issue. This also gives a point of reference should there be any concerns in the future or if you have to deal with a different contact. The more you can tell a supplier about what you want from them, the more likely you are to receive it: don't presume they'll just know!

Just as you evaluate your customers, you need to evaluate your suppliers, too: how well are they meeting your needs? It may be that you need to change suppliers as your business changes. The supplier that was fine when you started out may not be able to give you the volumes you need once you've grown, or the pricing structure you require to grow your profit margins, or may not have the speed of delivery you need.

Each supplier should be evaluated on an ongoing basis against your needs:

- How often did they deliver on time?
- How often were there any shortfalls and were you informed beforehand?
- Was there always someone on the end of the phone you could speak to?
- Is their ordering service better, worse or the same as when you started using them?

- Are they available for technical help and support and, if so, can they always answer your queries?
- Does their rep contact you enough on the phone or in person?
- Have they been competing with you by selling direct through websites or shopping channels?
- Does the training they offer meet your needs?
- Do they support you with point-of-sale or promotional items?
- Do they drive customers to you through consumer promotional activities?

For certain suppliers, you may want to consider having an exclusivity clause, whereby they don't supply other stores within a certain radius. Negotiations and contracting with suppliers is covered in more detail in Chapter 8, which looks at the topic of purchasing.

YOUR COMPETITORS

All businesses have competitors – it's up to you to recognise yours and monitor them, analyse their activities and take action to reduce any risk they represent. In retail there is usually a lot of competition. You need to look at what makes your offering special and different, and therefore what your means of competitive advantage is.

IDENTIFYING YOUR COMPETITORS

It's important to realise that competition comes from many areas. As with so many other aspects of business, the more you know, the more able you are to reduce any risk competitors may pose. You need to know almost as much about a competitor's business as your own – that way you can plan for how you can effectively compete.

Listed below are the types of competition you will come across. You need to think how you will uncover and then deal with the threats they present, and so reduce their risk. Not all your competitors will have exactly the same type of offering as you, so the first thing you need to work out is what type of competitor they are. Broadly speaking, there are five types of competition.

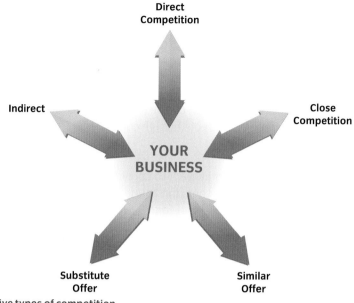

Direct
Competition

Indirect

Close
Competition

YOUR
BUSINESS

Substitute
Offer

Similar
Offer

Five types of competition

Direct competition

In most businesses, how you compete with your direct competitors
is the main issue. It is when the offer provided by directly competing
businesses is so similar that it's difficult for customers to see any
appreciable difference. You could liken this to Pepsi and Coke: both
companies will say they are different but essentially they are seen as
providing the same type of product.

As already mentioned, it's important to have a competitive advantage
and that your customers recognise this as a means of differentiation.
Just as you complete a SWOT analysis on your business (as discussed
in Chapter 1), you should carry out a thorough and ongoing SWOT
of your main competitors. Otherwise you won't know what they
offer, what they are up to or how they have changed, and therefore
you won't know if you have maintained or lost your competitive
advantage.

 **OVER
TO YOU**

Choose three of your direct competitors and list the main points of
difference between them and your business, then alongside each
point write down how you can compete.

Close competition

This is where the offerings are similar but are not seen as the same by a customer. For example, Rolls-Royce and Bentley may be direct competitors, but Rolls-Royce and Mini are not, although both are brands of car that provide transport from A to B.

In a customer's eyes, Marks and Spencer and Primark may be close, but not direct, competition – the offering could be argued to be the same but it's the quality and price that are different.

OVER TO YOU

Choose three of your close competitors and list the main points of difference between the competitors' businesses and your business, then alongside each point write down how you can compete.

Similar offer

This will be dependent on how you have chosen to market your offer, such as a product or piece of equipment.

Two retailers selling products for which the price and the quality are fixed, such as newspapers and magazines, can only compete on the level of customer service or the range of other products available.

OVER TO YOU

List three competitors that offer similar products or equipment to your business. List the main points of difference between you, then alongside each point write down how you can compete.

Substitute offer

Competition may come from alternative sources, such as websites or stores selling 'professional' products or equipment. With these competitors, customers are led to believe that they can achieve similar results as the professionals by using equipment they buy or hire for themselves.

OVER TO YOU

List three competitors that offer substitute products or equipment. List the main points of difference between them and your business, then alongside each point write down how you can compete.

Indirect competition

This is competition from any source that places a demand on your customers' money. It could include household bills, school uniforms, a summer holiday, Christmas presents, car expenses, clothes, shoes and so on. In other words, anything else that a customer could or should be spending their money on. This is where marketing your offering as a luxury can backfire; other purchases may be seen as more important or essential by your customers.

OVER TO YOU

List 10 things customers need to spend their money on before they can spend it with your business. Think of the essentials you need to spend your own money on – household bills, food, clothes and so on.

HOW CAN YOU COMPETE?

There are three basic ways of competing: price, differentiation and niche (or focus).

Price

If you compete on price you may be charging for your offering at the cheaper end of the spectrum. This can be a risky strategy – you must be sure you'll be able to keep your costs down to still be able to make a profit. Unfortunately, what can sometimes happen is that businesses buy cheaper goods that are not as good quality, and customers become unhappy with their product or service and go elsewhere.

You also run the risk of creating a disloyal customer base – one that stays only as long as your price is cheapest and soon leaves when there is a special promotion elsewhere, leaving you with a lot of unsold stock (which you had to buy to get the low price).

The benefit of competing on price is that you are likely to have lots of customers – but it is up to you to keep them with new services and products. The expression 'pile it high, sell it cheap' applies to this strategy.

It can work: Lidl and Aldi compete on price and have a well-established business model delivering cheaper food and other products in cheaper-to-run buildings with cheaper shelving and display units. They have a loyal customer base – Lidl's tagline is 'Where quality is cheaper'. In tough economic times they may find they gain customers defecting from other supermarkets… but when times are good again those 'temporary' customers might remain.

Differentiation

With this strategy, you compete by being different from other businesses with a similar offering. You aim to be unique in a way that your customers recognise as important to them. Because of this you can charge – and they will pay – a premium price. This strategy requires investment in understanding customer needs and delivering on them. Differentiation is often based around quality – quality of service, quality of product, quality of surroundings (think classy restaurant vs high street burger chain). Quality costs, though, so you must be as certain as possible that you are providing what customers want and that there are enough of those customers to make it pay.

Using supermarkets again to illustrate the point, this strategy would be represented by Waitrose and Marks & Spencer. They don't have the range or the lower prices that Tesco, Sainsbury's, Asda and Morrisons (known as the 'big four') offer, but they compete on great service and excellent quality.

Niche or focus

This strategy involves having a very narrow field, so there are fewer competitors but also fewer customers. In the world of food, a niche (or focus) business would be a delicatessen; in the field of clothes shops it would be a school uniform outfitter or dance clothes supplier. This approach is the ultimate in segmentation and can be based on cost leadership or differentiation.

Whichever strategy you choose, you also need to decide if you are aiming to be a market leader, a challenger, a follower or a **nicher**.

Market leader

Being recognised as a market leader often means being an early adopter – being the first with new technology, products or services. This is an expensive option; normally new things are expensive, as suppliers charge a lot when launching a product so they recoup their costs as quickly as possible. However, being first will give you a great competitive advantage – you will be the only one offering the new thing so customers will have to come to you. You'll need to build on this; don't just sit back and let your competitors catch you up, particularly those in a position to challenge you. These competitors will watch every move you make. Cite customer recommendations in the trade and consumer press, on your website, in your blog, in your tweets, in chatrooms; in fact, in any media you can think of to spread the word that what you have is great and that you are the only one offering it.

? JARGON BUSTER

Niche/Nicher: a narrow focus of offering delivered to a narrow focus of customer. In America they say 'nitch'/'nitcher'.

Challenger

The challenger competitor watches the leader very carefully because they want that top spot. The challenger and market leader often swap places as they are very similar in offering and delivery, and both watch their markets and act on innovations, products, services and so on. One business may be the first to come out with something new but the other will be the first next time: think Microsoft and Apple. Leaders and challengers are seen as being at the top end of the market and customers often pay a premium to be the first to have something from them.

Follower

This competitor sits back and watches the top two fighting it out for market share, both spending money on new technology as they both want to be the first to offer anything new or different, both competing on promotions, team training, recruitment and the like. Followers are seen as being 'middle of the road' by customers who only want to pay average prices.

The follower adopts the follow-everyone-else, or me-too, strategy; it allows the top two businesses to fight for customers and develop new areas of customer interest. When the market has grown, it will jump in with a similar (me-too) product, equipment or service provided by a cheaper supplier who has copied the original idea, and attract all the potential customers who couldn't afford the original, and possibly some of the leader's and challenger's customers who want to try the cheaper offer. The follower piggybacks on the leader's and challenger's promotional activities to grow a market. This can be a very successful strategy as there is reduced risk and reduced cost.

Nicher

Arguably, this business isn't really a competitor, but it could be if its narrow field of operation were to cross over with something that your business does.

MAKING YOUR BUSINESS STAND OUT

Differentiation or competitive advantage must be viewed through the eyes of your customers – if they can't see the difference between you and your competitors then the difference doesn't exist. The starting point for recognising and then building on your means of differentiation is knowing what your competitors offer; if you don't know that then you can't compete with them. You need to measure or compare what you offer against their offering.

The starting point for understanding differentiation is to come up with a list of criteria against which you can measure your business's competitors and yourself. Judging the 'look' of another business, or what you have heard through the grapevine, isn't enough. Being good at business means many things in addition to being good at your trade. One of them is being good at finding out things about your competitors. There are many ways of doing this, but sending in mystery shoppers (see page 26) is the most popular method. Mystery shoppers need to have a list of issues to look for; the same list should be used for all the competitors they visit. It's also best to use just one mystery shopper, as you then remove the element of personal differences from the data obtained. The mystery shopper should be given a sheet like the one below to complete after each visit.

COMPETITORS' ABILITY TO MEET CUSTOMER SERVICE NEEDS				
SERVICE OFFERED	COMPETITOR 1	COMPETITOR 2	COMPETITOR 3	YOUR STORE
1. Range of products				
2. Quality of products				
3. Customer service				
4. Overall ambiance				
5. Welcome				
6. Knowledge levels of staff				
7. Disabled access and facilities				
8. Parking access				
9. Value for money				
10. Value for money				
TOTAL	/	/	/	/

This specific type of research should be carried out on your direct competitors at least once a year, or four times a year if your business has a seasonal element. If a new competitor comes into your market, they should be visited when they open and again after the opening offers have finished and the team has settled in.

OVER TO YOU

Carry out research on your top three competitors: list what you believe their strengths and weaknesses are and compare them to your own. Then complete the competitor SWOT analysis chart (see page 66) for each one – list where there are opportunities for your business and where there are threats.

COMPETITOR SWOT ANALYSIS

COMPETITOR NAME:_____

COMPETITOR STRENGTHS	COMPETITOR WEAKNESSES	OPPORTUNITIES FOR YOU	THREATS TO YOU

Store all your competitor research data in a file – mystery shopper reviews, competitor advertisements, flyers, price lists, vouchers and so on. Make sure it's easily accessible so it can be reviewed and added to. Keeping the main pieces of information about a competitor on one profile sheet is useful so it can be easily seen and acted upon.

COMPETITOR PROFILE

COMPETITOR: _____

COMPETITOR INFORMATION:	Address: Alderney Gifts
	        2 High St, Castletown,
	        Localshire, CT1 4NL
	Owner: Margaret Guide
	Senior sales x 1

	Sales assistants x 4 Tel No: 01234 456789 Delivery driver x 1 Email: info@themaincompetitor.org.net Storeman x 2 Website: www.themaincompetitor .org.net
PRODUCT RANGE	Jewellery Kitchenalia Cards Candles Puzzles Books Games Gadgets
FACTS	Number of team members: 8

	Opening hours: Mon–Wed 9.30–7.00,
	                Thurs–Fri 9.30–10.00,
	                Sat 8.30–6.30, Sun 10.30–5.00

LOCAL PERCEIVED REPUTATION	Limited range, relatively expensive, cluttered, untidy, no cohesive layout.
THREE THINGS YOU LIKE ABOUT THEIR BUSINESS (AND WOULD LIKE TO OFFER YOURSELF):	High margins Sunday opening Welcoming staff
THREE THINGS YOU DON'T LIKE ABOUT THEIR BUSINESS (AND YOU COULD DO BETTER):	Limited range Poor use of retail space Website difficult to navigate

When you have learnt about your competitors you need to turn the information into something tangible to compete with. Once you've identified what you think your key points of differentiation are, and your strengths in comparison to your competitors, you need to use the segmentation information gathered earlier to communicate the advantages to your customer base. Put simply, your aim is to identify how you provide a better service, and then make sure that your customers know all about it.

 KEY TO SUCCESS

Knowledge is key, but action must follow – if you don't act, it's a waste of time.

Caroline James runs a small ladies' fashion shop in a high street in a market town. Her competition has traditionally been the national department stores and chain stores that sell their stock at higher prices than Caroline.

A national chain which sells ladies' fashion at lower prices, which will compete directly with Caroline's business, is to open nearby. Caroline realises that she will need to take some action to prevent the new competition from taking her business and decides to take a two-pronged approach. She will look to source new suppliers for her existing range at more competitive prices and to extend her range into men's and children's clothing so that she can increase her customer base and, hopefully, increase the average spend as her existing customers buy the new products as well as their usual purchases.

Caroline carries out research into potential suppliers and identifies the following:
- Wholesalers will offer 'ends of ranges' at greatly reduced prices. These are the units left over after the major retailers have bought their stock.
- Manufacturers will have 'overmakes', which are the units produced in excess of those ordered on a contract to make use of the materials available. They will also have 'seconds', which are units with minor faults that fail the quality control processes of the original retailer. For instance, if a button is missing from a blouse, the chain store retailer will reject the blouse; Caroline may be willing to buy the blouse at a greatly reduced price.
- Surplus stock buyers or 'jobbers' buy bankrupt stock, customer returns, ex-catalogue stock and ends of ranges from retailers.
- Disposal auctions, where surplus and bankrupt stock is sold to the highest bidder. These may be online or held in auction rooms.

She decides to continue buying from her regular supplier to ensure continuity of stock and to make contact with the sources she has identified so that they will alert her to opportunities that she may be interested in.

Alexander Styles intends to open an independent shoe shop in Grantchester. He is undecided on the best location and whether to aim for the high-end customers or a more mass-market, low-price operation. He decides to search the internet for potential competitors in the area and finds that there are seven shoe shops in and around the town centre.

Of these, one is advertising 'fine footwear', three are offering high street brands and three are offering budget lines. Alexander visits each of the seven shops as a potential customer to find out what their standards of customer service are, the type of retail experience they are offering, the payment methods they accept, the associated products they offer and how they sit in their surroundings.

He finds that the shop selling 'fine footwear' is located slightly out of the town centre to the west while the other stores are all in the town centre itself. He considers that the customer service in all the shops is only average at best. He also finds that the more expensive shoes on sale in the 'fine footwear' shop are not of a particularly high quality, not offered in a sufficiently wide range of sizes to meet the needs of the potential customers, and that the layout and merchandising of the store is tired and out of date.

Alexander decides that his shoe shop should:
- be located to the east of the town centre
- offer high-price but high-quality products
- offer a wide range of sizes
- employ more, better paid and better trained staff to ensure the best possible level of customer service
- use display and shop fittings of a West End standard
- be called 'Style Footwear of Grantchester'.

Alexander's mission statement is 'To offer quality shoes with quality service'.

WHERE TO GO FOR MORE INFORMATION

The following sources will be helpful in keeping you up to date with what's happening in your sector – suppliers, competitors, industry trends, benchmarking reports and other information specific to your sector, such as skill gaps and recruitment issues:

- Sector Skills Councils/standard-setting bodies:
  - Skillsmart Retail, www.skillsmartretail.com.
- Trade magazines:
  - *Retail Week*
  - *The Grocer*
  - *The Retailer*
  - *Retail Technology*
  - *Drapers*
- Trade associations:
  - *British Retail Consortium*
  - *Association of Retail Trade*
  - *National Retail Federation*
  - *Retra (Radio, Electrical and Television Retailers' Association)*
- Market research companies:
  - Mintel, a market research agency offering primary data and reports to help identify market opportunities, trend analysis and market size: www.mintel.com
  - MORI, a market research and opinion polling company: www.ipsos-mori.com
  - A range of market research companies can be found at: www.approvedmarketresearchcompanies.co.uk.

CONCLUSION

In conjunction with what you've learnt from Chapter 1, you can now recognise the key people relevant to your business, and see the areas where they could have a negative impact. You can also measure the level of risk your suppliers and competitors represent. In addition, you should now recognise how valuable a customer you are to your suppliers – you need to build on that when negotiating with them for goods, as they don't want you to go elsewhere. You will have a clearer picture of who your customers are, the various ways you can keep them, and how you can segment them to make your communications and offering more targeted. You may also realise that some of your segments aren't profitable. If so, you have some decisions to make – do you keep those customers or not? If the answer's yes, there needs to be a sound reason for doing so – perhaps you get lots of new customers through their recommendations? You should also understand the concept of gap analysis and how you can measure what you think is happening against what actually is happening. This is a useful technique to use across your business – assume nothing and prove everything.

CHAPTER 3
MARKETING AND SALES

INTRODUCTION

The previous chapter has explained how the knowledge gained about your customers and competitors from market research is crucial to the success of your retail business. However, you need to do something with that knowledge, in relation to the way you promote your business, for it to result in actual sales. Income from sales is vital to your business and its ultimate success.

This chapter looks at the key issue of how you can translate marketing activities and other forms of customer communication into measurable sales. It delves into how to choose the most effective marketing communication activities and how to analyse the success of your chosen strategy. It also explores what you need to do to create a sales plan that will help you achieve the sales you need, and how you can ensure that your marketing and promotional activities not only support this plan, but that their costs are realistically reflected in it.

MARKETING COMMUNICATIONS

Marketing is defined by the Chartered Institute of Marketing as 'the management process responsible for identifying, anticipating and satisfying customer requirements profitably'. It is a vast area, which covers any part of your business that impacts on your existing or potential customers. Areas that you have already looked at in Chapters 1 and 2, such as PEST analysis, customer satisfaction and so on, are part of marketing. Then there is what's called the marketing mix (covered in detail later in this chapter), which outlines the key tools and methods that should be combined when planning how best to promote and market your products and services.

The term 'marketing communications' (MarComs) includes any means used to communicate with existing or potential customers. The aim is to do one or more of the following three things:

- To **inform** – This is where you aim to give information: what a new offering is, what the benefits are, how much it costs, when it will be available and so on.
- To **persuade** – This is where you aim to create a positive impression and perhaps change perceptions, dispelling any negative views or opinions about you, your offering or your business. You may also take the opportunity to be negative about the competition and provide a fertile base for a positive change of behaviour in your target audience in the future.
- To **reinforce** – This is where you aim to convince existing customers that they have made the right choice in coming to you, to extend customer loyalty, secure future sales and encourage customers to act as advocates (ie likely to actively recommend you to their network of friends and acquaintances).

Refer back to the work you did in Chapters 1 and 2 on identifying your means of differentiation and the areas in which you stand out from the competition. In MarComs terms, these are the things you need to turn into key messages – the views of your business that you want to promote. It's important that your staff understand what the key messages are, what they will achieve for the business and the role they themselves play in communicating them. You need to ensure that you communicate these key messages to your team as well as to customers, so that any MarComs deliver a uniform message.

The tone and methods you use when communicating your MarComs messages to customers may be personal or non-personal:

- personal MarComs occur when you are in face-to-face contact with your customers
- non-personal MarComs occur when you are not in face-to-face contact with your customers, for example on your website.

The method you choose depends on what you want to achieve. The non-personal approach is more suitable for general marketing where you want to reach a lot of people and the personal touch is not required. You may use it to raise awareness in the local media of a new business, moving premises, a charity open day or to promote a new offering that is relevant to lots of different types of customers. The personal approach is better for targeted messages to smaller numbers of people; it is ideal for a specific marketing message that is relevant to fewer customers and perhaps needs an element of explanation or demonstration. Whichever you choose, the important thing is that you are clear and consistent about the key message(s) you want to get across. Remember the three aims – to inform, to persuade, to reinforce – and use them to focus your message.

THE MARKETING MIX

The marketing mix is made up of a series of components deemed essential to a comprehensive marketing campaign. Each of the seven areas has its own mini-plan, yet all are interrelated and together achieve the main objective.

The seven Ps of the marketing mix are:

- **Price** – This is the amount of money your customer gives you in return for your offering. But pricing is so much more than that. Price is seen by consumers as an indicator of how you compete: in their eyes, low price = low quality; high price = high quality. The price you choose to charge is communicating a message about you, your business, the type of customer you have or want and the likely levels of customer service they will receive, as well as the quality of the offering itself. The key is to be seen as value for money by the customers you want. Some people would argue that expensive is good value if the quality of the item or service justifies it. It is important to be competitive in your pricing and have a clear place in the market alongside your competitors. You need to ensure that, whether you set your prices slightly above or below theirs, the correct balance of quality and value for money is maintained.
- **Product** – This is your offering. The term 'product' came from when marketing was used mainly in FMCG (Fast Moving Consumer Goods), and referred to an item that moved quickly off the shelves, such as bread, alcohol or cigarettes. It has now come to mean anything sold to a customer. The whole of your business is built around the strength of your offering, so it is absolutely key that you get this right. Think: what does each of your offerings say about you, the types of customer you serve and how you compete (are you a market leader, challenger, follower or nicher, as described in Chapter 2)?

- **Place** – This is where a customer can buy your offering. This may not be a tangible place that customers physically visit (like a shop) but could be a dedicated sales phone line or a website. The place also communicates a message about your business: what is yours saying about your likely competitive advantage, levels of service and customer base?
- **Promotion** – This really means any communication you have with a potential or existing customer to promote you, your business or your offering. But what do you want to communicate? That you have just opened, or are about to move, that you have a new product or service, your special deals, or that you are holding a charity event and want everyone to come? All communications are an opportunity to promote your business, and how you conduct them will also communicate a message. What do your promotional messages and events say about your business?
- **People** – This relates to anyone acting on behalf of or representing your business: face-to-face, on the phone or by any other means in a transaction with a customer. It applies to you and members of your team. How they speak, act, dress and deal with customers all communicate who you are as a business and where you are positioned in the marketplace. It also indicates quality, reliability and likely value for money. What messages are you and your team members projecting about your business?
- **Physical evidence** – This is anything that the customer comes into contact with and bases their opinion of your business or offering upon: anything that they can touch, see, smell or hear. For example, if an accountant gave you a business card that felt thin, was a bit creased and crumpled and had a coffee stain on it, you would assume their business wasn't too good. That is physical evidence. What are your price lists, business cards, company name, the age and state of your work car or van, sales area, toilets, dress code, promotional literature and so on saying to customers about you and your business?
- **Process** – This is anything your customers go through in their dealings with you, from the very first moment to the very last. For instance, what is the process for obtaining a refund? Methods of payment? Deposits? Are children welcome? How important are customers in your processes – are they at the centre of all that you do or an afterthought? If your answerphone message says you'll call them back within 30 minutes, do you? Are your opening hours suitable for them or you?

Jay Woodworth (known as Woody) has a large collection of vinyl records and spends a lot of his time surfing the net looking for rare items to add to his collection. He has a full-time job as a civil servant which he finds boring. He is thinking of giving up his job and starting a small business buying and selling records. He has seen a small shop situated in a side street off the main shopping street and has enquired about the rent, rates etc.

Woody feels comfortable operating online and decides that he will design a website, offering vinyl records for sale. He is undecided whether to also open the shop or to operate the website from home.

He decides to put together a list of the pros and cons of opening the shop or operating from home.

Shop		Home	
Pros:	Storage space	Pros:	No rent or rates
	Passing trade		Security of stock
	Customers able to see and feel the stock		Flexible hours
Cons:	Cost of rent, rates, light and heat	Cons:	Lack of space
	Fixed opening hours		Lack of passing trade
	Need for staff to cover holidays, sickness etc		Delivery and payment issues

Woody comes to the conclusion that he should open the shop and also operate the website from the shop. This will enable him to have a worldwide presence via the website while having personal contact with customers in the shop. He feels he will be able to discuss with the customers what they are looking for and be able to provide a personalised service, sourcing rare records. This will give him a reputation within the vinyl collecting community which will bring in further trade to both the shop and the website.

Marketing objectives

Nothing should be done in terms of marketing your business through the seven Ps without objectives being set; without a goal or a target you can't evaluate the success of a strategy. Just because something seems like a good idea is not a good enough reason to do it. Objectives are normally based on facts and figures – the number of website hits, customer spend per transaction, number of transactions per timescale, number of new customers per timescale, percentage of offering sold to number of targeted customers, number of new customers who bought goods and so on. Analysis of outcomes

SMART objectives
are those that are:
Specific, **M**easureable,
Achievable, **R**elevant
and within a set
Timescale.

against objectives is straightforward if the objectives set were
SMART – this gives you a framework on which to hang the objective
so it can be measured. It makes you really think when setting
objectives in the first place and is a good discipline to get into.

Sales objectives will be covered towards the end of this chapter, but
are predominantly based on required sales figures.

The key measurements for analysis of outcomes are cost per response
(what it cost you to get that potential customer) and percentage
response (out of 100 potential customers, how many ordered or
booked with you?). Asking the question 'How did you hear about us?'
or 'How did you find us?' is important, as the feedback will indicate
which of your MarComs is the most effective.

SETTING MARKETING BUDGETS

Another name for budget is financial plan: you need to have the
money planned for and in place for all the activities you intend to carry
out. The importance of setting aside a realistic amount of money
for the implementation of any plan cannot be overestimated. Lack
of finance for implementation of a marketing plan is one of the main
reasons new businesses go bust; they simply fail to recognise the
value of marketing activity and don't invest enough in it. No budget =
no business. It's not difficult to estimate what monies are required
if you cost all your plans correctly and everything goes well. What is
difficult is foreseeing changes in market conditions (another reason for
comprehensive PEST analysis; see Chapter 1), or disasters happening
outside your control (such as storeroom flooding). Set aside a
contingency amount for unforeseen circumstances – but remember
that this is not a pot of money for you to dip into just because you have
not planned your budget adequately.

Your marketing budget will be set, along with the money to implement
all other plans, in your main business plan (see page 39). Once it's
set you need to stick to it, otherwise your main business plan will be
incorrect. You can see therefore how important it is to have a clear
understanding of what you want to achieve and what it'll cost before
you can put together the business plan. An existing business may
draw up the main business plan based on sales forecasts and allocate
the money available from the profits across all areas, and you'll have to
work within those parameters.

Part of your planning process will be to investigate the different
methods you can use to communicate your messages, and where the
resources for this are to be found – do you get an external agency in to
carry out your marketing activities, which may cost more but will free
up your time and be less stressful, or do it in-house and keep down
costs (accepting that your time is, of course, a cost)?

TYPES OF MARCOMS

There are many different types of MarComs. Some are paid for, such as advertising, printed literature or events; some are lower cost or free such as press releases, e-marketing (website offers, email and SMS campaigns) and viral marketing. Which ones you choose will depend on a number of factors – most importantly, the budget you have available and the demographics of your potential customer base. Look back to the work you did in Chapters 1 and 2 on profiling and segmentation, and think about which MarComs are likely to be the most effective for each of your different market segments. For tech-savvy 20–40-year-olds, communication through social networking may be most effective, while an advert in your local magazine might reach an older, retired audience.

OVER TO YOU

Identify your two or three key segments and think about which channels of MarComs would work best for them.

Choosing which MarComs are most appropriate for your business is likely to be a time-consuming and thought-provoking process. Key points to consider are:

- What is your budget?
- What do you want to say?
- When do you want to say it?
- Who do you want to say it to?
- Where are they?
- When can they see/hear it?
- What action do you want from them?
- What do you want to achieve/what is your objective?

It is unlikely that there will many choices available to you once you have answered the above questions – in particular in the light of the answer to the first one.

CASE STUDY 2

You have allocated a reasonable amount of money to run a campaign to promote the new, increased evening opening hours of your business. The new opening hours come into force in two months' time, so you want to time your communication for the week before. You want to get this message out to all the young professionals who live within a five-mile radius of your premises, as

Continued

your market research questionnaires indicate that most of your customers are not prepared to travel further than five miles for your type of offering. As your target audience are likely to work during the daytime, you want your campaign to reach them in their leisure hours, as this is when they are more likely to use your services. Therefore, you would like them to read the message at home. You want to include a specific call to action with the information about the opening hours: a cut-off voucher that they can present at your business for a discounted product (valid for a limited period of time). This will encourage new customers to try out your business and reward existing customers. Your aim is an increase in sales of 20 per cent as a result of this campaign and the longer opening hours – and you want to be able to measure how much of the success is down to your campaign.

You decide that a direct mail activity is most likely to succeed in targeting your main audience: a flyer advertising the new opening hours, with a discount voucher at the bottom. The cost is determined by the leaflet's design and print costs plus delivery mechanism. You know that Royal Mail will deliver to all houses within your specified postcode areas for a reasonable cost; however, to specify which particular addresses you want to deliver to (those containing young professional households), you will have to pay extra to purchase a list of addresses from a list owner or broker. You need to weigh these costs carefully against the expected uplift in sales that the direct mail would generate.

A joint MarComs activity with a non-competing company that shares a target audience could be a way of keeping costs down. Once you have answered the questions above, you should have a clear idea of who you want to reach and how, which will enable you to judge whether your marketing goals are sufficiently aligned with those of another company to make a joint campaign workable.

MarComs can be split into different areas, which are now considered in turn. It is worth remembering that some areas may overlap with or complement each other, so think about all the different outlets you could be using to get a marketing message across.

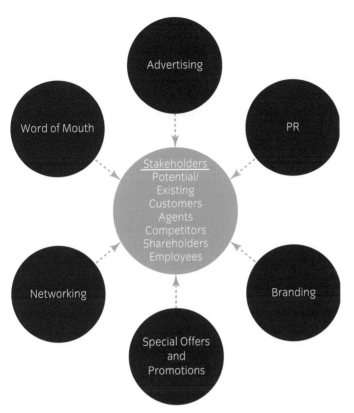

Areas of MarComs

ADVERTISING

Advertising is generally accepted to be any form of MarComs for which you pay to call the public's attention to your offering in a public, media-based forum. Historically this was mainly in newspapers and magazines, on radio and television, in cinemas and on billboards, but advertising is now also available through e-marketing – on websites with paid-for banner ads and links, and via email campaigns. Advertising delivered directly to your customers in a targeted way is often referred to as direct marketing. This could be direct mail – flyers or brochures sent out to customers' addresses – or electronic, such as SMS or email campaigns. Advertising can be an expensive option as there is also the cost of design and production, plus the possible cost of using companies that supply contact databases. Using a database company does save a lot of time, though, and they can sometimes also offer address lists in socio-demographic segments. This is more expensive but, as it will enable you to target your market more precisely, is arguably more cost-effective.

PUBLIC RELATIONS (PR)

PR means creating, maintaining or improving a favourable relationship between a business or person and the public. PR is used mainly to raise the profile of your business or you as an individual; it is not a directly sales-related activity. PR includes sending media releases to the trade and consumer press, as well as to other media, to get your message over, as well as writing blogs, dealing with social media and face-to-face occasions such as press launches, exhibitions and conferences.

You can also include PR on your business's own website (maybe under 'News' or 'Hot off the press'), on YouTube, on your Twitter, Facebook and LinkedIn pages, and in email and SMS alerts sent out to your customers in the guise of an update. The benefit of PR is that it generally doesn't cost anything to put into the public domain – but it does cost to write, design, proofread and upload the material, and if you use a PR agency that costs too. As with using any other kind of external agency, you have to weigh up costs against your time. There often isn't enough money in the budget for a PR agency but there may be some for a technically minded person to upload your words onto your website and e-marketing channels.

Different channels will deliver information in different ways and at different speeds. Only the briefest of information can be given in a 'tweet' on Twitter, but it is immediate and can be reinforced often and added to frequently. To get the same information out via traditional media would take days, or even weeks or months if you were to send it to a monthly or quarterly trade magazine. You can also send out an e-newsletter or e-media release to your customer database where you can say whatever you want and perhaps even include an offer or two. A quick SMS could encourage your customers to view your website for news: 'Something exciting on our website – visit www...'

You can use PR across a range of different media. For example, if you won a 'best local business award' you could:
- tweet that you have won an award
- add a photo with 200 or so words to your Facebook and LinkedIn profiles
- SMS customers with the weblink to your Facebook and LinkedIn profiles
- create a press release or e-newsletter and email it to all your customers
- upload a photo and write-up onto the front page of your website under 'News'
- email a press release to local consumer and trade journalists.

Don't forget traditional media – being able to communicate and build strong working relationships with journalists from your local and trade media will be very useful to your business. The local media (press, radio and TV) can give your business, its offering, its team and its customers coverage and exposure in your community. Media exposure will reinforce to existing customers that they are going to the right place and will encourage potential customers to consider coming to you – it may even motivate them enough to pick up the phone, visit your website or pop in. Exposure in trade media can give you credibility within your business area (for example, with suppliers); it could also annoy your competition, which you may or may not want to do. It is newsworthy to the trade press when you have success in your local area, and if you do well at a trade event such as British Retail Awards, local media will want to know and will often promote you and your business as local celebrities. Remember to adapt your message depending on whether you are contacting local or trade media.

Media releases

When writing a media release for press, radio or TV, there are a few golden rules to adhere to, but the main one is KISS – Keep It Short and Simple. Media releases are a way to communicate your message to an audience via a journalist. This means you are actually writing for two audiences: the journalist (who has to see the benefit to his audience), and the audience (the readers, listeners or viewers) themselves. There is no point writing a rambling exposé of why a particular offering is fantastic if the journalist will not even read it.

Part of a journalist's job is to give information of interest to the audience; if he is in charge of a specific area such as the local business pages, that will influence what he chooses to write about.

Always put yourself in the place of the person you are writing for and read your release as they will – remember that your own judgement is biased! When writing about things you are passionate about you may start rambling. It helps to first write your information in bullet point form. Don't look at it for a day, then revisit it and shorten it. Revisit and cut more the following day, or at the very least a few hours later, until you have the bare bones of what you need to say to your audience.

KEY TO SUCCESS

It is your responsibility to tell the media about any success – they are not mind-readers!

KEY TO SUCCESS

If you write about your business as a centre of local excellence, that you open until 10 pm every evening, that you have just won an award for 'Best customer care' in the region, that you have been in business for 10 years and are about to take on three new team members... that gives a journalist many angles to write about and is extremely interesting. But if you write that you have a new product that is great and that everyone can get 10 per cent off their first order, that isn't very newsworthy by comparison.

Having a set format to follow is extremely helpful as it helps you to structure your information into a form that journalists will be much more receptive to. The first thing is to get their attention through an attention-grabbing headline, often referred to as the 'hook'. It obviously has to have relevance to the story, and must be creative, but should also be very brief – preferably so it can fit on one line in the font you are using for the headline. The fewer words and more white space a headline has, the more likely people are to read it – they may have read it before they are even aware that they have done so.

After the hook comes the main message, or body, of the piece – this is where you get the information across. This might be one paragraph, or two or three, but it must be short, easily digestible and in a font size that makes for easy reading (no less than 14 pt; 16 pt is even better).

A picture paints a thousand words, so always use a photo or image to enhance the story. This must be of print quality – check what the requirements are prior to taking photos. If images don't look professional when reproduced this will have a negative impact on your communication, and journalists are unlikely to use poor-quality photos.

At the bottom of the release, state what you want the audience (the journalist) to do; in other words, what is the **call to action**? Do you want him to ring the business, visit your website, pop in or email you? Whatever you want him to do, ensure that all the information required is there and that any instructions are clear to everyone, not just to you!

Indicate where the release finishes so the journalist knows that any other information is for his information only, such as your contact details. Journalists are very busy but the promise of a good story can sometimes bring them out to see you – and the offer of a freebie or something special just for them can also help. If they do come to you, ensure you have prepared a factsheet to give them so they get all the information you want them to have even if they haven't asked for it.

Prepare a bulleted list of information that will become the basis for a consumer media release (you can use the example on page 98 to organise your information):

- List the points you feel should be included in your hook. Decide on the main thrust of the release and what needs to be in the headline.
- State the points you feel should be included in your main message. Stick to the basics at this point, nothing flowery.
- List the types of images that could portray your message. What are the choices of images that you could send that add value to the story? List and prioritise them.
- State the points you feel should be included in your call to action. What do you want the journalist to do after reading, hearing or seeing your information?
- Using your chosen points, summarise your hook in draft form. Be creative when summarising the main point or points.
- Using your chosen points, summarise your main message in draft form. Now is the time to think in sentences and put the bullet points together. Get rid of any points that mean the same thing – be brutal!
- Describe your chosen image. Ensure that the journalist knows what the image is, where it was taken, who is in it and their names in the correct order with the correct spellings. If you are sending the image by email, ensure you give the email a title relevant to the release. If posting, make sure your contact details and other information are firmly attached to the back of the photo.
- Using your chosen points, summarise your call to action in draft form. When you are clear what action you require, list the necessary information.
- Remember to indicate that the release has ended. State 'Release ends' at the end of the release in the centre of the page.
- Include your contact details for the journalist below 'Release ends'. Give your name, contact address, telephone number and email address, even if they are the same details as written in the 'call to action' or the main body of the release. The journalist can then find your details immediately without having to trawl through the text should he want to contact you about the release.

Now repeat the exercise with information relevant to your industry colleagues and peers – things that you could include in a trade media release – such as attending a trade show or event, meeting a well-known figure in your industry, attending a specific course or announcing you are taking on a new product or piece of equipment.

PRESS / MEDIA RELEASE

	POINTS THAT YOU WANT TO INCLUDE	COPY THAT YOU WANT TO INCLUDE
HOOK		
MAIN MESSAGE / MAIN BODY		
IMAGE		
CALL TO ACTION		
	RELEASE ENDS	YOUR CONTACT DETAILS FOR THE JOURNALIST

You can use a chart like this to help you prepare information to include in a press/media release

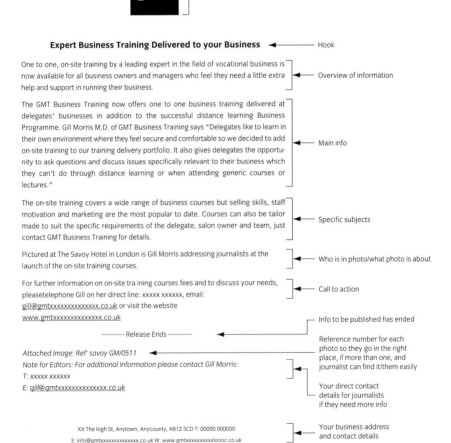

gmt ◄———— Branding

Expert Business Training Delivered to your Business ◄———— Hook

One to one, on-site training by a leading expert in the field of vocational business is now available for all business owners and managers who feel they need a little extra help and support in running their business. ◄———— Overview of information

The GMT Business Training now offers one to one business training delivered at delegates' businesses in addition to the successful distance learning Business Programme. Gill Morris M.D. of GMT Business Training says "Delegates like to learn in their own environment where they feel secure and comfortable so we decided to add on-site training to our training delivery portfolio. It also gives delegates the opportunity to ask questions and discuss issues specifically relevant to their business which they can't do through distance learning or when attending generic courses or lectures." ◄———— Main info

The on-site training covers a wide range of business courses but selling skills, staff motivation and marketing are the most popular to date. Courses can also be tailor made to suit the specific requirements of the delegate, salon owner and team, just contact GMT Business Training for details. ◄———— Specific subjects

Pictured at The Savoy Hotel in London is Gill Morris addressing journalists at the launch of the on-site training courses. ◄———— Who is in photo/what photo is about

For further information on on-site tra ining courses fees and to discuss your needs, pleasetelephone Gill on her direct line: xxxxx xxxxxx, email: gill@gmtxxxxxxxxxxxxxx.co.uk or visit the website www.gmtxxxxxxxxxxxxxx.co.uk ◄———— Call to action

———— Release Ends ———— ◄———— Info to be published has ended

Attached Image: Ref' savoy GM/0511 ◄———— Reference number for each photo so they go in the right place, if more than one, and journalist can find it/them easily

Note for Editors: For additional information please contact Gill Morris:
T: xxxxx xxxxxx
E: gill@gmtxxxxxxxxxxxxxx.co.uk ◄———— Your direct contact details for journalists if they need more info

XX The High St, Anytown, Anycounty, AB12 3CD T: 00000 000000
E: info@gmtxxxxxxxxxxxxxx.co.uk W: www.gmtxxxxxxxxxxxloooc.co.uk ◄———— Your business address and contact details

Example of a completed trade press release

NETWORKING

Networking is a means of personally promoting your business and yourself, but not directly to customers. It is used to build relationships, make contacts and promote your business with other businesspeople, the aim being to get recommendations and help each other.

Networking can be carried out within your industry so you get the opportunity to meet existing and new contacts who can refer business to you. It can also happen outside your industry, at a general business event, where you might meet a printer, accountant, solicitor or builder who can give you a good deal or recommend what you do to their customers.

Conferences and exhibitions are great opportunities to network. You can start the process even before you go if you're able to check the organiser's website to see who has signed up – you can create a hit list of people you want to speak with. There is normally a delegate list given out in your conference pack on arrival, detailing the attendees. Take some time to go through it and make a list of who you want to meet; you can also use this list to follow up with 'great to meet you' emails and phone calls, and longer-term marketing communications. Breakout sessions, refreshment areas and lunch are good opportunities to meet and mingle – ensure that you wear your name badge prominently. Take sufficient business cards with you in a smart holder (with space to store cards you're given), wear a smile and remember that people will be wondering if you can help them as much as you are wondering if they can help you. As a means of promotion this is cost-effective as long as the audience is, or could be, relevant to your business. Attending a trade conference is usually affordable – the organisers want as many delegates as possible to be able to attend. There are added benefits for you in attending, as they are a means of keeping up to date with your industry and help with your continuing professional development (CPD).

Other types of networking events are less formal and smaller, and are often held early in the day as breakfast meetings – these are popular as you don't have to take too much time out of your working day. There are also some business supper clubs but these are not normally as well attended. There is usually an interesting and relevant speaker at these smaller events, but mainly they are opportunities for everyone to introduce themselves to each other, hand out business cards, talk about business in general, learn from each other and get recommendations.

KEY TO SUCCESS

Picking up market information through simple acts of conversation with customers, suppliers and even competitors can deliver very useful results when added to the marketing plan.

Whether it is a large or a small event, be clear before you attend what you want to achieve and have the necessary paperwork handy. Networking is usually more about seeing lots of people for a short period of time than fewer people for a long time, although this can also happen. Generally, business is discussed in detail at a follow-up meeting.

As well as joining local business clubs such as your local Chamber of Commerce, you might want to consider joining non-business-related, and even charitable, organisations such as the Rotary Club (RIBI) and Lions Clubs International, or general sports and other types of social clubs. They, too, are ways of networking with people in your community who could help you. Your industry will have trade websites and associations that offer yet more networking opportunities, both online and face-to-face; check out your Sector Skills Councils/standard-setting bodies, trade associations, and school and college alumni organisations.

Of course, you can also network online; most noticeably, at the time of writing, via LinkedIn. This is a business networking site that has been called the 'Facebook for suits', where you can grow your contact list and be seen by others very quickly.

For details of organisations that run networking events in your area, contact:

- Rotary International in Great Britain and Ireland: an organisation of more than 55,000 men and women who, as members of over 1850 Rotary Clubs, volunteer their time, talents, professional skills and energy to improving the lives of people in their local communities and others around the world: www.ribi.org.
- Lions Clubs International are an international network of men and women who work together to answer the needs that challenge communities across the world. www.lionsclubs.org.
- A free directory of UK business networking groups and clubs: www.networkingclubs.co.uk.
- The British Chambers of Commerce have regional networking meetings for their members but often you can go as a guest. See their website for membership details and how to find your local group: www.britishchambers.org.uk.
- For online business networking, visit www.linkedin.co.uk.

BRANDING

Branding is a way of packaging what your business stands for, sometimes referred to as your 'brand values'. For example, the brand values of the John Lewis Partnership are quality, service and that their products are 'Never knowingly undersold'; everything they communicate to customers and potential customers reinforces those values. In addition to the key marketing messages that you want to get across, in Chapter 1 you also listed the brand values you want people to associate with your business and how you could communicate those values. Branding communication is important as it helps to increase awareness of your business and what it stands for. Consequently, how your brand is communicated must be consistent, to avoid confusion in the minds of customers. Making sure that you always use the same font style, logo, colour(s) and a similar style of images is a good start. You might wonder what it will cost for you to create a visual impression of your brand values and what it might cost to reinforce those values. Well, whatever the costs of design, print and electronic media, plus exhibition stands, brochures and so on… it's bound to be less than if you were to get your branding messages wrong (for example, as a food outlet that becomes notorious for a food-poisoning incident) and had to combat negativity.

When designing a website, you should reflect your brand in the use of font, colour and images. The website may be used to sell products directly to the customer or to encourage them to visit your shop. Look at sites such as www.next.co.uk, www.marksandspencer.com and www.debenhams.com; these each reflect the brand image of the parent store.

It is important that your retail unit also reflects your brand image. The 'unit' does not just mean a physical shop – as mentioned above, it includes your website if you provide online retailing. Competition for customers is severe and shops put a great deal of thought and money into designing product displays which encourage customers into the shop – and also encourage them to make impulse purchases. Your 'shop window' – whether physical or on your website – should set the stage for the retail theatre that lies within. It should suggest to the customer what they can expect and focus on the entire experience. The shop window display needs to capture the attention of potential customers so it must be innovative, well-balanced and use colour and props to create a strong theme. When the customer enters the shop they should find a well-designed interior which encourages them to follow a path around the shop that will take them past as much of the merchandise as possible.

Clever use of retail theatre will increase footfall, enhance the customer's shopping experience and improve sales. Visual merchandising is a separate skill, so you may need to use an outside agency to help with your design, but understanding its importance is essential for every member of your team.

SPECIAL OFFERS AND PROMOTIONS

These are generally used to attract the attention of existing and new customers to your business. The reason behind all promotions is to sell, and that should never be forgotten. The sale may come well down the line after information, education, awareness and so on have all been achieved, but it is still the ultimate goal. Personnel and cost resources need to be planned for, and all team members need to have ownership of any promotion to be able to give it their all and make the most of the event (this is where internal promotion comes in; see page 101). Properly planned and implemented promotions can be a highly effective way of driving sales for your business. There are several different types of promotions and special offers, as outlined below.

Generic promotions

Of the many ways to promote your business, generic promotions are among the most popular. They are general in their appeal and the assumption is that they will mean something to most people. Generic promotions fall into four main areas:

- **Supplier-led** – What promotions does your main supplier have planned? (For example the launch of a new product, whereby they would give you an introductory offer to encourage you to take it on in reasonable numbers and to pass on the savings to your customers.)
- **Seasonal** – What seasonally specific promotions is it appropriate to offer? (Easter eggs, Christmas trees)
- **Monthly** – From your individual business targets and requirements, what promotions specific to a particular month would you like to offer? (February – Valentine's Day)
- **Ad hoc** or 'as and when' – What promotions can you offer to respond to external local influences? (sporting event)

OVER TO YOU

With your team, set aside 30 minutes to brainstorm three ideas for generic promotions that you could run.

Targeted promotions

Targeted promotions are those where the promotion or communication is targeted to a specific group, or similar groups, of people to achieve a particular goal. You have already identified these specific groups in the activities you carried out in the market segmentation and customer profiling sections in Chapters 1 and 2. Carrying out targeted promotions is a great way of getting value out of the time and effort you put into getting this research. Targeting promotions is like firing an arrow at the bullseye – addressing a specific interest group directly. You don't want to hit any other groups, as they would bring minimal results. Your efforts and spend should be targeted as much as possible at those who are most likely to buy.

For example, it would not be a cost-effective promotion to send information to clients over 65 years of age about a new line of games consoles, or to promote a range of electric blankets to the under-20s.

OVER TO YOU

With your team, set aside 30 minutes to brainstorm three ideas for targeted promotions that you could run.

Event-specific promotions

Event-specific promotions are designed around specific occasions rather than results-driven offerings; it is the event itself that is being promoted. These events might be internal – within your business – or external, either within your local community or further afield.

In the case of internal business events, this could mean a celebration of the anniversary of the business opening or winning an award, unveiling an extension, or revealing new decor or a refurbishment. External events are of interest to all in the local community, which means that your existing and potential customers could be exposed to them. Often these are run in conjunction with others – perhaps a council-organised carnival, tourist board promotion or local radio roadshow.

Another form of external event could be working with a charity. This is a win:win situation as you get to raise your profile as a caring business as well as raising money for that charity. Or you might work with other local businesses who share the same type of customer base as you – they can become your event promotion partners. These could be small local food shops, hairdressers, shoe shops, cafés, bars etc. You would share costs and manpower for the promotion and both have an equal amount to gain, such as promoting each other's offerings to each other's customers. It is important to ensure in this case that both businesses are able to get what they want out of the event – you should both be able to raise the profiles of your businesses, and get your key marketing messages across.

OVER TO YOU

With your team, set aside 30 minutes to brainstorm three ideas for event-specific promotions that you could run.

WORD OF MOUTH

This is the holy grail of MarComs, as it costs you nothing but is highly effective. It is a by-product of the success of your business as experienced by your customers, and you get it by delivering excellent service. MarComs can help you attract potential customers, but it's how you treat them that dictates whether you get the word-of-mouth benefit. Word of mouth is an incredible tool. It's like **viral marketing** – the good news just continues to spread in an ever-increasing circle of potential contacts. Of course, negative word of mouth, where customers have received poor service and tell others about it, works in the same way but has the opposite effect!

PLANNING AND EVALUATING MARCOMS ACTIVITIES

In the previous section you started to think about the costs involved in carrying out different MarComs activities. This section looks at the planning and evaluation of any marketing activity you are considering – from an email campaign to a targeted promotion – using analytical tools to gauge which will be the most beneficial to your business before you employ them, and also to appraise their effectiveness afterwards. You do need to look at the planning and evaluation side of any MarComs activity as this is vital to its success. A set process to carry this out should be used every time; enthusiasm, although a great asset, can get in the way of objective analysis. Having a clear process prevents unconstructive enthusiasm getting in the way of good planning and management, and ensures that ineffective, and therefore expensive, campaigns are not considered or implemented.

ASSESSING THE PRACTICALITY OF A MARCOMS ACTIVITY

Before you go ahead and commit to any MarComs campaign, you need to ask yourself the following questions:

- What type of MarComs activity is envisaged?
- What exactly needs to be done to carry it out?
- Who will do what needs to be done?
- When must they do it by?
- How long will the activity/campaign run (is it a one-off communication or an ongoing promotion)?
- How much will it cost in terms of money (the actual costs but also the implications of any lost revenue if personnel are doing something else)?

- What external resources are required and at what cost (printers, caterers and so on, and also personnel who need to be allocated the task of dealing with and managing external resources)?

All the potential activities across all the different MarComs areas you have identified should be added to an ongoing activity cost chart (see page 106) that records the answers to the above questions. You can use this chart to compare the cost implications of all the different activities that you are considering, and give them a **traffic light key** rating based on their cost-effectiveness.

To complete the activity cost chart:
- List all the potential activities that you are considering in the first column.
- In the second column, put in the timescale for each activity – is it a one-off event that will take place next month or a sustained campaign that will run over six months?
- Explain in detail what needs to be done to run each promotion. You need to think of everything that will be required, large and small. Compile this on a separate spreadsheet, putting the main headings only on this chart in the third column.
- List any team members who would need to be involved, when and for how long. Compile this on a separate spreadsheet, putting the main headings only on this chart in the fourth column.
- Describe any external resources involved, such as equipment, tables, chairs, caterers, florists, waitresses, representatives from promotional partners, suppliers and so on. Compile this on a separate spreadsheet, putting the main headings only on this chart in the fifth column.
- List the anticipated cost of each promotion. This includes all the set-up costs, costs of external resources, and any revenue that you will be losing out on while your staff are involved in running the activity. When you have listed everything required, you then need to cost it all and come up with what it will cost you to run the promotion. Add this figure to the sixth column.
- Assign a traffic light status based on how much it will cost to run each promotion. (Red sticker = high costs; amber sticker = average costs; green sticker = low costs.) Add this information into the final column of the chart.

ACTIVITY COST CHART

POTENTIAL ACTIVITY	TIMESCALE	WHAT NEEDS TO BE DONE	WHO IS INVOLVED	EXTERNAL RESOURCES	COST	BENEFIT	⬤
1 Support local charity event		Take a stand at local charity event in aid of Cancer Research UK	1 member of the team	Rent 2 × display stands and plants	£300. £100 for stand, to include all refreshments, £100 for leaflet printing and 'goody bags' and £100 for 1 team member being out of office for the afternoon	Green	
2 Half-price one-page **advertorial** in local paper (last-minute offer)		Agree, design and approve advert, meet journalist and agree copy and photos	Business owner	Designer and copywriter local paper do this	£1,000. Cost of advert (local paper not usually this expensive for one page last minute)	Red	
3							
4							
5							
6							
7							
8							
9							
10							

TRAFFIC LIGHTS KEY: RED = STOP   AMBER = WAIT   GREEN = GO

? JARGON BUSTER

An **advertorial** is an advertisement in a publication designed to look like an article

Put the potential promotions that you listed in the previous three Over to you activities (generic, targeted and event-specific) and any other MarComs ideas that you have generated into the table and complete the other columns. Which activity or activities offer you the most cost-effective solution?

EVALUATING THE BENEFITS OF A MARCOMS ACTIVITY

You also need to be able to compare the benefits to your business of each potential activity. You can use an activity benefit chart (see page 108) to organise this information.

To complete the activity benefit chart:
- In the first and second columns, list all the potential activities from the activity cost chart and the traffic light status you allotted them based on cost.
- Describe the aim of each promotion. What benefit to the business are you trying to achieve with the promotion? Increased sales from existing customers? Sales or bookings from new customers? Increased awareness? Use the third column to summarise this information.
- State whom the promotion is aimed at. Who is the target audience for each promotion? Who do you want to see it or be involved with it? Put this in the fourth column.
- Describe the likely effect of the promotion. What do you think the effect of each promotion will be? Existing customers spending more money? Getting more new customers? Selling more? Summarise this in the fifth column.
- Describe how this will affect your business. If the promotion goes well, what will the effect be on your business? 7 per cent more new customers? 15 per cent of existing customers increasing their spend by 20 per cent? 17 per cent more products sold in a six-month period? Put your conclusions in the sixth column. The effects you choose should be measurable, so that you can judge the success of the activity against them.
- Assign a traffic light status based on the anticipated benefit of running each promotion. (Red sticker = small benefit; amber sticker = medium benefit; green sticker = large benefit.) Add this information into the final column.

ACTIVITY BENEFIT CHART

POTENTIAL PROMOTION	COST	WHAT IS AIM?	WHO AIMED AT?	LIKELY EFFECT	EFFECT ON YOUR BUSINESS	BENEFITS
1 Support local charity event	Green	To increase awareness and gain local PR	Our target audience aged 40–75 who support local charities	Being seen as part of local community and one of the 'good guys'	20 per cent increase from word-of-mouth recommendations	Green
2 Half-price one-page advertorial in local paper (last-minute offer)	Red	To promote a new product with a special offer/voucher	Everyone, as the product is health-related	Awareness of new product and sales	15 per cent more sales from new business	Amber
3						
4						
5						
6						
7						
8						
9						
10						

RAFFIC LIGHTS KEY: RED = STOP   AMBER = WAIT   GREEN = GO

The activities that give you a double green traffic light on cost and likely benefit present themselves as viable activities to take forward. There will, however, also be cases where ideas for promotions turn out to be amber (needing something changing) or red (requiring either radical changes or abandonment). There may be occasions where amber ideas can contribute effectively to your overall marketing communications objective – for example where the projected benefit is medium to low (amber or red) but the cost is also low (green), or where the projected long-term benefit is low but the activity will support a quick win, which can be built on once customers have been retained or a new service introduced.

↳ **OVER TO YOU**

Evaluate the same activities again, but this time based on the likely benefits to your business of each. Complete the activity benefit chart for the activities you put into the activity cost chart. Are there any clear winners? Where are you going to target your resources?

MEASURING AND ANALYSING THE IMPACT OF MARCOMS ACTIVITIES

When you have gone through the process of paper evaluation of your promotional plans you should have a very clear idea of which are likely to be successful. The only thing that remains is to implement the plans and to analyse their impact.

There are various tools you can use to measure, analyse and compare the success of your promotions:

- If your objective was to increase sales by a set amount, you will measure the actual sales figure against the predicted amount.
- If your required return on investment (ROI) was £X profit, you will measure the amount of revenue gained minus the costs incurred.
- There are often intangible elements to any promotion, which can be difficult to measure but anecdotally you and your team should have an idea regarding word-of-mouth benefits, increased awareness and profile, or former customers being enticed back.

Analysis of the overall campaign should happen at the end, when everything has finished and you've had a chance to measure the results against your objectives. Ongoing analysis can be part of the planning and implementation stages – consider what's going well, what could be better, what's not so good, and why. However, it is generally accepted that the final analysis is the most important.

ANNUAL MARCOMS ACTIVITY CALENDAR

Using the tools given in this chapter you will have decided which activities are worth going ahead with. You don't want them all listed on separate pieces of paper that might get mislaid, damaged, or overlooked by key team members. They should be kept in one place – on an annual activity calendar. This not only helps to ensure that you have planned activities in a logical order, but you will also be able to view the components of your plan alongside other key business activities and events, and see how these might support the implementation of your plan, or if you might miss any key selling windows.

You will find it useful to place the calendar where everyone in the team can see it at all times. Any new information should be added immediately you are made aware of it (for example supplier promotions, so you don't miss out on special offers). The calendar should also be used to ensure that you are aware of when external resources need to be ordered and delivered (such as printing), rather than trying to get everything done at the last minute. It may be helpful to put staff holidays on this calendar too, to avoid running complex events when you have fewer people to manage the preparation or delivery.

BUSINESS NAME:

_____

_____

JAN	FEB	MAR	APR

MAY	JUN	JUL	AUG

SEP	OCT	NOV	DEC

Annual activity calendar

Jacaranda Florists has been trading for two years and, while sales are steady, the owners feel there is an opportunity in the areas of corporate events and upmarket weddings. During July and August, the owners sit down and draw up a marketing plan for the year commencing 1 October.

Category	Strategy
Target market	Top-of-the-range corporate events and upmarket weddings
Positioning statement	The florists of first choice for luxury
Offering	Luxury bouquets and arrangements hand-produced by experts
Price strategy	Price 25% above the closest competitor
Distribution	Shop and internet
Sales strategy	Increase sales by 40% above current year; hire an events liaison person to be responsible for promotion
Promotion strategy	Develop a campaign focusing on the offer and the position, including: networking with event organisers and wedding venues; advertorials on local radio and in local newspapers; advertising on local transport; and posters in the windows
Market research	Collect customer feedback and identify new market opportunities

Jacaranda Florists' marketing calendar October 2011–September 2012

Oct	Nov	Dec	Jan	Feb	Mar	Apr	May	Jun	Jul	Aug	Sep
PROMOTING CORPORATE EVENTS											
			PROMOTING WEDDDINGS								
	CHRISTMAS										
			VALENTINE'S DAY								
				MOTHER'S DAY							
					EASTER						
						CHELSEA FLOWER SHOW					
							DIAMOND JUBILEE				
									OLYMPIC GAMES		

Pick out the activities that were double green on your activity benefit chart (see page 108) and add them to the activity calendar in the appropriate place. You will have to think which activities suit which season or month. Ensure that no one month or season has too many activities while others don't have enough; also take into account your business's busy times and when team members are on holiday. You might find it helpful to do it in pencil first!

SALES

Your marketing activities have achieved their aims – they have brought potential customers to you. There now needs to be a completion process: sales. Selling is a skill that requires training and practice. It also depends on you thinking like the customer. This section covers a range of sales channels and techniques that you can use – the choice of which will depend on the needs and preferences of your customers, and the channels you have available. A sale is the end action of a long process, and as one process is completed it should open the door to others, if what you offer is what the customer wants and does what you've said it will do. Selling to a customer once is not what you should aim for; building a relationship with a customer who then buys from you regularly and recommends you to others is the goal.

ROUTES TO MARKET

Whereas in the past the bulk of a business's sales would have been over the counter, changes in technology and the way that we shop mean that any business nowadays has to consider multiple routes to market. This section looks at the main types.

Face-to-face selling

This is when you are in front of your existing or potential customer, either on a one-to-one basis or in a group. One-to-one could be someone coming into your premises and asking about what you offer, or you might have made an appointment with them. Group types of face-to-face sales are more likely to be at an exhibition or promotional event where you have a group of people listening to you or watching you demonstrate something new and exciting. The key to this type of selling is that your interpersonal skills have to be top quality. Skills such as listening, making eye contact with the person opposite you, or with everyone in a group, and being knowledgeable, approachable and professional – yet with a smile – are so important. Your customers will make a judgement on your offering based on your appearance, so you need to consider that too. You should never adopt the 'I must get a sale at all costs' approach; if you're too pushy you may make one sale but you could lose a repeat customer forever.

Telephone sales

Telesales, as this is often called, can refer to anything from calling a customer to see if they need any of your services or products, to massive organisations that employ multinational teams of dedicated sales operatives. In reality, the owners of most small businesses call customers themselves, with perhaps one or two people in the office also keeping in contact with customers – making sure they are happy, seeing if they need anything and making them aware of what's new or any special offers that they think the customer might want based on their past purchase history. As the name suggests, this is a phone-only medium, and so the way you speak on the phone is critical. Key points to remember are that you should always smile when you speak, as it gives your voice a better quality; use language the customer understands; be aware you may be interrupting the customer (and avoid doing it!); and always have a reason to call. If there is no actual reason, the call should be a 'courtesy call' – an opportunity to assess the customer's satisfaction with your offering or service.

Internet sales

These are any sales made via the internet, which may be exclusively through your website or with minimal involvement with an actual salesperson. A salesperson may contact a customer through e-marketing, emails, blogs, e-newsletters and so on, directing them to the offer on the website. Alternatively, the customer may have come across your offering using search engines like Google or Yahoo. This type of selling is generally thought to be cost-effective as any involvement from a team member (and therefore cost) is either removed completely or minimised. The initial cost is the cost of developing a website that is customer-friendly, easy to navigate, has a good content management system (so you can make alterations easily), is search engine optimised, offers easy and secure payment options and that interfaces with other marketing tools (so all information on your customers is collated) – and this is not cheap. When investigating the cost of a website you will need to spread the amount over a year or even several years – it is a longer-term investment.

Other sales

These are sales that have come in without you necessarily instigating them or where a long time has passed since your initial contact. They are often called ad hoc or unsolicited sales. These sales are good to receive as they arguably haven't cost anything to get – and as you hadn't planned for them they are a nice bonus! However, if you only have enough stock for what you plan to sell, these other sales could put a strain on your stock levels and stock control mechanism. Keeping additional stocks for ad hoc sales is costly, and this is where good relationships with your suppliers, and their ability to deliver very quickly, are extremely helpful.

However you sell your goods or services to your customers – whether you're contacting them or they're contacting you – it's important that all orders are processed efficiently and effectively. It's also important that you and your team are aware of the opportunities of cross-selling and up-selling.

You can see that there are different ways for you to sell, but if your business is customer-facing you are most likely to use face-to-face selling, although you may also sell direct to your customers through your website.

You are face-to-face with your customers most of the time when they buy anything, but they may also buy products through your website on an ongoing basis, coming to you for advice. Beware of stocking products they can buy from nearby competitors – or, even worse, direct from your suppliers – through shopping channels and/or the internet. When suppliers compete with you for your customers' retail business it may be time to change them. Look again at how you rated your suppliers in the power and risk analysis in Chapter 2.

SALES SKILLS AND TECHNIQUES

Business owners and staff often don't feel comfortable selling, or even think they are no good at it. Remember that selling is a skill and that if you've not had training in that skill you won't know how to do it, just as you wouldn't expect a Level 2 technician to carry out work at Level 3 if he hasn't been trained. Getting training is important, as it will give you confidence – although there is nothing like knowing a product inside out and upside down for enhancing your selling skills. Those who just need some support or tips can often learn from more experienced or confident colleagues through observation. However, if you need more help, formal training may be required. This is generally delivered either on-site by a consultant trainer or tutor, or off-site at a training company's premises or a regional venue. Some people prefer the training to be delivered at their place of work as they feel more comfortable in their own surroundings; others prefer to get away and feel they learn better in a different environment. Online learning is also available, but for a discipline such as sales, where role play is often a crucial part of the training, learning may be more effective when face-to-face. There will be some sales training companies specific to your trade and you'll find them via trade journals, exhibitions and possibly Sector Skills Council websites.

You may also like to visit the following websites:
- City & Guilds sales training: www.cityandguilds.com.
- The Institute of Sales and Marketing Management, for approved courses and ideas: www.ismm.co.uk.

There are some recognised methods of selling that you are likely to use.

Consultative sales method

The preferred way to sell is to use this technique – which is actually not you selling, but rather your client buying from you. The consultative sales method works through consultation with a customer and coming to an agreed solution, rather than you dictating what they need to buy. Customers need to understand that what you are offering is a solution to their needs, and you need to understand precisely what the customer wants so you can provide the correct solution. Consultation is about discussion and exchange of opinions – in other words, talk to your customers, listen to what they want and then give it to them.

Here is an example of a good consultative sales method interaction:

Salesperson: You look like a man with a mission!
Customer: Yes, I'm determined to get my garden dug over ready for this weekend.
Salesperson: Oh, that sounds like hard work, are you doing it all yourself?
Customer: Yes I am, there's no one else that can really help me.
Salesperson: I can rent you a motor rotary/digging unit for a couple of days, would that help you?
Customer: How much?
Salesperson: Well, not much compared to your bad back... only £35.
Customer: It's a deal, thank you!

In contrast, this is a bad consultative sales method interaction:

Salesperson: You look like a man with a mission!
Customer: Yes, I'm determined to get my garden dug over ready for this weekend.
Salesperson: Oh, that sounds like hard work, are you doing it all yourself?
Customer: Yes I am, there's no one else that can really help me.
Salesperson: Rather you than me!

Thorough knowledge of your offering and market

Knowledge of what you offer is crucial; it gives you the confidence to speak to customers, and that, in turn, gives your customers confidence in you. It is also the professional thing to do – it reflects well on your business, aids recommendations and referrals and gives a competitive advantage. The key to this is an in-depth knowledge and understanding of what you are offering, what makes it special and what makes it different to your competition. Your unique selling proposition (USP) is exactly that – unique – and you need to appreciate how you can get that across to your market.

The two go together – a thorough knowledge of your competitive offering and of the market you are selling into. It is even more essential to have this knowledge when your offering is specialist rather than generalist.

Up-selling

This is when you persuade a customer to buy something in addition to what they have just bought, or bought previously, and for more money. It's a technique that should be used with care, as no customer wants to feel they are just a vehicle for making money. However, most customers are pleased when told about something that will make them a saving if they buy more, or that if they spend just a bit more they'll get a better-quality product that will last longer.

Cross-selling

This is when you offer a customer something that links in some way to whatever they have just bought. An example might be car insurance with a special offer on house insurance (the link being insurance), or if someone has just bought a conservatory they might also buy solar panels, or it could be a haircut with a special offer on hair straighteners.

Discounting and free products

Discounting and giving away free products are used for four main reasons: to reduce levels of stock, to help with cashflow by getting money in quickly, as a thank-you for a purchase or as an incentive to buy. The level of discount you set will depend on the reason for offering it. It may be that you choose to sell at cost or even below cost price (even though you will lose money, this will free up storage space for new stock). If you try to sell at a less heavily discounted price and fail, you will have to discount it a lot later and make even less – it's a gamble. Another part of the gamble is that discounting or giving away free stock may devalue the offering, or your brand, in the eyes of your customers. You need to weigh up the risks against the original reason for discounting.

Good businesses generally give their salespeople a certain amount of leeway to do what they feel is right at the time to close a sale. It may be helpful to have a written policy on the subject that all the team know about and can access.

 CASE STUDY 4

James Barker owns a shop selling beds and soft furnishings. He employs Jordan McKay as a salesman to sell beds. Jordan uses a consultative sales method to sell products to his customers, going through a series of open questions to find out which products will best meet their needs while attempting to up-sell a more expensive option.

Continued

Jordan needs extensive product knowledge as he offers customers choices between divan beds, which come in non-drawer, two-drawer and four-drawer versions, and frame beds, which come in choices of wood, metal, leather and frames containing TVs. He also needs to ascertain whether the customer needs a single, small double, double, king or super king sized bed. There is also a choice of mattresses; pocket spring, open coil spring, memory foam, latex or orthopaedic.

Jordan will be attempting to provide the customer with a choice which meets the customer's needs, within their budget, while making the best sale for the shop. James pays Jordan a commission on each bed sold based on a percentage of the selling price.

James has decided to keep his soft furnishings separate from his bed sales and employs Lucy Anderton to serve customers in this section. She sells by keeping all the available products on display so that the customers can make their own choice, while she is available to answer any questions they may have. James pays Lucy a bonus at the end of the month if total sales on her section exceed the plan.

Commission and incentives

Some people will do their utmost to sell all day every day; some need a monetary monthly or quarterly incentive to do well in the first place; others will respond better to one paid retrospectively as a thank-you for doing well, for example in the form of an annual bonus. Commission may be paid on sales but it needs to be in the budget, as it is a cost of sales. Commission is not normally paid until the salesperson has brought in enough income to cover their costs. The business owner needs to look at what the costs are to make a sale and then set targets – commission payments are made when those targets are achieved. Most sales jobs are made up of a basic salary (the amount the salesperson will earn every month regardless of the sales they bring in) and commission on top. Commission varies from business to business and from industry to industry – your trade body and associations will be able to give you advice on what is considered the norm.

In all of your sales activity, you should remember to put yourself in the customer's shoes for the good of your business. A hard sale might give you short-term profit, but at what cost? If you've been pushy you may lose that customer and the associated long-term business, as he or she will not want to deal with you again, will not recommend you and, at worst, will actively discourage people from dealing with you. No customer wants to be seen as just a pound sign: think about how you like to be treated yourself.

SALES PLANS

Your business plan and other subsidiary plans were based around the returns on investment you wanted to achieve and what level of income was required to fund your business. Income comes from sales and you will have listed your sales targets. Refer back to the cost calculations you did in Chapter 1 and use these to make sure your sales targets are sufficient and achievable. The key to achieving these targets is to have a detailed and realistic sales plan in place. Your sales plan pulls together all of the marketing and sales activities covered so far in this chapter into a structured, costed plan for achieving your aims.

A sales plan should be created alongside your main business plan and other subsidiary plans. It is vitally important, as it's the only plan to do with bringing money into the company – all the others are to do with spending it. Leaving this until your business is underway is financial suicide. At the beginning of each financial year your sales plan should be adapted for the coming year to meet new challenges.

In essence the sales plan deals with how many of what will be sold, when, at what cost, at what profit and at what margin. It will also include how the sales objectives or targets will be met, by whom, what activities will be required and what they will cost. It will also attribute any commission levels and payment timescales to particular salespeople if applicable. It lists when money should be available to be spent on or by the business.

The sales plan is usually created by the business owner, although input from an accountant is always a good idea. Excel spreadsheets are great tools for putting sales objectives and targets together; things can readily be changed and the impact of a change on other figures is easily seen. The sales plan is for your eyes only (and your accountant and bank manager). You may want to show part of it to your sales team – the part where their targets are set – but it's best if this information is in the form of a separate document. The sales plan will form part of the supporting information for your business plan, whether it's for a start-up or for expansion.

Structure of a sales plan

Following on from the guidelines on writing a business plan in Chapter 1 (see page 39), this section describes what you need to include in your sales plan. Your sales plan is a dynamic document that you should refer to often and update to ensure it's always relevant.

- Title page – 'Sales Plan'; date it
- Contents page
- Introduction page
- Executive summary page

- Body of the plan:
  - Objectives – This is one page, where you state what is it that you plan to achieve in sales within the timescale of the plan, normally a year. Each objective should be SMART, for example '15 per cent increase in sales this year from last year's sales figures, across all lines that give us a profit margin of 55 per cent and above. This equates to £X per annum.'
  - After the objectives comes the detail of **how** you intend to achieve your objectives; this includes what you are going to concentrate on selling. Here you would itemise the parts of your offering that give you at least that profit margin. Which customers do you want to focus on? Itemise the customer segment(s) you are going to concentrate on for each part of your offering. Explain how you intend to compete – adapt your competitive and environmental analysis (SWOT and PEST) from your business plan and show what your competitors offer against each of the parts of your offering you intend to concentrate on. Also add whether there are any opportunities or threats that may have a positive or negative effect on you achieving your objectives.
  - Promotions – Itemise and cost what you intend to do to ensure you get the interest from customers and potential customers to meet your sales objectives: advertising, leaflet drops and any promotional activities, plus team target and commission setting and training.
  - Sales methods – These might include direct selling, sales via your website, incentives, up-selling, cross-selling…
  - **Sales forecast** – This is a forecast of what you intend to sell every month. Because this is regularly updated it is best done as a spreadsheet so the totals update when you add information.
  - The sales budget, or financial plan for sales, is broken down by month – how much money will come into the business each month? This amount is what you base your business expenditure on. If your income from sales is less than you have planned for in your budget, you may have problems paying your bills.
  - How will you measure the success or otherwise of your sales plan? Measure and analyse results against objectives – what worked and why, what didn't and why.
  - Carry results over to the next year's sales plan.
  - Last year's sales figures – List the amount sold per month and per annum, against each part of your offering.
  - Costs – What it will cost to achieve your objectives per month and per annum.
  - Appendices – Additional material such as examples of competitor sales activity, suppliers' promotions and so on.

? JARGON BUSTER

The **sales forecast** details and breaks down the sales you hope to achieve from each of your offerings. It is updated regularly – as soon as you have sales figures information.

Sales forecast spreadsheet

The spreadsheet shows:

	Jun-13	Jul-13	Aug-13	Sep-13	Oct-13	Nov-13	Dec-13	Jan-14	Feb-14	Mar-14	Apr-14	May-14	Annual Total	Current Month Ending mm/yy	2012
Cat 1 units sold													0		
Sale price @ unit															
Cat 1 Total	0	0	0	0	0	0	0	0	0	0	0	0	0	0	
Cat 2 units sold													0		
Sale price @ unit															
Cat 2 Total	0	0	0	0	0	0	0	0	0	0	0	0	0	0	
Cat 3 units sold													0		
Sale price @ unit															
Cat 3 Total	0	0	0	0	0	0	0	0	0	0	0	0	0	0	
Cat 4 units sold													0		
Sale price @ unit															
Cat 4 Total	0	0	0	0	0	0	0	0	0	0	0	0	0	0	
Cat 5 units sold													0		
Sale price @ unit															
Cat 5 Total	0	0	0	0	0	0	0	0	0	0	0	0	0		
Cat 6 units sold													0		
Sale price @ unit															
Cat 6 Total	0	0	0	0	0	0	0	0	0	0	0	0	0	0	
Cat 7 units sold													0		
Sale price @ unit															
Cat 7 Total	0	0	0	0	0	0	0	0	0	0	0	0	0	0	

Enter your Company Name here. Fiscal Year Begins Jun-13. 12-months Sales Forecast. Sales His[tory].

Using the sales plan

You will update your sales forecast every month and compare the actual figures to the planned figures, so you can see if you are ahead or behind the planned sales income and take appropriate action. For example, you might cut back on expenditure if you are behind and increase your sales effort to make up the shortfall. The sales plan is a dynamic document that changes depending on the actual results.

You will use the projected figures for additional, separate tasks that sit alongside the sales plan, such as estimating required stock levels and working out the sales targets for the team and what commission you can afford to pay them. These figures will need to be updated in line with any changes in your sales plan. The targets and commission rates may be adapted depending on the results – usually a below-plan sales quarter will be followed by an increase in sales activity and targets for the following quarter. Weekly checks against the plan will guide you to take action if sales are down on budget; waiting for a whole quarter to find you are down a lot may mean it's late to recoup anything. Once you have been in business for more than a year you can measure a month or week against the same month or week from the previous year, or even focus on a particular day! There are annual fluctuations that need to be planned for; for example, in some businesses there is a dip in sales in the summer when customers are on holiday.

Think of your sales plan as a map for getting from A to B – from your position at the start of the financial year to profit at the end. You'll then use the individual parts of it – budgets and forecasts – as a guide to income and expenditure. Properly used, a sales plan allows you to use your income when it's most needed and helps you to control your business's flow of cash in and out.

WHERE TO GO FOR MORE INFORMATION

Visiting particular websites will be helpful in keeping you aware of what's going on in e-marketing and networking. Contact your trade bodies and associations to maximise networking opportunities. Check out the websites that offer free advice on writing your sales plan with templates and examples; there is also lots of general advice to be found on sales and marketing in general.

- Social media – Facebook: www.facebook.com.
- Micro-blogging – Twitter: twitter.com.
- Professional networking – LinkedIn: www.linkedin.com.
- Information on writing a sales plan with useful templates:
  - www.businesslink.gov.uk
  - office.microsoft.com
- For general advice on sales and marketing, the Business Link website is very useful: www.businesslink.gov.uk

CONCLUSION

Having worked through this chapter, you should have the tools to understand and evaluate how all of your marketing communication activities feed into your ultimate goal: increased sales. Selling is a vital part of your business. A sale is the outcome you need to keep your business going; therefore everything you do should lead to sales either now or in the near future. Sales are the one thing that bring money into your business and, just like all other parts of your business, they should be planned. As you have seen in this chapter, a well-thought-out MarComs strategy will provide the bridge between your offering and your target market. Being good or even great at what you do is not enough – you must use your MarComs decisions wisely to get this message across to customers earlier and in more effective ways than your competitors. It is this aspect of promoting your business that will drive sales – and, ultimately, your success.

CHAPTER 4
THE CUSTOMER RELATIONSHIP

INTRODUCTION

This chapter focuses on the vital relationship between you and your customers. You and every member of your staff have responsibility for creating the right environment so that customers feel comfortable, valued and likely to return. You can do this by setting up a customer service culture that permeates your business; this is known as customer relationship management (CRM). You'll gain ideas and see examples of how to run satisfaction surveys and understand the results, appreciate the benefits of superior listening skills, the various ways of communicating with customers, dealing with complaints and generally how to go the extra mile to keep customers and encourage their loyalty. After all, every customer that you lose you give to your competitors. If you are working as a sole trader, the advice in this chapter is especially applicable, as you have to take on all the team roles to ensure that you are giving excellent personal customer service.

CREATING THE RIGHT IMAGE

There are many parts of your business that customers come into contact with in their dealings with you, so when considering building relationships you need to consider all the people involved. It's not enough for you to have a great relationship with customers if your team members don't – if your assistants are rude or the person answering the phone isn't helpful, or the cleaner is noisy and gets in the way. You need your customers to have a positive experience in all their dealings with your business – not a neutral one, and definitely not a negative one. Ask yourself: 'Are any pieces of my customer care jigsaw missing or not as good as they could be?' As you know, one small missing piece has the power to spoil the whole jigsaw.

Just as with a jigsaw, a missing piece in your customer care can spoil the whole

CREATING THE RIGHT FEELING

How your customers feel about you and your business is based on a number of issues, all of which affect their relationship with you. Such issues include their preconceptions based on other businesses like yours or on hearsay, their past experiences with you and your team, their initial contact with your business and their ongoing experience each time they come to you.

Having customers with a positive attitude towards you will pay off, as they are more likely to enjoy their experience, spend more with you, return, recommend you to others and generally become an advocate of your business. In businesses where word-of-mouth recommendation is vital, having customers with this positive mindset is priceless. A dissatisfied customer will tell between eight and 16 others in person that they are dissatisfied; with access to social networking sites, they can tell thousands.

Once your customers start feeling neutral or negative towards your business you will have to work much harder to get them to feel positive again. It costs you more in time and effort to take a customer from negative to positive then it does from neutral to positive, but if they are already in a positive state of mind about you – from a great phone call or warm welcome in person – then the cost to you is minimal. So it makes sound commercial sense to ensure that every member of your team is on board with customer service. Ninety-one per cent of dissatisfied customers never purchase goods or services from the company again, but if their issue is resolved quickly, 85 per cent of them will be repeat customers.

Negative >>>>>>>>>>>>>>> Neutral >>>>>>>>>>>>>>> Positive +

Always take your customers on a journey away from feeling negative and towards feeling positive about your business

As your business grows, remember that team training is necessary to ensure that everyone's definition of customer service delivery is the same and that everyone carries out your customer service to the same level and in the same way. This should be done as part of staff induction – even if there are only two or three of you involved in the business, you are still a team. Ongoing training should also be carried out to ensure standards don't slip and that you maintain a consistent approach to customer service. Customer feedback, gained via satisfaction surveys (see Chapter 2), will also highlight any issues that need to be raised and discussed during team meetings.

OVER TO YOU

Create a list of your team members who come into contact with your customers, either in person or by phone, email or text. This may include some or all of the following in larger businesses: receptionists, accounts staff, salespeople, technical support workers, delivery people ...

GETTING FIRST IMPRESSIONS RIGHT

First impressions do count, and the old saying is true: 'You don't get a second chance to make a good first impression.' There can be a tendency in some businesses to put the least experienced, lowest-cost employees, who often have a lack of training in people skills, on the shop floor or have them answering the phone. This is a bad move, as customers can be put off before they even get to experience your great offering. Think like the customer and be sure that the person who is welcoming your customers is doing it right.

However, this is not the only person involved in giving first impressions – how do the rest of your team measure up? Do they stand around looking bored or chatting to each other, or are they scurrying about so much that the customer feels like an intrusion? It's not just how your staff behave, it's also what they're wearing – do they all look smart and professional or merely comfortable and relaxed? How do your team members greet customers and what does that say about your company? Do all of your team treat customers in the same way? Have you invested in training your team in customer service, and are you keeping their training up to date?

Think, too, about the first impressions your business environment is communicating. If you have premises, do they look good from the street – also known as 'kerb appeal'? If you have offices, the same applies: what message are they communicating? If you have company vehicles, these also communicate a message; are they saying 'old and a bit tired', or 'modern and doing well'? How well are the vehicles driven? A badly driven van or car with your logo emblazoned on it will immediately communicate the wrong message.

Adrian Ratcliffe buys an existing, but failing, gift shop on the seafront. Included in the purchase price is the stock. On taking over, Adrian feels that much of the stock is of poor quality. The fixtures are over-crowded, with cheap items such as buckets and spades, flip flops, etc displayed on the pavement outside the shop and with no **adjacency**. Fixtures are untidy because stock is regularly knocked over by customers trying to negotiate the narrow aisles and because it is impossible to clean the fixtures or the floor.

Adrian sees the potential of the location of the shop if the impression given to customers can be improved. His first act is to hold a sale, giving 75 per cent discount on all stock for a two-week period. At the end of the sale, he disposes of the remaining stock to a surplus stock dealer and announces a launch of the new business. He installs new fixtures which give customers more space to browse, buys higher quality stock and displays only a few of each item.

As a result, Adrian has to replenish the fixtures regularly to ensure continuity of availability, but feels this gives him an insight into his best sellers. He also feels that removing the outdoor stock improves his kerb appeal and the new layout of the interior improves the shop's image. After two months' trading he finds that the shop is attracting fewer browsers, who don't buy anything, and an increased average spend from customers.

? JARGON BUSTER

Adjacency is the skill of putting products next to or near other products which the same customer may want to purchase.

On the same theme, what does your website communicate about your business? Is it easy to navigate with the minimum number of clicks? If so, it implies you know what you're doing and don't waste time. In design terms, how does it look? Does that look match your business branding and target audience? Do you want to be seen as funky and modern? The answer might be yes if your business is a music store but probably not if you're a traditional tailor. First impressions also apply to any electronic communications, no matter how brief, such as email campaigns and SMS (text) messages.

All your first impressions, and ongoing impressions too, should reflect your business brand. Are you trying to appear hyper-professional? Friendly and more laid back? Customer focused? A market leader? If you look back to the branding and target market work you did in Chapters 2 and 3, you will be able to ensure that your communications are relevant.

Imagine that the best customer you could possibly have is coming to your business in two days, then two weeks, then two months. Write three separate lists of all that needs to be done to impress that person in those timescales. Walk up to and around your premises or vehicle, and try to see it through the eyes of the customer – after all, you know what's there, so you sometimes miss things, like the cobweb on the ceiling or the flaking paint on the front door. The two-day list will consist of things that can be done quickly for maximum visual impact: general tidying up, sweeping outside, removing weeds, cleaning everything on show, adding flowers, checking that the water cooler and coffee machine are full, making sure magazines are up to date, putting new towels and soaps in the toilet, emptying all the bins and so on. The two-week list will consist of all of the above plus more time-consuming things, such as a coat of paint or rearranging furniture. The two-month list gives time for heavy-duty changes as well as the more cosmetic, so may also include structural alterations: removing walls, opening up areas, changing the equipment, resurfacing the driveway, and so on.

**? JARGON
. BUSTER**

Pareto's Law, or as it is sometimes called, the 80/20 rule, applies to a number of business functions. The classic example is in sales: 80 per cent of sales come from 20 per cent of customers. Also, 80 per cent of profits come from 20 per cent of your offering. It may also be the case that 80 per cent of your time and effort is spent on the weakest 20 per cent of your offering.

LOOKING AFTER KEY CUSTOMERS

From your analysis in previous chapters you will know who your most profitable customers are. It makes sense that they in particular are looked after and made to feel special. This certainly does not mean that the less profitable ones don't deserve good customer service – they do; they *all* do. It just makes sound business sense to expend more effort on the things and customers that give you the greatest return. Analysis of your customer spend in relation to your time and effort will show if the 80/20 rule, or **Pareto's Law**, is true in your business.

It will at the very least demonstrate where effort matches sales and where it doesn't, which is vital information when it comes to planning. You may decide that certain key customers need looking after more closely, as your business simply can't afford to lose them. These customers are known in some businesses as 'key accounts', and you may decide it's worth dedicating a considerable amount of your time, or the time of one of your senior team members, specifically to looking after them. But that time and effort has to be carefully weighed up – in other words, it has to be worth it.

The basis on which this judgement is made is normally financial – if the customer brings considerable income into the business and it would negatively impact on your turnover and profit if you were to lose that customer, then looking after them in this way is worth it. Customers who leave you will also undoubtedly turn to one of your competitors. You must differentiate the way you look after these customers compared to the trade or industry norm so they feel special and understand how much they and their custom are valued. How you do this depends on your normal business practice, but would normally include:

- going the extra mile to provide more personal attention and look after their needs with exceptional customer service. This may involve a dedicated person looking after them, called a Key Account Manager (KAM)
- a more frequent contact or call cycle – make contact with them often
- payment terms of 60 or even 90 days instead of the usual 30, which helps their cashflow
- tailored or special offers based on their order history and designed specifically to meet their needs – these are unlikely to be matched by your competitors.

🔑 **KEY TO SUCCESS**

Your time is something you can't buy more of, so ensure that you and your team spend it profitably.

CASE STUDY 2

Susanne Carmel owns an exclusive fashion store in the West End of London. She has two staff members who deal with day-to-day customers, while she maintains a list of clients who she deals with personally.

When buying stock, Susanne has her personal clients in mind and, while she buys a range of clothing for general sale, she buys individual exclusive items which she believes her clients will be interested in. When the stock is due to arrive, she contacts the client who she considers the item will suit and invites them to visit the store to be the first to have an opportunity to buy.

Susanne records every purchase made by her client list, and every suggestion that she has made that has not led to a sale, so that she can more accurately forecast their needs when buying. As a result, the clients on her list rely on her judgement and will always approach her first when they need that special item.

CUSTOMER RELATIONSHIP MANAGEMENT (CRM)

CRM is part of your marketing and is a business-wide strategy for managing relationships with existing and potential customers. At its most basic, it's a plan for finding out who your customers are, what they want, when they want it, what price they are prepared to pay for it and what it takes to keep them. If customers come under the key account management system, your KAM would be in regular contact with them, so would foresee and deal with any problems or issues.

IMPLEMENTING CRM

From the very start of your business you need to ensure that your whole team is involved in CRM; the correct management of relationships with customers has to be applied by all the people involved in the customer service jigsaw mentioned at the start of this chapter. This even includes non-face-to-face team members such as warehouse, dispatch, purchasing and accounts staff. Everyone has useful knowledge, but it is only when all viewed together through a CRM process that you can see how powerful this can be. For example, if your accounts person doesn't share with your sales representative that a customer owes money, goods might go out when they shouldn't; conversely, if accounts don't know that sales have given a customer 60 days' credit instead of 30 days, they might mistakenly issue a stop on any orders going out.

In smaller businesses there should be one person responsible for gathering customer data from all the team and assimilating it into meaningful information to be shared and acted on. Obtaining information but not acting on it is a complete waste of time.

Most businesses have customers whom they have not dealt with for a long time, and if you don't have a CRM process you might not realise it and so not know who they are – after all, it's unlikely you can remember all your customers and their spending habits. You will probably only find out that you have lost them when you discover they have not been to you for ages and that they have probably gone to one of your competitors, and you will – irrationally – feel upset because you felt they were yours. However, customers are not yours by right; you have to earn their custom. Unfortunately, business owners often forget their existing customers in the rush to get new ones, presuming that their existing customers will never leave. This is a very unwise strategy – as already stated, it costs more to get a lapsed customer back than it does to keep them in the first place. Feeling unimportant is a major reason for customers leaving.

Unfortunately, by the time you find out they have not ordered or been in contact for a while it's too late. The CRM process should highlight customer buying patterns so you can make contact with them before you lose them.

Salesperson	Customer name	Account No.	Phone No.	Sales in year 1	Sales in year 2	Sales in year 3	Sales in year 4 to date	Date contacted	Contacted by whom?	Result	Action
Mary	ABC Supplies	ABC1	01234 567891	£66,928.55	£35,944.50	£1,500.00	£0.00		MH		
Mary	Northbridge	NOR 1	01234 567891	£67,639.97	£29,508.08	£97,148.05	£33,000.00		WM		
Mary	Graphite	GRA1	01234 567891	£31,090.35	£13,011.11	£44,101.46	£29,400.97		HA		
Mary	MNG Display	MNG1	01234 567891	£15,091.52	£28,874.83	£43,966.35	£29,310.90		MH		
Mary	Wimbledon	WIM1	01234 567891	£20,151.55	£8,954.94	£29,106.49	£15,000.00		WM		
Mary	ABC Print	ABC2	01234 567891	£17,526.49	£9,230.42	£0.00	£12,837.94		HA		
Mary	City Tools	CIT1	01234 567891	£19,390.37	£3,653.06	£21,043.43	£11,362.29		MH		
Mary	Staples	STA1	01234 567891	£15,980.01	£6,791.70	£22,771.71	£25,181.14		WM		
Bill	Oxford Press	OXF1	01234 567891	£11,998.73	£10,240.34	£22,239.07	£14,826.05		HA		
Bill	Totnes Plastics	TOT1	01234 567891	£14,858.71	£6,499.65	£15,356.00	£16,238.91		MH		
Bill	Phone Key	PHO1	01234 567891	£9,934.84	£6,832.55	£10,876.00	£9,178.26		WM		
Bill	Mirrors	MIR1	01234 567891	£10,761.33	£5,834.67	£10,092.00	£8,064.00		HA		
Bill	Car Support	CAR1	01234 567891	£11,333.38	£4,005.15	£13,687.00	£12,225.69		MH		
Bill	Glassware	GLA1	01234 567891	£12,154.33	£3,127.23	£13,500.00	£15,187.71		WM		
Hassan	Potts 4 U	POT1	01234 567891	£12,038.28	£3,058.53	£11,283.00	£8,064.54		HA		
Hassan	Creme	CRE1	01234 567891	£9,784.55	£3,678.71	£10,450.00	£1,975.51		MH		
Hassan	South Skills	SOU1	01234 567891	£10,542.85	£2,891.00	£10,000.00	£955.90		WM		
Hassan	XYZ Supplies	XYZ1	01234 567891	£8,825.22	£3,153.62	£935.00	£985.89		HA		

Example of a CRM spreadsheet

When calling customers, you might say 'This is a courtesy call to see if everything is okay; is there anything you want or need?' but with lapsed customers you may wish to start off with an apology for not contacting them before and then ask if there is anything you can do for them. Be careful not to sound insincere when you are apologising – customers can tell if you are, and virtually nothing will push them towards your competitors quicker than them thinking you are insincere! Keeping the customers you want to keep is something that needs to be worked at – don't take them for granted. Every communication between you and them should be memorable for the right reasons, regardless of the size of their order.

Most CRM is software-based and there are many extremely cost-effective systems in the marketplace. If that option is outside your current budget, even an Excel spreadsheet of customers, which highlights their spending history, is incredibly useful. You can quickly see which customers would normally be buying from you and how much they would be spending. You can also add comments about when you last contacted them, the result of that call and the next action to take. An example of this type of spreadsheet is given on page 131.

The spreadsheet shows which accounts belong to which salesperson. It allows for comparisons to be made between the accounts of the same salesperson (or the only salesperson, in a sole trader environment), and also the accounts of all the salespeople (as would be applicable for larger companies).

A lot of information can be pulled out of the spreadsheet. In the example above:

- Looking at the first account, ABC Supplies, you can see clearly that they have drastically cut their business with the company in the past few years, to such an extent that, so far this year, they have ordered nothing.
- Northbridge's orders with the company this year are not as good as they were in year 3. Then they were at a record level, which suggested that their business was performing well, but it dipped drastically before that in year 2 and it looks to date as if it could dip again in year 4.

Finally, the company would need to do something with the information gained from the spreadsheet. In the case of ABC Supplies there should have been an urgent follow-up call, or even a visit, as soon as the decline in year 2 became obvious, to find out whether their business was suffering or whether they'd switched supplier. It would appear from the figures that they didn't make that follow-up call, so couldn't address the fall in sales. If this follow-up is left until year 4, it may be too late to get the business back. In the case of the Northbridge account, the company did see the dipping trend earlier and got the relationship back on track with the customer. It now appears that Northbridge's custom will surpass previous orders – a result of excellent customer service.

IT makes it easier to organise and automate sales information with all the other business functions that are customer-facing such as marketing, customer service and technical support.

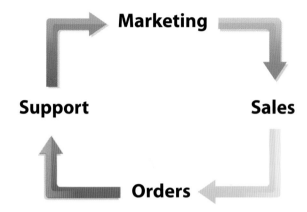

CRM is an ongoing cycle of customer support and marketing resulting in more sales

These websites will give you an overview of CRM software:
- http://www.sage.co.uk
- www.microsoft.com.

A key issue with CRM is making the customer feel important and special to you and your business. This can be done in many ways, but one particular way costs nothing – it just requires a little time and some concentration: listening.

LISTENING SKILLS

Listening to customers shows you are interested in them and what they have to say, which makes them feel special and positive about you. The opposite is also true; you have probably experienced how negative you feel towards someone who doesn't listen to you, whether when in a shop or in conversation with a member of your family or a friend. Certainly most of us as teenagers have screamed at our parents 'You never listen to me!' What we are after is active listening, where we feel the other person is taking in what we say and responding. Ensure you listen to your customers – it not only makes them feel special but you'll also know you have the correct facts from them, so it's win:win.

KEY TO SUCCESS

Active listening is different from hearing – it is a skill that helps to build solid relationships, prevent misunderstandings and make others feel valued.

There are barriers to listening:

- Talking – if you are talking, you can't listen.
- Thinking about something else – if you are distracted, you are not concentrating on what the person is saying.
- Making assumptions – thinking you know what a customer wants just by looking at him, or relating what he is saying to a similar experience you have had or someone close to you has had.

To make sure you listen properly you need to:

- Ask your chosen questions – it's best to have a list of questions handy, then you can't forget anything and you are not distracted by trying to remember which question comes next.
- Listen to the customer's answers – listen, and show you are listening: maintain eye contact, nod and make encouraging noises and statements such as 'I see', 'okay', 'I understand', 'hmm', 'ah', 'yes', 'go on' and so on.
- 'Listen' to non-verbal communication – this is about watching what a customer's body language is saying to you: does he seem relaxed or stressed, calm or uptight?
- Aim for 20 per cent talking and 80 per cent listening – leave your customer to do most of the talking; ask your questions then keep quiet and listen to the answers.
- Record – make brief notes so you have information to come back to; don't rely on your memory. However, don't write so much you forget to look at your customer and listen to him!

CRM is not just achieved face-to-face, it's about all the communication channels, including the ease (or otherwise) of navigating your website, your emails and SMS messages, and – arguably the most important – phone conversations with customers and potential customers. It's important that the right messages are communicated in the correct way, otherwise you will have to deal with negative feelings and all the expense of either losing a customer or managing a longer customer journey to them feeling positive (see page 140).

Speaking skills and phone customer service

Anyone can speak on the phone... can't they? People take making and receiving phone calls for granted, as it's something they have probably done for many years. However, business calls differ from personal calls – they are part of the overall CRM. Your manner and perceived attitude when speaking with existing or potential customers are vital, but phone skills are often overlooked. It's important that your business is viewed as positive and professional – from the first phone conversation with a potential customer, right the way through to reinforcing to existing customers that they have made the right decision in choosing to deal with you.

The importance of positive phone communication

Consider the points below, which should make you and your team aware of the power you hold when you make and receive business calls:

- Making a call is like making a visit to a customer.
- Taking a call is like receiving a visitor.
- Putting a caller on hold is like asking a visitor to wait at the door.
- Transferring a call is like introducing two people.
- Leaving a message is like making a call or a visit to a customer.
- Taking a message is like receiving someone else's visitor.

The quality of your voice plays a vital part in communicating your business message to customers. These points all apply in face-to-face conversation too, but are particularly important on the phone, where you are relying on your voice alone to make an impression:

- The volume of your voice has a huge effect. If your voice is too loud or booming, customers may perceive you and your business as boisterous at best, pushy or aggressive at worst. If your voice is too soft and quiet, they may feel you are likely to be timid and not knowledgeable.
- If the pitch of your voice is too high or too low, it may be difficult for customers to understand you and this may leave them feeling confused about your business.
- If you speak too quickly, customers may miss vital information and may also feel that any service they receive from you will be rushed and not personalised. If your speech is too slow, they may think that you are unknowledgeable and may suspect the quality of offering delivered by your business.

- If the clarity of your speech is poor and slurred, customers will also presume that you and your business are slack and operating at the lower end of the quality scale; conversely, well-pronounced delivery in a clear voice will give the impression of a well-organised, high-quality business.
- If your voice is dull, boring and monotonous to listen to, customers will assume that you and your business are dull and boring too.

Smile when you speak: this makes your tone of voice lighter, which appears more friendly and approachable. Although you may not be aware of it, a smile travels down the phone line.

A few further tips:
- Speak clearly and distinctly to ensure that you sound approachable yet professional.
- Use changes of tone to emphasise any points you need to make and to demonstrate that you understand what customers are saying.
- Decrease the speed of your voice at important points and pause slightly afterwards to allow the information to be absorbed – the customer might even be making notes.
- Raising and lowering the volume of your voice gives it interest and can help to add emphasis.

KEY TO SUCCESS

Give phone customers your EAR; be Enthusiastic, Attentive and Receptive.

Customers judge a business they have never been to on the strength of its communication. This may be via your website or through promotions but at some time they will probably phone for information. Communication on the phone is never good when the phone is answered in a rushed, distracted or generally unprofessional way.

You need to assess the quality of your phone communication skills and those of all the members of your team who answer the phone, whether they do it all the time or only occasionally. A good way to do this is by keeping records of phone calls made by you and members of your team over a set period of time. You can use the phone call summary sheet provided below to assess how well you and your team respond to customer calls.

Each member of your team should complete a form each time they have answered a call. This exercise will really make them think about what they are communicating to customers, in terms of both the actual information and the subliminal messages customers pick up on in voice and attitude, which can affect their perception of the quality of your offering.

The form must be completed as soon as possible after each conversation, while it is still fresh in the mind. There is no point in lying; encourage your team to be honest when completing the form. You may find it useful if another person listens occasionally to give objective feedback on the communication.

For assessment purposes, a phone call can be broken down into four parts:

- background information
- the start of the conversation
- the middle of the conversation
- the end of the conversation.

Fill in each section of the form as follows:

- Team member's name – Write your name at the top left of the form.
- Customer – Write the customer's name in the top middle section of the form.
- Date – Fill in the day of the week and the date to avoid any confusion.
- Time – Fill in the time of the call. Make the time of day clear by using 'am' and 'pm' or 24-hour clock.
- Type of call – Was it a potential customer seeking information, or an existing customer wanting information or an appointment?
- Did you introduce yourself? – This is a matter of courtesy.
- Did you speak clearly and slowly? – Your listener should have had time to follow and digest what you were saying.
- Did you allow the customer time to speak? – Ensure that your listener had time to ask questions and clarify things.
- Did you smile when talking? – This lifts your tone of voice so it's lighter and more friendly.
- Did you review/confirm the customer's need/reason for calling? – This shows you were listening.
- Did you use the customer's name appropriately throughout? – Older customers may prefer 'Mrs' or 'Mr' rather than being addressed by their first name.
- Did you avoid using jargon? – Customers do not necessarily have your level of knowledge, so use words they will understand.
- Did you sound friendly yet professional? – What subliminal messages did your voice send out?
- Did you speak appropriately to the customer? – Judge this in relation to their age and how he first spoke to you.
- Did you sign off politely? – 'Thank you for your call/enquiry/interest in our business/products.'
- Did you ask the customer if he needed anything else? – 'Is there anything else I can help you with?'
- Did you ask if you had answered all the customer's questions?
- Comments – Add any additional comments that will be helpful to you and others in the future.

PHONE CALL SUMMARY

TEAM MEMBER'S NAME: _____   CUSTOMER : _____   DATE: _____

TIME : _____   TYPE OF CALL : _____

START	Y/N
Did you introduce yourself?	
Did you speak clearly and slowly?	

MIDDLE	
Did you allow customer time to speak?	
Did you smile when talking	
Did you review / confirm the customer' need / reason for calling?	
Did you ask for & use customer's name appropriately throughout?	
Did you avoid using jargon?	
Did you sound friendly yet professional?	
Did you speak appropriately to the customer?	
Comments:	

END	
Did you sign off politely?	
Did you ask the customer if they needed anything else?	
Did you ask if you had answered all their questions?	

Comments:

A phone call summary sheet can be used to record details of every call answered by your team

OVER TO YOU

Photocopy the phone call summary form so there are enough copies to cover all the incoming phone calls for a week. Divide the number of calls received as evenly as possible throughout your team. Ensure everyone gets to observe everyone else at least twice and give feedback. At the end of the week, compare the results across the team:

- What types of calls came in?
- How many of each type were there?
- What were the busiest times of day?

Continued

- What were the busiest days of the week?
- Were your views of how you handled the calls the same as the observer's?
- On average, of the 12 questions, how many did each team member mark as 'Yes'?
- On average, how many did the observer mark as 'Yes'?

The information taken about the types, times and dates of calls is helpful when it comes to deciding your opening hours and what knowledge is required to effectively answer customer queries.

This information should also be assimilated into customer care training both for front-of-house staff and any other members of your team who interact with customers on the phone. In addition, it should be used to analyse skill gaps in your team and determine additional training needs. Customer care training, of which this is a part, is normally delivered when a new member of the team joins, but it should be an ongoing process, too.

MEASURING CUSTOMER SATISFACTION

You've just carried out self-analysis on your customer service phone performance, using phone call summary forms; you also need to get an outside perspective on your customer service. This outside perspective is even more important to the growth and continued success of your business if you are a sole trader, as you only have one pair of ears and eyes judging your performance – yours.

In Chapter 2 you looked at how to design and use customer satisfaction surveys (see pages 52–60). If you don't know how satisfied your customers are, you don't know how well your business is doing or how susceptible you are to losing them to a competitor. If a customer gave you two out of four for a friendly welcome but marked a competing business as three or four out of four, he probably won't stay your customer for long. Regular questionnaires keep you up to date with how your business is viewed by your customers. By using the same questions across a series of questionnaires, **trends** can be easily spotted and addressed appropriately. The responses should also be measured against the results of the mystery shopper reviews of your competitors (see page 79), so you can see where your business sits alongside your competition.

**? JARGON
: BUSTER**

Trends can be observed from information collected over a period of time (for example into one spreadsheet). They demonstrate where you are getting better, staying the same or getting worse in terms of performance.

Look at the customer satisfaction survey questions you came up with in Chapter 2 (see page 60). Based on these:

- identify the standard questions you need answers to on a regular basis
- come up with four specific questions about issues you want answers to now.

Customer satisfaction questionnaires should be given to all your customers; try not to miss anyone out, as all responses are valuable. If your customers deal with you on a regular basis they would only receive a questionnaire every now and then; if they only deal with you on an occasional basis they may complete one every time.

This type of regular questionnaire will ensure that you are aware of any upward trends in satisfaction, which you can then build on to become even stronger. It will also highlight any downward trends so you can address the issues before they do any damage to your business. Growth comes from building on your strengths and addressing weaknesses. Ongoing questionnaires also allow you to canvass opinion on specific issues, through the ad hoc questions you add at the end, which can save you from making expensive mistakes. Remember: your offering should be all about what your customers want, not what you want.

IDENTIFYING TRENDS

Customer satisfaction questionnaires give you a snapshot of information taken over a very brief period of time. The average time taken for a customer to complete such a survey is 30–60 seconds. They are based on one person's view and that view is impacted on by a number of variables outside the influence of you or your business. These variables can make a customer react differently from day to day. Variables might be specific to that customer (such as being in a bad mood because of a disagreement at home or at work) or generic to everyone (such as bad weather, traffic jams, or no parking spaces available).

Because of the circumstances and variables for each customer it is important to have:

- Enough completed questionnaires to give a rounded view of all satisfaction levels. You really need questionnaires completed by at least 10 per cent of all the customers who deal with your business during the period of time the questionnaires are set.
- Responses to the same set of standard questions asked at regular intervals over a period of time, ideally four times a year.

When information from individual satisfaction questionnaires is compiled into a customer satisfaction trend survey that covers the whole year, the information shown gives a much broader overview and depth of data, and allows you to see where the business might be going.

Trend spotting is a valuable management ability – it allows you to flag up issues so you can deal with them. Spotting trends is not just about seeing negative issues and how to deal with them; it's also about spotting positive trends, promoting them and building on them.

Information from customer satisfaction surveys should be transferred to an annual trend survey sheet. You can start to see trends as soon as you input the second set of data but they are not normally reviewed in depth until there is a year's worth of data to evaluate. However, if you notice after the second survey that something is going badly wrong, you should of course deal with it immediately.

CUSTOMER SATISFACTION TREND SURVEY

STANDARD QUESTIONS	1st	2nd	3rd	4th
Efficient staff handling of your booking	TOTAL AVERAGE			
Friendly and knowledgeable staff				
Look and feel of the store/business				
Quality and range of products				
Value for money				
How likely are you to recommend this business to a friend or colleague?				
Opening hours meet your needs				

TOTAL: ADD ALL THE RESULTS FROM YOUR QUESTIONNAIRES FOR EACH PERIOD

AVERAGE: TO FIND THE AVERAGE DIVIDE THE TOTAL BY THE NUMBER OF ACTUAL SURVEYS FOR THAT PARTICULAR TIME

Keep the completed customer satisfaction questionnaires together in a safe place until as many customers as possible have completed them within the set timescale, say three months. Then set aside some time to fill in the trend survey sheet as follows:

- Add up all the scores, question by question, until you have seven sets of number totals, one for each standard question. Add them to the top of the rectangular box next to the relevant question marked TOTAL.
- Add up the number of respondents for each question.
- Divide the totals by the number of respondents. Put that figure in the bottom section of the rectangle marked AVERAGE.

Example: TOTAL figure for first question (107) ÷ number of respondents (43) = AVERAGE (2.49).

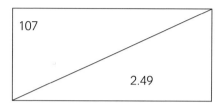

Each column represents a set of quarterly questionnaire scores: column 1 is for the first quarter questionnaire, column 2 for the second quarter, column 3 for the third quarter and column 4 for the final quarter.

After each column has been completed, compare the results against the previous column or columns and note whether the average for each question is up or down. If it's gone up it means there is an improvement, if it's stayed the same it means there is no improvement but it's no worse, and if the average has gone down it means things have got worse and action needs to be taken immediately. If the average goes down, as a business owner you must resist the urge to be confrontational, angry or upset with your team members. You must realise that if things are going wrong there will be a reason – usually that they need more support to do their jobs properly, which will require training. It will help if you remember that your team don't wake up every morning determined to sabotage your business and that mistakes are just that... mistakes. Your role is to ensure that your team have the skills and tools to do their job properly. If they don't, you must look to yourself first to see where you went wrong and where you could have supported them more.

After each survey has been completed, keep it for comparison purposes against future trends when you reuse some of the standard questions. You may wish to consider putting the results up in the team space so all team members have access to the data.

Your should use the information from the customer satisfaction trend survey sheets on an ongoing basis, when planning promotions, publicity, training requirements and budgets, SWOT analysis and so on, plus a host of other business projects where customer satisfaction information is central to the planning process. This is an essential business tool; care of your customers and knowledge of how well your business performs through their eyes is useful on an ongoing basis.

QUALITY CONTROL

Quality control is a process by which you make sure you get what you wanted. It might be for something as basic as the outcome of a telephone call, all the way through to developing a new website. Quality control is really about managing the quality of your customers' experience through every step of their journey with you – ensuring every piece of your customer relationship jigsaw fits together seamlessly.

There are two key phrases, which are often used interchangeably, that sum up quality control and the related issue of quality assurance:
- Quality assurance makes sure you do the correct things, in the correct way, in the first place.
- Quality control measures the results of your actions.

Questionnaires, informal chats and mystery shopper feedback are all tools for managing quality. Training, as stated in the last section, is an important aspect of quality control; people need to know how to do something before they can do it correctly. As a business owner, never assume that someone knows how to do something; it's your responsibility to ensure they have the training and support required so you know that they know how to do it.

Keeping your finger on the pulse of how satisfied your customers are with your service is great, but no quality control mechanism and trend analysis can ever avoid out-of-the-blue and seemingly random complaints. The next section looks at how to deal with these.

CUSTOMER COMPLAINTS

Do the very words 'customer complaints' send shivers down your spine? Some people react with fear and trepidation when a customer has a complaint. But remember, complaints are merely another form of communication between you and your customers, and they need to be addressed as part of the CRM process.

Think like the customer! How do you react as a consumer when you feel the need to complain? Do you complain or do you vote with your feet and leave because you don't want to make a fuss? If you leave, you don't give the service provider a chance to put things right – they may not even be aware that the business or their team are doing anything wrong, and so they can't improve their service. If you were that service provider you'd want to know what was wrong, or perceived as wrong... wouldn't you?

KEY TO SUCCESS

Never assume: it makes an ASS out of U and ME.

KEY TO SUCCESS

For a competitive advantage you may wish to put your business through the ISO 9001 quality management training programme and promote the fact that you are committed to great customer service. There are numerous companies that offer this training – an internet search for 'Quality Management ISO 9001' will bring up plenty of options.

How many complaints do you get from your customers? How many don't complain to you and simply leave or, even worse, tell others about their dissatisfaction? In other words, how many opportunities to improve do you miss? Because that is what complaints are: they are opportunities to improve your business and your customer care skills.

Why do some people feel threatened by the word 'complaint'? Why do some members of the team presume it is a manager's job to deal with complaints? If a complaint is dealt with appropriately straight away, the damage is much reduced – as consumers, we know that if a service provider puts something right and does so promptly, we may actually feel better about them than we did before.

DEALING WITH COMPLAINTS EFFECTIVELY

People often make assumptions that all complainants are going to be ranting and raving, red-faced and unreasonable, when in fact that is far from the truth. If customers are dealt with appropriately, the acts of complaining and dealing with that complaint can, and should, create a positive win:win situation. The customer is satisfied and the business learns how to be better. As complaints are such golden opportunities to improve, do ensure that systems are in place to record them. A complaints-capture process is simple to create but, as with all systems, needs to be used, analysed and the data acted on; capturing complaints is only the start of the process.

Having a complaints-capture process enables you to spot any emerging complaint trends. Complaints are generally related to one of three things: you/your staff, your offering/service or your business environment. The vast majority of complaints are from people who feel that part of the service was not what they expected – and they don't want anything other than to prevent it happening again. In other words, they are giving your business an opportunity to put it right for the next time. If you ignore their concerns, however small, you will lose their custom – no-one likes to be ignored.

You need to listen quietly to the customer's complaint, not interrupt, keep eye contact, look concerned, and react positively. In this way you will turn complainants into advocates. Most complaints are easily put right. It is important that each team member takes ownership of customers' concerns and does something about them, rather than adopt the 'hot potato' attitude and try to offload them to you as business owner.

Here is a step-by-step guide to dealing with complaints:
1 **Do not hide!** Avoiding the customer will not get the complaint resolved.
2 **Listen actively** – Show that you are concerned about the customer and what he is saying by maintaining eye contact, not

interrupting, making encouraging noises, nodding your head and saying things like 'I see', 'uh-huh', 'go on', 'I understand' and so on. Being listened to helps to calm people down; they know you are taking them seriously if they can see they have your attention.

3 **Repeat** – Repeat back to the complainant what he has said and review what you've heard to make sure you have your facts right. For example, 'Can I just repeat back to you what I understood you to say, as I want to make sure I have this right?'

4 **Say sorry** – The customer is waiting to hear you say the word 'sorry' and when he does he will calm down much more quickly. Even if what has happened is not your fault you should still say sorry – but use wording like 'I'm so sorry you are upset' or 'I'm so sorry you feel that way'. Neither of those statements is taking personal responsibility for anything that has happened.

5 **Ask what the customer wants** – Normally customers don't want anything, other than for what has happened not to happen again. They also don't want to be taken advantage of and they need to be listened to. However, ask what the customer would like as a means of making it up to him. Often he will ask for less than you'd give, so let him be in the driving seat at this stage.

6 **Reach agreement** – If it is in your power to agree to what the customer has asked for, you should do so immediately and gather any details that may be required to fulfill that: delivery address, contact number and so on.

7 **Refer to line manager** – If you are the business owner you'll have the authority to deal with anything. However, if staff members are not in a position to agree to what the customer would like, they need to refer the situation to you or, in larger businesses, their line managers. Train your team to be courteous and say something like 'I don't have the level of authority required to sanction that, so will get my line manager, who will be able to help you' and apologise for the customer having to wait.

8 **Thank the customer** – It sounds a little twee, but you should thank the customer for complaining. Say something like 'Thank you for bringing this to my attention; if you hadn't done so we wouldn't have known this was happening, so we are very grateful for you taking the time to point it out to us.'

9 **Make sure it happens** – Ensure that what you agreed to does happen, exactly as agreed and when you said it would. Getting it wrong at this stage will bring back all the customer's bad feelings.

10 **Follow up** – Allow some time, not too much though, for the resolution to be delivered and then make contact to ask if everything was okay and to thank the customer again for bringing the issue to your attention.

Create a list of typical complaints in your business and role play a conversation based on the steps above, showing how one of these complaints could be addressed and resolved.

You are often better thought of by your customers when you deal well with a complaint than if the complaint had never arisen. Most resolutions take one of the following forms, although your business might be different:

- Product-based – Where the complainant wants a specific discounted product, either the same one they were complaining about or a different/additional one.
- Service-based – Where the complainant wants a discounted additional service, either the same or a different/additional one.
- Money off – Where the complainant wants a discount on his or her next purchase.
- Freebie – Where the complainant wants something for nothing.

An example of a complaints capture form is given below. Each member of your team should complete one of these for each complaint they deal with. A nominated team member should keep them safe after the complaints have been dealt with. This doesn't have to be you, but it does have to be someone organised and responsible. Capturing complaints in this way helps you to be better at CRM and serving your customers.

Fill in the form as follows:
- Add the team member's name to the top left, then the customer's name and the date the complaint was raised.
- Tick the box that best describes the type of complaint: whether it is about a member of staff, the offering, the service or any part of your business environment. If none of those are applicable, tick 'other' and state what the complaint was.
- Customer preferred solution – Write down what the customer says they want, for example 'I think I should have a free/different/new…'
- Business suggested solution – Write down the possible solution you are suggesting; this may be the same as the customer's preferred solution or it may be something different, depending on the situation.
- Agreed solution – A solution needs to be agreed and then it needs to be written in along with agreed terms: timescales, personnel involved, the days of the week you can/can't offer the solution, the offering that can/can't be involved…
- Agreed terms – What levels of discussion and negotiation took place? Record these, so there is no comeback later as to what was offered and what was not.

COMPLAINTS CAPTURE FORM

TEAM MEMBER'S NAME: _____   CUSTOMER NAME: _____   DATE: _____

WHAT IS COMPLAINT:

COMPLAINT TYPE: ◯ PERSON   ◯ OFFERING   ◯ SERVICE   ◯ ENVIRONMENT   ◯ OTHER PLEASE STATE

Description:

CUSTOMER PREFERRED SOLUTION:

BUSINESS SUGGESTED SOLUTION:

ESCALATION REQUIRED:

AGREED SOLUTION:

NEXT STEPS / FOLLOW UP:

- Next steps/Follow-up – Who is involved in the solution? Record the agreed timescales for the solution to be delivered, such as within two weeks. Is confirmation in writing required? When the solution has been delivered, follow up – ascertain if the customer is happy with the solution.
- Escalation procedure – If a team member feels that he can't deal with the customer satisfactorily, he will need to adopt the escalation procedure – briefing the appropriate person, such as his line manager, to take over.

Using these forms to record each complaint enables you to get complaints out from under the carpet and helps you assess what your customers think is wrong with the business. As you are in business to meet the needs of your customers and make a profit from them, it makes sense to listen to and act on their complaints or concerns, not to ignore them. If one customer speaks up and complains it is rare for there not to be others thinking the same thing. However unpalatable it can initially appear, dealing with complaints really is an opportunity to put things right and make your business better.

While it is important to deal with each complaint individually, in order to make the customer happy, it is vital that the information on the complaint capture forms is collated so that an action plan can be formulated to avoid the same complaint being repeated. You need to deal with the causes of complaints, not simply the complaints themselves.

Create a clear and transparent refunds and returns policy which all your staff fully understand. This will often be based on your competitors' policy; if they accept returns of non-faulty items within 28 days of purchase, you may feel that you need to have the same policy. The important thing here is that your policy can be better than the law requires, but not worse. The legislation on accepting returns is dealt with in Chapter 9.

CASE STUDY 3

Denise Lawson owns a baby and maternity shop and holds regular monthly staff meetings. At a recent meeting held after Denise returns from holiday, staff report that they have noted that there seems to be an increasing number of complaints about a particular model of pram. Jane, who works Wednesday to Saturday, reports that she has had three prams returned over the last month because the folding mechanism has buckled. Alison, who works on Monday and Tuesday, says that she has also had one example of the same fault with the same model. Denise asks what action they have taken and both have returned the prams to the manufacturer for repair. They comment that all four customers had been unhappy with this, as they had been left without a pram, but store policy is to allow refunds up to 28 days from purchase, and all four had been bought several months earlier.

Denise is disappointed that her staff appear to have dealt unsympathetically with the customers by applying the store policy without considering the inconvenience of the customer. She points out to them that under the Sale of Goods Act products that are not fit for purpose, as the prams clearly are not, breach the contract with the customer. The shop has a choice whether to repair or replace the prams, but this must not cause the customers 'significant inconvenience'.

Continued

Denise decides to contact each of the customers, apologise for the way their complaint has been handled, and ask them to visit the store at their earliest convenience to choose a replacement pram. She realises that these could be long-term customers, buying pushchairs, cots, playpens, toys, etc for their children, and that losing their custom for the sake of a faulty pram would not be good business.

She then contacts the manufacturer to advise them that she is dissatisfied with the quality of the particular model of pram and ask them to collect the remaining stock and give her credit for the prams already returned.

Denise also starts a complaints log where all customer complaints are recorded so that she can be aware of any trends and all her staff can be made aware of complaints occurring when they are not working.

 OVER TO YOU

Based on your own business, or personal experiences and observations, complete a complaints capture form for each of the following types of complaint: offering, service, staff member and business environment.

Reviewing all the complaints forms at the end of every week and at the end of every month will help you identify any trends that are emerging – is there a pattern to the complaints that you are receiving, and if so, what can you do to address it? Not capturing complaints can be disastrous for your business – having the information and not doing anything with it is madness!

Having gone through the activities above you will see that complaints are not something to be scared of, but are really a means to improve your service and the skills of your team members. Remember:

*You can please **some** of the people **all** of the time.*
*You can please **all** of the people **some** of the time.*
*BUT you can never please **all** of the people **all** of the time.*

However, it's good business practice to try!

As you will have seen from the surveys and informal interviews (such as face-to-face chats and phone conversations) you have carried out

 KEY TO SUCCESS

Knowing what your customers are unhappy about is even more important than knowing what they are happy about – it is what they are unhappy about that can cause them to leave and give their money to your competitors. A complaints capture form gives added value to your CRM – as long as you act on the information.

with your customers, good customer relationships are based on many factors. A key consideration in this relationship, from the customers' perspective, is for you to go beyond what they expect of you and to surprise them with the lengths to which you are prepared to go to keep them – this is covered in the next section.

EXCEEDING EXPECTATIONS

You should aim to give all your customers more than they expect to receive – ie, to exceed their expectations. The way you achieve this can take many forms. You might give customers more time than they thought they would have with you, better-quality goods or materials, quicker delivery, more back-up and support than expected and so on. In all your dealings with customers, think: 'What else can I do to make their transaction with my business better?'

Going the extra mile can also be delivered by a business in a formal and recognised way – you may want to consider training in, and offering, a recognised standard of customer service. See page 131 for sources of information on customer care qualifications.

The Institute of Customer Service has carried out research to identify the most important elements of service delivery according to customers. Their results are:

- timelines
- appearance
- courtesy
- quality and efficiency
- ease of doing business
- problem-solving.

OVER TO YOU

Table 1

Criteria (up to 10 points for each)	Mark yourself	Customer's marks
Timelines		
Appearance		
Courtesy		
Quality and efficiency		
Ease of doing business		
Problem-solving		
Total (out of 60)		

Mark yourself and/or each member of your team out of 10 for each element, then get a customer to do the same.

WHERE TO GO FOR MORE INFORMATION

As this chapter has shown, the biggest single factor in improving your business's relationship with your customers is the care and support delivered by you and your team. The following organisations can support your internal customer service training by providing qualifications and information.

- City & Guilds offers a wide range of qualifications in customer service: www.cityandguilds.com.
- The Institute of Leadership and Management (ILM) offers qualifications to equip you with the skills to get the best out of your team in all areas, including customer service. Visit www.i-l-m.com.
- The British Standards Institute (BSI) publishes the British Standard Code of Practice for Customer Service. This sets out best practice guidance for dealing with internal and external customers: shop.bsigroup.com.
- For real-life customer service case studies, visit the Institute of Customer Service (ICS): www.instituteofcustomerservice.com.
- For a good general overview of customer care for business, take a look at these Business Link web pages: www.businesslink.gov.uk.

CONCLUSION

Your customers bring in the money to your business that you use to pay your bills and salaries – they are the most important people to your business (after all, a business with no customers is not a business!) and you need to look after them. Improving relationships with your customers and exceeding their expectations will build customer loyalty. This will help to prevent not only you losing customers but also them giving their money to your competitors: every customer you lose is gained by one of your competitors. The activities have shown how everything needs to work together to form your customer relationship management (CRM) strategy. Your whole team needs to be on board with excellent service and this should be part of staff induction and ongoing training.

While customers are arguably the most important people to your business, without you and your team there is also no business. The next chapter looks at the working relationships between you and your team, which are as important as those between you and your customers. Ultimately, it's through you and your team that your service is delivered.

CHAPTER 5
WORKING
RELATIONSHIPS

INTRODUCTION

As you know from the previous chapter, the relationship between you and your customers is paramount, but the relationship you have with your team – be that one person or many – and the relationships they have with each other is as important. This chapter looks at the various ways you can work and communicate with your team, and your style of leadership. You lead the business to success but you also have to manage the issues, the day-to-day running of the business and the people involved. As you grow your business, this will increasingly involve managing, mentoring, motivating and empowering your team. It also explores the concept of the 'internal customer' and how recruitment issues can be addressed to benefit your business.

WORKING IN A TEAM

There are many aspects of working in a team, and all are important for it to succeed. The most important is that the team should achieve more together than the individual members would on their own. This is often shown as:

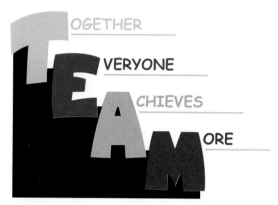

Together everyone achieves more acrostic

And is also known as synergy:

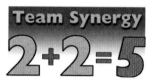

Team synergy sum

When a team is working well, everybody in it gets on with each other, and they support, encourage and help everyone else. Teamwork involves working together as a single unit rather than as different segments. Think of the best sports teams – yes, some contain individuals who are brilliant, but generally a well-honed team will beat a group of individuals who put themselves and their own glory first.

COMMUNICATION

There are many ways in which you communicate with your team and its members communicate with each other: written (by email, by text, through social media), verbal (face-to-face on a one-to-one basis, face-to-face in a group, on the phone) and through body language. You need to recognise that all people, including you, adopt different styles of communication depending on the situations they find themselves in and based on their previous experiences.

Understanding that there are different styles of communication will help you to react most effectively when dealing with your team members, particularly when you have to deal with a difficult situation with one of them. This understanding will also help you to recognise your own 'default' style of communication and to realise that you always have a choice as to which communication style you use.

Image modelling positive communication

There are four basic communication styles:

- **Assertive** – The most effective and healthiest form of communication is the assertive style. It's the way to get your point across calmly, without aggression and without putting anyone else down. This is how people usually communicate when they feel good about themselves, which gives them the confidence to put across what they want or need without shouting, being aggressive or generally being unpleasant to others, and also without playing office politics or manipulating situations or people.

- **Aggressive** – Aggressive communication always involves manipulation, either of a situation or of a person. Aggressive communicators may attempt to make people do what they want by making them feel guilty or by being intimidating and angry. Sometimes they act in this manner in an obvious way, sometimes more furtively; either way, they want to get their needs met and they will do whatever it takes to achieve it. Although there are a few arenas where aggressive behaviour is required (such as in certain sports or times of war), it will never work in a business or personal relationship. Even in war and aggressive sports there is often heavy reliance on team spirit, working together and strong leadership.

- **Passive** – Passive communication is easy-going and compliant, going with the flow, not wanting to upset the apple cart and hoping to avoid confrontation at all costs. Those using this style don't talk much, question even less and may actually do very little. They don't want to rock the boat – they have learnt that it's safer not to react and better to merge into the background than to stand up and be noticed.
- **Passive-aggressive** – This, as the name suggests, is a combination of styles. A passive-aggressive communicator avoids direct confrontation (passive), but attempts to 'get even' through manipulative (aggressive) behaviour. If you've ever thought about wanting to get even with someone or that someone needs to be 'taught a lesson', you've stepped pretty close to the devious, sneaky and backhanded world of the passive-aggressive. This style of communication is disruptive and often leads to office politics and rumour-mongering.

The only healthy communication style is assertive. However, in reality most people use a combination of these four styles, depending on the situation they find themselves in. The ultimate goal of communication is to get your needs met, so most people choose whatever style has worked best for them in a given situation in the past. If you take a really good look at yourself, you'll see that you've probably used all of these methods at some point in your life.

**OVER
TO YOU**

Which type of communication style do you think you use most? Now ask your friends and family which style they think you use most. Are the answers the same?

What are you communicating?
The important issue as the owner of a business is to recognise that your team members will communicate differently in different situations. For example, if people feel threatened they will communicate differently from when they feel secure. As a small business owner it is part of your role to set the best environment for effective communications, regardless of how you might feel. This means that when you are in a bad mood, for whatever reason, you must try not to show it because you may communicate to your team that there is a problem.

You come into work late after a meeting with your accountants that your team are aware of. You are clearly in a bad mood, announce 'I don't want to be disturbed!' and lock yourself in your office. What your team are likely to take from your communication is that there may be a problem with money. What you are actually in a bad mood about is that you got a parking ticket, even though the meeting itself went really well, but your team don't know that. Think about how this could affect team morale.

Everything you do or say communicates a message to the people you work with, whether it's the tone of your voice, the look on your face, the perceived 'tone' of a hastily written email or text, or your body language. You can see how body language (also known as non-verbal communication) communicates a message. When you look out of your car and see people talking to each other, even if you can't hear them you will still be able to tell the mood they are in by their body language – and so can your team, with you. Be aware of all your means of communication. Visit this website for more information on body language and the signs to look out for: www.h2g2.com. If you should want to take it even further, neuro-linguistic programming (NLP) is a useful thing to study – it will improve your self-awareness and ability to interpret other people's non-verbal communication. For more information visit www.anlp. org.

Communication styles can vary between different cultures, so be 'culturally aware' of the norms of the cultures among your team and customers – try to judge them by their standards, not by yours. For example, in some cultures it is considered rude to look people in the eye; in others the action of averting your eyes is seen as shifty.

CO-OPERATION

Co-operation is a vital part of teamwork and is something most people are taught from an early age – sharing toys, playing nicely and so on. 'United we stand, divided we fall' is a recurring theme throughout history, but co-operative spirit may be lost when the environment is not conducive to teamwork. If this happens, team members will start to act in their own best interests – the total opposite of what teamwork is about achieving. This is especially likely to happen if they feel threatened or demotivated for any number of reasons. For example, when a new person joins the team, as there is a change in the team's dynamics (this is covered in more detail in the recruitment section of this chapter); when team members do not understand the plan or goal for the business; or when they feel like outsiders, unimportant and insecure. Lack of co-operation within a team can also happen if they all feel they are being pitched against each other – if you operate a rewards-by-results system, you may be inadvertently encouraging an 'everyone for themselves' type of attitude rather than a healthy level of competition.

Collaboration and co-operation happen when everyone works together to reach a common goal or objective and put the team's needs before their own. A culture of co-operation and support helps to prevent conflict, or at the very least minimises the chances of it happening and its effects. This will have a positive effect on your bottom line as it saves time being wasted on conflict resolution.

It's worth noting that fostering an ethos of co-operation cannot happen overnight, and you will need to be persistent and persuasive until it is in place. Reaffirmation once it is achieved is also important. This might be done through internal rewards for the person with the most referrals or recommendations, or external recognition – entering your local Small Business Awards, perhaps the 'Best Customer Service in a Small Business' category. Think about running team-bonding events, whether they are external courses or light-hearted social events. It doesn't really matter how it's achieved as long as a unified, bonded team is the outcome.

Creating a balanced team

Teams need to have a variety of roles – and it's not just about different job titles. As your business grows, you need to look at the balance of these roles in the people that you're taking on. In a nutshell, you need to be aware of the basic differences between each role and what they each bring to the team so you don't end up with too many people of the same type, which can cause conflict and lack of achievement. For instance, if you have too many ideas-driven and excitable people but no thoughtful or planning people, this would be like a football team with too many strikers and no defenders.

You can categorise people into three role types, based on their main focus:
- those who do
- those who think and solve problems
- those who are people-oriented.

A useful way of understanding how particular skills fit into this picture is to look at the nine essential team roles as defined by Dr Meredith Belbin in the 1970s. You may be able to relate the following descriptions to people you've worked with before, or your tutors at school or college. See also: www.belbin.com.

Table of Belbin roles

Shaper
Lots of energy and action, challenging others to move forwards. Can be insensitive.

Completer/ finisher
Reliably sees things through to the end, ironing out the wrinkles and ensuring everything works well. Can worry too much and not trust others.

Implementer
Well-organised and predictable. Takes basic ideas and makes them work in practice. Can be slow.

Plant
Solves difficult problems with original and creative ideas. Can be a poor communicator and may ignore the details.

Resource investigator
Explores new ideas and possibilities with energy and with others. Good networker. Can be too optimistic and lose energy after the initial flush.

Monitor/ evaluator
Sees the big picture. Thinks carefully and accurately about things. May lack energy or ability to inspire others.

Teamworker
Cares for individuals and the team. Good listener and works to resolve social problems. Can have problems making difficult decisions.

Co-ordinator
Respected leader who helps everyone focus on their tasks. Can be seen as excessively controlling.

Specialist
Has expert knowledge/skills in key areas and will solve many problems here. Can be uninterested in all other areas.

Overall

Doing

Thinking/ problem-solving

People-oriented

Belbin roles

It is quite likely, though, that as a small business or sole trader, you are covering the skills of most of these roles yourself, even though some may not come naturally to you. But if you plan to grow your business you will need to be aware of your own strengths and weaknesses in these areas so you bring in others who will complement your skills, not conflict with them.

Recruitment is generally based on any applicant having the correct level of qualifications and experience required, and that is quite correct. But let's say you have two applicants with identical skill levels: one is a jovial, larger-than-life character with a big personality, who has great ideas; the other is shy and quiet but with great attention to detail and the ability to get things done. Both are technically equal but you'll need to think which one will best suit you, any other team members and your customers – and therefore your business. For example, if you have lots of doers but not enough thinkers, for example, let that guide you.

According to Belbin's theory, to achieve the best balance, there should be:

- a co-ordinator or shaper to lead
- a plant to stimulate ideas
- a monitor/evaluator to maintain honesty and clarity
- one or more implementers, teamworkers, resource investigators or completer/finishers to make things happen.

Getting the balance in a team right is vital. Teams work best when there is a balance of the main roles, when team members know their roles – even if they may have more than one – and know what is expected of them, work to each other's strengths and together manage any weaknesses. Getting your team balance right improves team morale and working relationships. It will also help you to achieve team and business goals much more quickly, as the different roles can work on different aspects at the same time.

In small businesses you will probably not be able to afford the luxury of having someone exclusively in the role of specialist. However, a specialist may be an existing team member who also has other skills or could be an external person, for example a consultant who is brought in as and when needed. For a list of consultants, visit the Federation of Small Business: www.fsb.org.uk.

Also see www.lifestyle.co.uk and Business Link, www.businesslink.gov.uk.

AGREEING GOALS

You have seen throughout the chapters in this book that setting goals and objectives is important, and when dealing with relationships at work it is the same. If everyone in your team knows what they are to achieve, when, how, at what cost and with whom, they will work better. The SMART acronym works here and gives you a goal or objective to measure success – or otherwise – against:

S – Specific
M – Measureable
A – Achievable
R – Realistic/relevant
T – Timed

Once you have written your business plan (see Chapter 1, page 39), you will create the top-level SMART goals to achieve the plan's objectives, which you will then share with your team. Involving your team in your business's goals will motivate them – they'll feel part of the business with all the feelings of security that brings; this will also encourage them to put forward their ideas. People are more likely to achieve a goal that they have been involved with from early on – and often achieve it quicker. Sharing goals can positively affect your bottom line, plus you get free ideas and input!

By breaking down the major SMART goals into team and individual SMART goals, you help to foster personal achievement, professional development, pride and co-operation. Achievement, and being seen to achieve, is a great motivator – and a motivated person will be more profitable. Verbal recognition, at the very least, must be given – and in front of everybody. Remember the saying 'Praise loudly, criticise softly'. If someone has done well it should be shared and they should be made to feel special; this motivates them and also the others watching.

Goals are not just for big plans; they are relevant for any situation where there is an achievable outcome. An example of a team goal might be:

To develop and implement Christmas promotions:
- *to brainstorm ideas and come up with four different promotions, which will be relevant to 90 per cent of customers*
- *to achieve a gross profit margin of at least 45 per cent*
- *to start taking pre-orders in mid-September*
- *to have stock in by mid-October.*

The different parts of the objective will be achieved by different members of the team, depending on their roles.

Any planning to achieve goals normally involves team meetings. The more effective the meetings, the more effective the process of achieving those goals will be. The next section looks at how to plan effective meetings.

EFFECTIVE MEETINGS

Team meetings are the time and place to share information, but they are also great motivators – they encourage discussion, debate and openness. In some businesses, they are often the only time all the team are together in one place for any length of time. However, sometimes communication in meetings isn't as effective as it should be, which can be a major ingredient in team dissatisfaction and demotivation. You need to communicate with your team in a way that is effective, efficient and has a positive effect. This applies whether there is just one additional person to you or many others.

Meetings can be:
- Ad hoc – This means they take place as and when needed, normally when something out of the ordinary has occurred which needs an immediate consensus view or when there is something specific to discuss, such as a sales promotion.
- Planned – As the name suggests, this is a planned-for meeting with an **agenda**.

Team meetings should be an effective and efficient means of communication between the team leader and team members, from team members to the team leader, and across the team.

Diagram showing the interflow of communication between members of a team and the team leader

How often a team can get together depends on a number of factors, such as whether team members have flexible working hours, or if you have a salesperson who is out on the road most of the time. But regardless of the size of your team – as long as there is more than one of you – there should be regular team meetings. Everyone should attend, and they should be looked forward to, planned, enjoyed and enable achievement of objectives. Regular meetings give everyone a chance to talk through any issue before it builds up into something caustic or destructive to the team or the business. They are also an opportunity, among other things, for updates, sharing knowledge, discussing trends and anything new, customer feedback and discussion of the types and number of complaints being received.

The best-case scenario is a meeting once a month. This allows issues to be addressed soon after they arise and means that everyone is aware of what is happening. However, if your ways of working mean that there can only be full team meetings every two or three months, make sure that between those meetings your team can come to you and discuss anything that is worrying them. It is then your responsibility to make sure you deal with the issue and share any relevant points with the rest of the team; it's likely that if one person is concerned about something then others will be too.

A well-planned meeting will ensure that all team members feel involved, important, relevant and motivated and look forward to the next one. You will get most from them when meetings are well planned – ideas are more free-flowing in an environment where there is plenty of time and positive energy between everyone. Unfortunately, in some companies, meetings are rarely held, are dreaded by the team and are seen as an opportunity for the boss to have a go at everyone. The main reason team meetings don't happen is they are not planned. Like anything else that is left to the last minute, they don't happen because everybody is too busy – or they do happen but are a waste of time. The advice in the following section will help you ensure that this doesn't happen to you or your team, and you will reap the business benefits.

PLANNING TEAM MEETINGS

A team meeting will achieve very little if there is no set agenda that lists the contents and order of the meeting. Learning how to create an agenda, which your team will be interested in and want to participate in, is an important business and people-management skill. It may be that, due to appointments and shifts, your team only comes together for these meetings, so you need to ensure this time counts and is productive for you all. Write meeting dates for the year on a calendar in the staff room so everyone is aware of them and can work around them.

It is a mistake to think that the meeting has to be chaired by you and just involves you speaking – it doesn't. For your team members to get the most from the meetings they should be actively involved and not passive participants. For this reason, if you have more than two in your team it is a good idea for each meeting to be chaired by a different person in rotation; this gives everyone the opportunity to manage the meetings and feel important. Alongside each meeting date, the chairperson's name should be written on the calendar so everyone knows who to go to with any queries or matters to discuss at each meeting.

Although the specific content will change from meeting to meeting, it's good if the basic meeting structure stays the same. That way everyone knows what to expect, what comes next, what they have to do and say, and so on. This means that the meetings are not seen as something to be worried, or even scared, about. The next section provides a best-practice model for getting the most out of your team meetings.

TEAM MEETING STRUCTURE

The overall length of a meeting should ensure that there is enough time for everyone to have an input, even if only a few words. The chairperson needs to be careful that the very vocal people don't take over and that the quiet ones can get a word in, so watching that everyone keeps to time is important. If you have enough people in your team, it's good to appoint a timekeeper for each meeting; again, this role can be rotated so everyone gets a chance.

The minutes of a meeting are the notes that are written down after each meeting as a record of what was talked about and what was agreed. At the beginning of a meeting, the minutes from the previous meeting are usually discussed briefly to identify any outstanding issues.

Here is an example agenda for a team meeting.
- Welcome from the chairperson – This is very brief; thank everyone for coming and for their hard work in the time since the last meeting. Allow 1 minute.
- Overview – This is where you give a general overview of what's been happening in the business since the last meeting. This ensures everyone is up to date with all the news, both good and bad, which gives them a feeling of involvement and importance. Allow 5–10 minutes.
- Team members' 'four whats' – Each team member in turn informs their colleagues about what they have been up to since the last meeting. This should be brief – perhaps only 4 minutes each – this timing is a good discipline for everyone to learn. The time is broken down into four 1-minute sections:
  - what they have done or achieved since the last meeting
  - what advantage to themselves, their colleagues or the business have they gained
  - what worries or concerns they have for the forthcoming month
  - what they need or want to do next (this may be regarding their worries or concerns, or to do with opportunities they have spotted).
  For example, a team member in a retail team may come up with the following:
  - I have brought the Autumn stock from the stock room and put it at the front of the shop.

- This will mean the new stock is in a prime position and will increase sales.
- I am concerned that the planned roadworks outside the front entrance will make it difficult for customers to access the shop.
- I want to produce a poster directing customers to the rear entrance.

- *Complaints update – Here you share with the team the information from last month's complaints log (see Chapter 4): how many complaints there were, and of what nature; whether there are more or fewer complaints than in previous months, what the possible/probable reasons were for the increase/decrease, and action planned in response to this. Trends over the last 12 months could also be covered. Allow 5 minutes.

- *Customer satisfaction update – This is where you review customer satisfaction levels. If it's a month where there has been a customer survey the results are discussed; if not, the discussion revolves around customers' informal comments and planned action. Allow 5 minutes.

- *Training update – Here you cover what training (if any) needs to be organised this month and any feedback from training taken in the past month. Allow 5 minutes.

- *Discussion point – This is chosen and introduced by anyone who is particularly interested or concerned about a subject and is discussed by everyone. It is usually a trade issue – perhaps a relevant article or something seen or heard about at a trade exhibition or event. All team members will be issued with the discussion point item a week before the meeting to enable them to read it and form their views. Each month's discussion point will be different, reflecting the differing interests of the team. Allow 5 minutes, or more if there is a lot to discuss.
  Two examples of topical discussion points in the retail industry might be the approach of Christmas and the effect that a proposed new shopping centre will have on trade.

- *Feelings form (see page 166) – For any small business owner, knowing how their team members are feeling is important; although you may think you know, this is an assumption. The form below is really for larger businesses but it can be adapted for smaller ones. The form is given to everyone at the end of the meeting, to be completed privately and anonymously within 2 minutes and handed directly to you. The form allows the team to express their feelings about their jobs, the business and their place within the team, and allows you to evaluate your team members' individual feelings and spot any negative trends.

- AOB – This stands for 'any other business' and includes any issues that are not on the agenda that a team member wants to raise and/or discuss. If any of the subjects raised are of an ongoing nature, they can be added to the next agenda. Allow up to 5 minutes.

- Close – The chairperson confirms the date of the next meeting, and who is to be the next chairperson and timekeeper. The rest of the details – customer satisfaction, complaints, training and

FEELINGS FORM

TEAM MEMBER'S NAME: _____   DATE: _____

This is how I feel about...

	Negative	$\rightarrow$		Positive
Being a member of my team:	1	2	3	4
My job role and responsibilities:	1	2	3	4
My relationship with other team members:	1	2	3	4
How my views are acted upon:	1	2	3	4
My long term prospects:	1	2	3	4

updates – should be agreed between the team; this helps with communication and co-operation skills.

*These five points may not always be included, or relevant, particularly in a small business. You can add them in as your business grows.

TIPS FOR SUCCESS

Preparation is everything when it comes to running successful meetings. Bear these points in mind:

- A week before the meeting, the chairperson should create the agenda and circulate it. This gives everyone time to prepare their 'four whats' and familiarise themselves with any topics to be discussed.
- You will need to liaise with the chairperson beforehand so they can make brief notes on what needs to be covered under each agenda item, making sure that nothing is left out.
- Follow the time limit for each agenda item during the meeting – it teaches everyone discipline.
- Be aware that the first time someone chairs a meeting they will be nervous, but reassure them that public speaking, even in very small groups, is an excellent skill to learn.

Getting the whole team involved in team meetings, by having each of them present their four whats and taking the role of chairperson in turn, is a real team motivator. It encourages feelings of security, importance, being recognised as being of value, feeling that they have a future and being involved. The next section looks at building relationships with your team through networking and seeing them as 'customers' – and how that can benefit your business.

NETWORKING WITH YOUR TEAM

In Chapter 3 you looked at various networking opportunities as a means of meeting fellow businesspeople who could recommend you and potential customers. In the context of this chapter, networking is more about the interactions you have with your team members. This is comparatively easy to manage in a small team, but as your business grows you must continue to meet with all your team members and ensure you show interest in all the different aspects of the business – this makes everyone feel of equal importance. Networking can also happen in situations outside of the work environment.

As already seen, team bonding is vital, and networking – or socialising – with team members can play a part. These are not just social occasions, so be sensible: a few drinks and a meal after you've all been working at or visiting an exhibition is fine; getting drunk and acting inappropriately is definitely not. The Christmas party or any other celebratory occasion should not be treated any differently – you are still on show, you are still leader of your team and you are still communicating your values and those of your business, so don't mess up. Your behaviour during any networking activity must always reflect that you are the business owner, the one who leads by example and, as discussed at the beginning of the chapter, that you communicate the appropriate message at all times.

Inviting a team member to accompany you to a networking event that is appropriate to their role and area of expertise is a good idea. They may have more in common with the other attendees than you, and you will find they have a positive effect. It also demonstrates your faith in them and their abilities, which is motivational.

A word of caution, however: never show favouritism to those who are more like you in personality or who are more responsible for bringing in the money. As described earlier in this chapter, a good team is made up of many roles and all are vital to its smooth running.

INTERNAL CUSTOMER MARKETING

You also need to think of your team members as customers, although they are internal to your business. Internal customer marketing (ICM) is when you market your plans to your team to get them on board and encourage them to take ownership of any changes. This can help to avoid resistance to change, by keeping everyone informed about what's happening and how it may impact on them.

As with external customer marketing, you need to identify your internal customers. You will need to segment them by the way they buy into any change you wish to implement, or any goal you want to achieve. It is helpful if you segment them as follows:

- those most likely to support change
- those neutral to change
- those most likely to oppose change.

As with external marketing, the three segments will respond to different communication messages relevant to their particular concerns, fears and/or needs. Networking events, such as the ones discussed above, are useful opportunities to share new ideas or plans with your team or individual members and should be used as part of your ICM plan.

ICM and planning for change

You must think like the customer, in this case, your team members. What are their concerns likely to be and what do they think are the likely implications? Before you implement anything:

- Be clear why you are considering change and what precisely that change will be.
- Ensure that the environment is co-operative, collaborative and positive; if so, your team will be more willing to accept change.
- From the segment most likely to support change, consider creating the role of 'champion' for the change.
- Bearing in mind the proposed change, carry out a skills and capabilities audit of your team. Implement any training and continuing professional development (CPD) as necessary.
- Communicate the change to the different target audiences (the segments) using messages relevant to them.
- Create an ICM plan with a realistic budget, and use it to communicate your messages.

It can be easy to slip into the mindset of 'me', 'my business' and 'my plans', but remember that everything you want to achieve you will most likely need to achieve through your team. To develop a good relationship with them inside and outside the work environment and to have them on board and positive about your plans makes it so much easier and more cost-effective than dragging them along with you reluctantly and negatively.

LEADING AND MENTORING

What do you do as a leader? You lead your team; there is no getting away from that. But how are you leading them, where are you leading them, and what do you want to them to achieve? Your answers to these questions will define how you lead.

Concept of leadership

For all leaders, including those in small businesses, how to lead well is not easy to quantify. Essentially it involves you having qualities that others will follow: you might be trustworthy, inspirational, have a compelling personality, amazing decision-making skills and a positive, can-do attitude. It is important to realise that your team, however many they are, are not following a management process – they are following you and all that you stand for and represent.

Your aim as a good leader should be to enable and encourage your team to achieve, through help, support and development. If you support each individual in your team, you help the team, you help your business and, in the larger scale of things, you help the economy. Of course, you need to have clear goals and objectives as to where you are taking your business so you know what your team needs to do.

↳ **OVER TO YOU**

Think about the people you have known who you consider to be leaders – what was it about them that made you think of them in that way?

The qualities of your leadership must include attitudinal aspects:
- commitment
- compassion

- confidence
- courage
- determination
- honesty
- humility
- integrity
- passion
- positivity
- sensitivity
- sincerity
- wisdom.

LEADERSHIP SKILLS

Anyone can develop the ability to lead; it is not just for people with money, power or big personalities. Leaders fall into many age groups and, although most leaders come to it later in life when they have skills and experiences to draw on, age is not the sole criterion. However, as with other roles, the more experience you have, the better you should become. Winston Churchill made some terrible decisions in World War One but later in life became a great wartime leader.

In retail, one of the major players is Sir Philip Green, who owns companies that are responsible for 12 per cent of the UK retail clothing market. He left school at 16 with no qualifications and became the ninth wealthiest man in the UK. He has a reputation as an aggressive leader who refuses to run public companies as they allow the shareholders to question his decisions.

Historically, one of the great retail entrepreneurs is Michael Marks, a Russian Pole who started a market stall in Leeds which he developed into a successful retail business. He sold half the business to Tom Spencer, forming the now world-famous Marks & Spencer. Tom Spencer's leadership style was in complete contrast to Michael Marks's. Spencer was a plain-speaking Yorkshireman, loud, burly, well organised and with a keen eye for detail, while Marks was a shrewd businessman, an accomplished salesman and a reserved character. The combination of two contrasting styles led the company to its success.

New leaders, particularly those newly promoted or newly recruited into a position of leadership, often feel that they should lead by being dominant. This may come from how they were led in the past; they perceive that to be the correct way. However, being dominant or being a 'boss' rather than a 'leader' is rarely successful. If you recruit for a supervisor or manager, be aware that a new leader can often be seen as an outsider when they join your established team – when they don't know the team members they can often misread situations and behave in an exaggeratedly dominant way. Relying on dominance can cause problems for a new leader, as a cycle of negative behaviours normally follows:

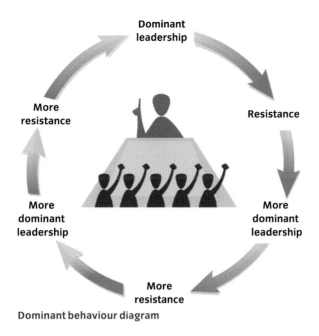

Dominant behaviour diagram

Team members rarely offer resistance to an idea that they have helped to develop and will have a sense of ownership (which is why internal marketing is so important). It's human nature to respond well to being appreciated, encouraged and recognised for your efforts; however, it's also human nature to react badly to being dominated, discouraged or having your views ignored. Negative reactions and resistance consume a lot of energy and time, as does dealing with the aftermath of all the negative feelings.

As with communication, leadership can be 'delivered' in many ways: the key is to adapt your style to suit a particular situation. That situation might be a one-to-one chat, a small team meeting, a large group, work-related, social, a sports group or supplier association. No single style covers all requirements. For example, the style you use just before the start of a promotional event will be high-energy, enthusiastic and motivational; the style used when discussing low sales figures will be more serious. Some people naturally understand which style is best; others learn by experience – you should only get it wrong once! Some never learn – and they are not true leaders.

As a leader, you should aim to:
- ask for and listen to the views of your team
- be enthusiastic and passionate about your team as well as your business
- be reliable, all the time
- recognise which leadership style will be most effective in any situation
- make sure all the styles you use reflect your personality

- continually develop your overall leadership style and measure its effectiveness through appraisals
- develop people
- inspire by example
- strive to earn the respect of your team
- treat everyone equally.

Dealing with people, and all that that involves, can be emotionally tiring. Good leaders have to be mentally strong. This doesn't mean that they have to be uncaring, but for the good of the team and business, they can't let their feelings cloud their judgement. Sometimes in business decisions have to be made that are not pleasant. Although you should always try for the win:win solution – good for the business and good for the team too – sometimes a win:lose solution is the only, or even the best, available option. For example, this might be deciding that the only way forward for the business is to bring in a machine, but as a consequence you need to make someone redundant because a job no longer exists. It could be weighing up the options of closing down the business or keeping it going but losing some jobs. In cases such as these, emotional strength as a leader will get you through because you can remain focused on the bigger picture and longer-term goal.

'Leadership' comes from an Anglo-Saxon word meaning the road or path ahead – knowing the next step and then taking others with you to it. It is really important as leader of your team that you concentrate on empowering them to thrive. This style of empowerment leadership is about serving the team, rather than the dominant, 'I'm-in-charge' style often confused with leadership.

MENTORING

Mentoring should be a crucial aspect of your leadership, as this is your opportunity to help and develop a member of your team. A team member who is mentored will grow and develop more quickly and therefore be more cost-effective than one who hasn't, although the time and cost of the mentor needs to be factored in. Mentoring may be carried out by yourself or other experienced colleagues. You might also consider retired colleagues who may be willing to give up a few hours to help. In some businesses a mentor is called a buddy, which sounds less formal, but they play the same role. Mentors are chosen either for a specific area of expertise (how to create appealing displays of products) or for more general support (confidence building). Often a team member who has passed through the mentoring process will himself go on to make a great mentor. As with everything else, the process of mentoring will need a plan, and in larger businesses a budget, as mentors may need training, evaluation and ongoing support.

MANAGING YOUR TEAM

As stated at the beginning of this chapter, your team are the most important resource you have. This is because they deliver your business objectives: they interface with your customers and your suppliers, they are the means by which your business grows, they are the face of your business and it's through them that you achieve what you want to achieve with your business. How you manage this vital resource is of the utmost importance. Any disruption to your business brought about by them being unhappy or demotivated at work, or at worst, leaving, will cost you in time, effort and money – and that doesn't even include any negative impact on customers or suppliers.

OVER TO YOU

Do you know how to manage? Or do you think you know? What experience do you have of being a manager and what do you have of being managed? On a scale of 1–10, how good do you think you are? Now ask people who know you – the family and friends you have bounced issues off before – how they would rate you. Do your ratings tally?

MOTIVATION

Your team members will work more effectively if you motivate and empower them. But how do you do this? First you need to understand what motivation is – it is the psychological urge all people have to 'do' something that gets them what they want or need, and this includes you too.

Using the motivation standard of Abraham Maslow's Hierarchy of Needs see page 174 you can see that our needs are shaped like a pyramid and that underpinning them all are our basic physiological and safety needs – what we need to survive. If we have no food or shelter, nothing above those bottom two needs matters.

As a manager you will get more involved in the next two levels of motivation:

- Social needs – The desire to belong and to love and be loved.
- Esteem needs – People's need to feel good about themselves, to receive recognition for what they have done and achieved, and to have some outward status symbol or sign of this recognition.

Social needs

These can be met at work by teamwork and through carrying out joint activities, where they also fulfil the need to belong to a group and to be appreciated. You need to be thinking about what you can do to ensure

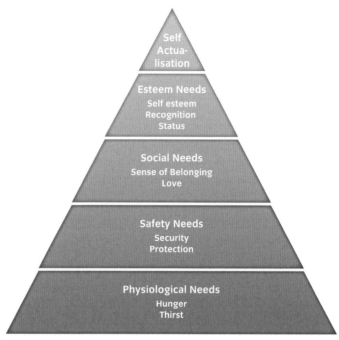

Maslow's hierarchy of needs

all your team members have the opportunity to belong and to feel appreciated.

Esteem

This is a key driver for people, although it is demonstrated in different ways by different people. Some want a new job or a different title, or a larger desk, or a better laptop or mobile phone. Generally, but not exclusively, people like to demonstrate their success to others through physical things; it makes them feel good about themselves and is a strong motivator. But different people are motivated by different things, so a catch-all recognition or reward will not motivate everyone equally; motivation is a personal thing. You should also bear in mind that some people's need for esteem is answered not by material drivers but by praise, by you validating their work and worth to you, particularly in front of colleagues.

 CASE STUDY 2

A young woman some years ago was unmaterialistic, under-confident and very shy. She responded incredibly well to a handwritten letter sent to her parents (with her consent) saying what a great part of the team she was and how valued she was and what she brought to the business. She gained esteem in the eyes of her family, which was something she had never had before; she became an even more valued part of the team after that, as she took on more roles due to her newly gained confidence.

You will need to spend time with each member of your team to uncover what motivates and drives him or her. Never assume you know; a set of golf clubs might be a great motivator for one member of your team but a spa weekend could be preferable for another, or an extra day's holiday, an early finish or gift vouchers might do the trick. If an incentive or motivator is not required or desired, it will not motivate; also, once the motivator has been received it no longer motivates.

Think about the following list of motivators and how you could use them with your team:

- promotion/different job title
- more holiday/more paid holiday
- better company laptop/mobile
- more responsibility
- more authority
- more interesting/exciting work.

Most people assume money is a motivator, but money itself does nothing – it is what money allows you to have or do which is the motivator. Here are some examples of how your team members may use any extra money:

- financial security – for example putting it into savings
- paying for a holiday/better holiday
- paying bills
- looking after loved ones
- treating loved ones
- buying clothes
- buying shoes
- buying jewellery
- travelling
- sport (for example equipment, or a season ticket to support their football team)
- moving house/home improvement
- planning a wedding
- getting ready for a new baby.

At the top of the pyramid of needs is self-actualisation. This is achieved when a person is totally happy with who they are, what they are doing, what they have, what they have achieved and are at peace with themselves. It may be that this is achieved when they have everything they want. This could be lots of money, a big house, a flash car and a jet-setting lifestyle – or it might be that the same person has given up everything, lives in a basic cottage in Scotland and shears sheep, but has everything that they need and want. Self-actualisation is different from one person to another, just as motivators are. What about you? What is your idea of self-actualisation? Will running your own business and taking control of your business life give you a better chance of satisfying your self-actualisation needs?

Val is the owner of Eastgate Garden Centre which she has operated for four and a half years with two staff who have been there since day one. They have always worked well together without any need for a formal team structure.

A two-acre field adjacent to the garden centre becomes available and Val discusses with her two colleagues the possibility of buying the field and using it to expand the business to operate a nursery, growing plants for the garden centre and for direct sale, and an area displaying garden furniture, garden ornaments and water features. They decide this is a good idea and agree that Dawn will manage the nursery, Rachel will manage the furniture area, while Val will concentrate on the garden centre with overall responsibility for the business.

Val decides to buy the field and learns from her solicitor that the land will be available for use in two months' time. She plans to hold a meeting with Dawn and Rachel to agree the best way to operate the newly expanded business. She wants to get policies and procedures agreed so that the three departments work to a framework while allowing Dawn and Rachel a level of responsibility for operating their departments within the framework.

Val lists the following subjects for discussion at the meeting:
- Delegation. Are buying, pricing, promotional activity and recruitment to be delegated to Dawn and Rachel?
- Leadership. Dawn and Rachel will have responsibility for their staff; Val will deal with the staff through the managers
- Motivation. Should there be a single bonus structure covering the whole business or separate departmental bonuses?
- Communication. Val will suggest a weekly management meeting followed by departmental huddles, and a monthly meeting of all staff to encourage flexibility between the teams for staff members

Now that the business has moved from a single team to a number of teams which overlap, there will be a need for much greater structure to prevent fragmentation.

EMPOWERMENT AS A MANAGEMENT TOOL

Empowered people generally feel more secure in their careers, and are more comfortable challenging 'norms', creating better solutions and thinking outside the box. They also feel valued and important, which in turn makes them more motivated and therefore more likely to do even better. This can start a cycle of doing well, being rewarded, being given responsibility and authority, and then doing even better, being rewarded again, given more responsibility and authority, and so on. ICM has a role to play in team members' empowerment; they have to be on board first with the general idea before you can empower them. The more things your team members can take responsibility and authority for, the more time you will have available to spend planning and growing your business. In Chapter 6 we'll look at how you spend your time and what you could delegate. Delegation is also a major contributor to motivation and empowerment.

There are two extreme ways in which people manage their teams – authoritarian and participative. There is always a range in between, but the pole you lean towards will depend on how you have been managed in the past and what you believe your team members' work ethic is. Are you the type of person who believes:

- that people will get out of doing work whenever they can?
- that you constantly have to check on their work to make sure they are doing it right?
- that you should secretly watch or listen to them to see what they get up to when you're not there?
- that the only way you can get them to do something is to force them with the threat of punishment?
- that they all prefer to be told what to do; avoid responsibility; are relatively unambitious and have no drive other than job security?

If you believe in all or most of the above then you lean towards being an authoritarian manager, which means a lot of your time will be spent controlling your team and being dictatorial. You are also likely to be strict and unforgiving, as you believe they are all just waiting for you to turn your back so they can stop working.

Or, do you believe:

- that work can be as natural a thing to people as play and rest?
- that people can manage their own work tasks, so they will achieve objectives without the need for you to control them or threaten them with punishment?
- that they will achieve objectives as part of their commission structure and rewards mechanism?
- that people usually want and often seek responsibility?
- that lots of team members have the ability to use their imagination, ingenuity and creativity to solve business problems without necessarily being in those problem-solving roles?
- that most people don't realise what they are capable of and few realise their potential?

KEY TO SUCCESS

The act of empowering someone is to give them responsibility and authority, whether for a small task or a key business objective. In other words, you give them the power to do what they think is right, having, of course, given them the skills to do so.

If you believe in all or most of the above then you are a participative manager and will produce better performance and results while allowing people to grow and develop.

If you have been managed badly in the past or seen bad management, you will have thought 'I don't want to manage my employees like that when I have a business.' But if you have had no other point of reference – you have not seen any other way of managing – you may find yourself repeating the bad practice however much you disliked being on the receiving end of it yourself. Reading through this section will help you to recognise negative traits and to take steps to change.

OVER TO YOU

Think about your first job and how you were managed, or even how you were treated by a teacher at school or college. Then create two columns and write down a list of what was good, and not so good, about the way the person managed you. When you have completed the list, see if you recognise any of your own qualities in the list – and which column they're in!

Profiling as a management tool

Having a profile of your team members is a useful tool – you may otherwise forget that they are individuals with their own sets of interests, goals and ambitions. If people don't achieve their goals or ambitions, or don't have interesting and satisfying jobs, they will become demotivated, and this could lead to them being unproductive, disruptive or even leaving. Finding out each of your team members' likes and dislikes, interests, passions, strengths and weaknesses will assist you in creating an environment for them in which they feel important, secure and of value. One of the ways you can do this is by ensuring your members get to do slightly more of the things they really love doing and slightly less of those that they are less keen on. You could also offer training in their areas of interest (such as evening classes in computer skills or French) to build on strengths and work on weaknesses.

CASE STUDY 4

Even small businesses can sometimes consider paying for or contributing towards training that is not directly work-related but helps to motivate and develop an employee. As an example, a business owner paid for a team member to have evening classes in Japanese flower arranging. She loved it, was very grateful and highly motivated by the fact that her manager had paid for something non-work-related.

TEAM MEMBER PROFILE

NAME:	Nina Carter
ROLE	Sales Assistant
RESPONSIBILITIES	Sales, customer service, till operation, merchandising
REPORT TO:	The manager
HOW LONG WITH THE BUSINESS:	6 months
MOTIVATED BY:	Job satisfaction
AMBITION:	To open her own retail business
HOW PREFER SUCCESS TO BE RECOGNISED:	Pay increase
MAIN AREAS OF INTEREST - PRODUCTS:	Games consoles
MAIN STRENGTHS	Communication skills
MAIN WEAKNESSES	Administration

TEAM MEMEBERS 100 WORD DESCRIPTION OF THEMSELVES BEGINNING WITH 'I AM AN IMPORTANT MEMBER OF THE TEAM BECAUSE...'

TEAM MEMBER: _____

TEAM LEADER: _____

DATE: _____

Profiles need to be updated as team members grow and develop. After each appraisal, the profile should be updated as the person will have progressed since the last appraisal; at the very least some of the items in the 'weaknesses' column should have moved to the 'strengths' column. Appraisals are an integral part of people management, and are discussed in the next section.

APPRAISALS

Appraisals are confidential meetings between you and your team members on a one-to-one basis. These meetings should take place four times a year. In some businesses they take place annually, but then they can become more of a financial review, and issues of training, strengths and weaknesses, and so on are frequently sidelined or ignored. This also allows issues or concerns to become major problems as they are not raised and tackled promptly. Appraisals involve some preparatory work on both sides, which allows you to gain an understanding of where you both are with regard to specific issues, and will enable the meeting to start quickly.

You should always start by appraising the team member with some positive feedback from their actions over the previous three months. If there are any negative issues they are then raised, but they too must be dealt with in a positive manner – 'What can we do together to improve?'; 'What can I do to help you?'. The required outcome of an appraisal is that there is an improvement in actions and a development of skills and attitude. It should not be and must never become a demotivational process that everyone comes to dread.

You should use the appraisal as an opportunity for feedback – ask if there is anything more you can do to help the team member perform better or ask if you are in any way hindering his performance. If a concern has been raised from the team member it should, where appropriate to the business and applicable to the needs of the individual, be acted on as soon as possible. It is important to react quickly as, having been made aware of a concern, taking no action shows the team member you have either not listened to him or are ignoring him, either of which is discouraging and may prevent future openness. If something cannot be achieved then an explanation should be given as to why not and a timescale given for when it will happen or be reviewed. Appraisals are like a discussion with a customer – listen to the information and act on it.

Managing the appraisal process

As part of the preparatory work for the meeting, give your team member a form on which they mark themselves out of 10 across a range of issues that are important to you and your business, such as timekeeping, knowledge, adaptability and working with colleagues (see the pre-appraisal marking form for an example).

To use the pre-appraisal marking form:
- The team member fills in their name.
- For each of the 'Selling and business skills' criteria the team member enters a score out of 10 for how they think they rate and adds comments justifying the score.
- For each of the 'Team and personal attributes' criteria the team member enters a score out of 10 for how they think they rate and adds comments justifying the score.
- The team member totals their score.

You should also complete a copy of the same form for the team member. At the meeting you would compare the values and negotiate to come up with an agreed number out of 10 (see negotiated appraisal marking form for an example of this negotiated appraisal marking form). Each of you should keep a copy of this final form to refer back to. You can use the complete set of team appraisal forms to map trends.

PRE-APPRAISAL MARKING FORM

TEAM MEMBER'S NAME: Nina Carter

SELLING AND BUSINESS SKILLS

SKILL	SCORE	COMMENTS
Knowledge of offering	6	Need to improve knowledge of new products
Retailing ability	7	Think this is quite acceptable
Time keeping	10	Never been late since last appraisal
Appearance	9	I think I look good most of the time
Administration	6	Not very good with figures
Wanting to be better	8	Quite happy with where I am now
Communication	9	I can talk to anyone about anything
TOTAL	55/70	

TEAM AND PERSONAL ATTRIBUTES

SKILL	SCORE	COMMENTS
CPD progress	5	Not sure what this is about
Helping and supporting others	7	I am good with people who need a bit of extra help
Creating own solutions	8	I am good at sorting out problems
Cleaning own work area	9	I am a very clean and tidy person
Being cheerful	10	I am always happy and cheerful
New skills this quarter	6	I am learning how to operate the till, I'm not quite there yet
Understanding team objectives	5	I reach my targets but others don't
Social interaction	10	I am a very sociable person, I get on with everybody
Levels of commitment	10	I am very committed to getting on and making a profit for the shop
Self belief	10	I have a great deal of self-belief
TOTAL	80/100	
		TOTAL: 135 /170

NEGOTIATED APPRAISAL MARKING FORM

TEAM LEADER's NAME: _____ TEAM MEMBER'S NAME: _____ DATE: _____

SELLING AND BUSINESS SKILLS

SKILL	SCORE	COMMENTS
Knowledge of offering		
Retailing ability		
Consultation Skills		
Time keeping		
Appearance		
Administration		
Wanting to be better		
Communication		
TOTAL	/80	

TEAM AND PERSONAL ATTRIBUTES

SKILL	SCORE	COMMENTS
CPD progress		
Helping and supporting others		
Creating own solutions		
Cleaning own work area		
Being cheerful		
New skills this quarter		
Understanding team objectives		
Social interaction		
Levels of commitment		
Self belief		
TOTAL	/100	
	TOTAL:	/180

Action plans

At the end of each appraisal meeting an action plan (see page 184) is drawn up between you and each team member, which addresses the issues raised. The action plan should be created by both of you together so each team member has ownership of their plan – that way it will be effective and motivating. Each team member will have a different plan based on the outcomes of his or her appraisal. It should include:

- the action to be taken
- the aim of the action
- who is responsible for the action
- when the action should be achieved
- the cost implications of the action.

You would normally start an appraisal with a review of the previous meeting's action plan and a discussion regarding what has been achieved. Using the action plan form as a guide, you'll check against what was agreed last time to ascertain whether what was supposed to be achieved has been, on or by the date given, at a cost of no more than was agreed. If anything has happened differently from what was agreed, the team member will need to explain why. You will then move on to ask if the aims of the action were met or not; if not, you need to agree what needs to be done now to meet them.

If the action plan has been organised correctly there will be very little to discuss regarding its content at the next meeting other than positive remarks such as all completed, on time, within budget, with all aims met. If, however, the action plan has been badly organised then the outcomes could be very negative – and the fault would belong to both of you as you both created and agreed the action plan. This introduces the team member to the concept of responsibility for their actions.

An action plan should be created at the end of every appraisal meeting:

- Enter the team member's name and the date.
- List any previous or ongoing actions and action information in the top section.
- Add any new actions to be taken from the current meeting (these will move up into the previous section after the following meeting).
- The team member and you, as team leader, both sign the form to indicate agreement.

INDIVIDUAL'S ACTION PLAN

TEAM MEMBER'S NAME: Nina Carter   **Date:** 30.11.11

PREVIOUS MEETING

PREVIOUS ACTION RESULTS	DATE ACHIEVED	COST	OBJECTIVES MET	OBJECTIVES NOT MET	WHAT NEEDS TO BE DONE?
Time keeping improved	13.10.11	Zero	Time keeping improved	None	

CURRENT MEETING

ACTION TO BE TAKEN?	OBJECTIVE OF ACTION?	WHO RESPONSIBLE?	WHEN ACHIEVED?	COST?
Nina to spend half day with office manager	Improve Nina's administration	Office manager	31.12.11	

TEAM MEMBER: _____   **TEAM LEADER:** _____

ASK factor assessment

Other things that change as your team members grow and develop are their attitude, skills and knowledge – the so-called ASK factors. Having wonderful skills with a superb level of knowledge is not enough without the correct attitude, and equally, having a great attitude is not enough without the skills and knowledge required to carry out a job effectively. What is therefore required is a mix of ASK factors, and you need to be aware of each person's ratings as this will help you to guide their CPD and career progression.

As with the negotiated appraisal form and action plan, these ratings should be discussed between you and your individual team members. It is demotivational for team members to have forms on which they are assessed without the opportunity to discuss them and to improve their ratings. As their CPD can be tracked with this mechanism, you can both see the benefits as they progress or, if not, take action to improve the situation.

Additions and alterations will need to be made to team members' ASK factor ratings; an ideal time would be after appraisal meetings. Rating everyone in terms of their attitude, skills and knowledge across a range of four criteria gives a clear overview of each team member. The four areas rated are:

- being part of the team
- offering
- customer care
- administration.

INDIVIDUAL ASK FACTOR ASSESSMENT FORM

TEAM MEMBER'S NAME: _____   TEAM LEADERS'S NAME: _____   DATE: _____

	ATTITUDE	SKILLS	KNOWLEDGE
TEAM MEMBER			
OFFERING			
CUSTOMER CARE			
ADMIN			

This information is obviously relevant and useful as part of an individual's assessment in the appraisal meeting but also when assessing recruitment, training and promotion or financial reward issues.

CONTINUING PROFESSIONAL DEVELOPMENT

CPD is defined by the Chartered Institute of Personnel and Development as 'a commitment to structured skills enhancement and personal or professional competence'.

The introduction to this chapter looked at your team being as important to your business as your customers, as without them there would be no business. As a business that makes money from the skills of your workforce, how you develop and grow them is vital to the success of it; without updating them you'll be trying to run your business with out-of-date skills and old knowledge. CPD can also give you a competitive advantage and certainly has a positive business benefit, which you should always bear in mind when looking at any time and money costs to deliver CPD, whatever your trade or industry sector.

CPD is a structured approach to the learning and development of skills for you and your team. In-house training, delegation and mentoring are all part of this process as they lead to greater mastery of skills, understanding and general development.

There are a number of professional bodies covering trade and industry in this country that offer support and guidance about their CPD requirements, for example SkillSmart Retail (www.skillsmartretail.com).

You do need to keep a record of your and your team's learning, development and up-skilling, as some of these organisations will demand to see it to validate the qualifications. However, it doesn't need to be complicated; just a list of what's been learnt, the difference it's made to the person and to the business, what they need to do in the future and the difference they plan to make to themselves and to the business. In this record you should also note the number of hours involved, as some trade organisations specify a minimum number of hours to be spent on CPD.

Below is an overview of headings you may wish to use in your record-keeping.

Last 12 months:
- What did you learn last year?
- What was the benefit to you?
- What was the benefit to the business in terms of value – money, customer satisfaction, referrals and so on?
- What ways of working have you changed as a result of your learning?
- How did you learn the new skills – training, shadowing, delegation?
- Who else has gained from your up-skilling?
- How many hours did you spend?

Next 12 months:
- How do you know what you need to develop?
- What subjects do you want to up-skill in?
- How do you intend to achieve the up-skilling?
- What differences will it make to you?
- What differences will it make to the business?
- How do you review your CPD?
- How many hours will you spend?

Responsibility for CPD

There is joint responsibility for planning CPD between team members and their line manager, which in the case of a small business will be the owner. CPD is not something that is imposed on a team member by the 'boss'; it is something team members have an interest in being involved in as it makes them of more value to the business and therefore more secure. The owner will have a more competitive workforce, which in turn makes the business more competitive, more likely to be financially viable and ultimately more profitable.

Where CPD fits in

As you learnt earlier, part of the appraisal meeting is the joint discussion of training needs and requirements, so CPD planning falls naturally into that process. If appraisal meetings are held every 3–4 months, this provides an ideal timeframe in which to set and agree CPD within the action plan, review its progress and then, through the ASK factor assessment, identify where it has made a positive difference. If there is a negative difference then you'll need to discuss what didn't work, why, and how things should be changed for the future. How you feed back negative information is crucial – you don't want to demotivate but you still need changes to be made. However, if you and the team member decided on the CPD plan together, you will bear some responsibility for its lack of success.

Note the use of the phrase 'lack of success' rather than the very negative and destructive word 'failure'. Constructive ways to give feedback are covered in the next section.

FEEDBACK AND COACHING TECHNIQUES

Feedback is an essential communication mechanism for you and your team members – it is a means to check that you have been understood and that you understand what is being communicated to you. Sometimes the feedback mechanism is within a structured situation, for example the appraisal, where both parties are expecting feedback and have prepared for it based on a previously agreed format. There are occasions, however, in business where situations arise where an informal feedback mechanism is required. Such cases are usually where something has gone wrong or where a team member may feel out of their depth, where support or encouragement is required. This type of informal situation may be dealt with verbally between you and the team member in the form of a chat, but to have a written format that can be filed for future reference is always preferable. In most feedback situations there are two aspects – giving positive feedback and giving negative feedback.

When giving negative feedback, it should be 'sandwiched' between items of positive feedback so the recipient has something positive to take from the meeting as well as the negative. Even negative feedback can be given in a positive way: 'I don't think you're as good at this as you could be, so this is how I propose to support you… what do you think?' It's important to realise that if things have gone wrong somewhere in your business it isn't always the obvious person's fault. When things do go wrong it could be the result of poor management decisions – for example, poor delegation or inadequate training programmes – in other words, your fault!

Feedback is often thought of as being used when things need to be improved, but a formal feedback situation when things have gone really well is very motivational. Not only is the team leader saying good things in this case, but it is being recorded and filed too. A simple feedback form, like the one shown here, can be used to capture your discussion.

TEAM FEEDBACK FORM

FEEDBACK TO: _Nina Carter_
DATE: _06.01.12_

FEEDBACK FROM: _Alison Cooper_
SIGNATURE: _____
SIGNATURE: _____

STRENGTHS	WEAKNESSES
Timekeeping, appearance, communication skills, social interaction and levels of commitment	Product knowledge, CPD and understanding team objectives

NEXT STEPS

Nina is to be mentored by the sales manager for six weeks to improve her product knowledge and her understanding of team objectives

---

When giving negative – or, as we prefer to call it, constructive – feedback, try not to point the finger, literally or figuratively. This can be interpreted as aggressive and is normally accompanied by blaming language. Open-palm gestures are not seen as aggressive and are normally associated with rational two-way discussion, as used in healthy negotiation.

Open palm; Pointing finger

Remember that the person receiving the feedback may be nervous and as a consequence may not take in the information in the way it was meant – they may hear only the bad points. It is important that you communicate your message bearing this in mind and use positive language, tone of voice and gestures.

Understanding what each of your team members wants is important, as you can then, between you, create a motivational cycle of achievement and rewards. Appraising your team of their performance and creating an action plan that they have bought into are excellent management techniques. Allowing them opportunities to realise their potential and be better than they thought they could be is one of a good manager's greatest pleasures – the fact that it breeds loyalty is a great bonus. Sometimes you recruit the people you need; sometimes they are there already but you haven't yet seen them.

RECRUITMENT

Carrying out the correct recruitment processes and procedures will save you time and money. It will also help to ensure you appoint not just the candidates with the right sets of skills and qualifications but also the right personality types to fit in well with the existing team and reduce the time taken for everyone to gel.

IDENTIFYING THE SKILLS NEEDED

When you are considering recruiting an additional team member, you must first evaluate your business's needs and requirements by carrying out a skills gap analysis (SGA) (see also Chapter 2, page 65). This analysis will flag up what skills your business needs to satisfy your existing and potential customers and enable you to compete profitably. This will be based on previous information-gathering activities such as customer satisfaction surveys, mystery shoppers, the complaints procedure and competitor analysis. The gap can be shown in many ways – two different examples are shown below – but the method chosen should clearly show where the gaps are between your existing and required skills. However, it's the information, more than how it's shown, which is important, so use whichever presentation method you feel comfortable with.

Example 1

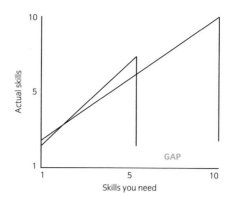

Example 2

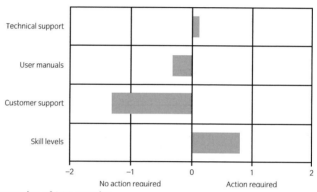

Two examples of SGA graphs

For more information and examples of gap analysis, visit www.enotes.com.

When the SGA has been carried out you'll need to match what is required by your team to what they already have – anything missing is a 'gap'. You then need to decide if the gap is best filled by reorganising your existing team members' responsibilities or by recruiting a new external employee or even a consultant.

Now is a good time to refer back to the work you did at the beginning of the chapter, identifying different Belbin roles. Combined with a gap analysis of the role(s) required you'll be able to uncover what type of person you need to complement you, your existing team and your business.

You have four main options:

- Don't recruit – This may be the cheapest option. By adopting a flexible approach to working hours across the team it can be more appropriate to rearrange and share responsibilities. However, be wary of overloading your present employees, which will lead to demotivation.
- Promote internally – In your appraisal processes, have you identified someone in your team who is ready to move up to the next level? If so, do they fit the requirements for the vacancy? If you do promote internally, you will also have to consider whether you need to get a new person in to cover the newly promoted person's original role.
- Outsource or contract out the role – Could you fulfil the requirements of this role more cost-effectively by contracting it out to one or more people, or through agencies? Although this may be a cheaper option in the short run, think carefully about what you might be losing in terms of control and skills within the business.
- Recruit externally – If you have identified a clear and urgent skills gap within your team – as a result of growth or someone leaving – bringing in a new member of staff may be the best long-term solution. If recruitment is needed is to replace someone, carry out an 'exit survey' with the person who is leaving to uncover any issues that may have caused them to leave and which need to be addressed.

In all of these cases you will need to define and review the responsibilities for the job – what are the essential qualifications or specifications needed (for a new post) and have they changed (for an existing post)? Seek views from the rest of the team about the job responsibilities and person specifications; also ascertain what you have learnt from the previous holder of the job (if relevant) and discuss what, if anything, needs to be changed within the team as a whole.

WRITING A JOB SPECIFICATION

When writing job descriptions be honest; don't hide any difficult aspects of the job. This is a chance to define the skills you require – which should include education, formal qualifications, trade experience, additional training and personal attributes – based on the information you have gathered in your SGA and any exit survey. It's helpful to use a job description form to organise the information:

- Enter the title of the vacancy and the date. The job title you advertise will influence the type of applicants you get and their expectations, so make sure it accurately describes the role and responsibility level, for example 'Experienced Sales Assistant'.
- Enter the typical roles and responsibilities of the vacancy. List what you expect the person to physically do and be responsible for. It may help if you envisage what you want them to do on a daily, weekly, monthly and even quarterly basis.

- State what qualities and qualifications you consider 'essential' in order for an individual to fulfil the role's responsibilities. List what qualities and qualifications the candidate absolutely must have to be considered for the position – if they don't have them, they will be immediately rejected – for example a Level 3 qualification in a relevant field. These are normally skills that take a while to acquire.
- State what qualities and qualifications you consider 'important' in order for an individual to fulfil the role's responsibilities. These are qualities and qualifications you really would like the candidate to have to be considered for the position. This might be a specific qualification or a particular skill, such as sales training. These are normally skills that could be gained in a reasonably short timeframe but if the candidate were to arrive with them already that would be ideal.
- State what qualities and qualifications you consider 'good to have' in order for an individual to fulfil the role's responsibilities. This list is less to do with qualifications and skills and is more the icing on the cake of your wish list – for example, has experience of accounts, is keen on a particular part of the job that the existing team members don't enjoy, will balance out the team and so on. These are normally issues that come into play should you be in the position where you can't make up your mind between candidates.

The form below is for your use only; it helps when you are first thinking about what skills you want from a potential employee and in what order of importance they come – what the essential, important and good to have skills are.

JOB DESCRIPTION

TITLE: _____

DATE: _____

ROLES AND RESPONSIBILITES

ESSENTIAL QUALITIES

IMPORTANT QUALITIES

GOOD TO HAVE QUALITIES

Writing things down in this clearly defined way helps you prepare an external job advertisement, and helps with internal recruitment when discussing opportunities at appraisals.

According to the Business Link website (www.businesslink.gov.uk), an external advert should include as a minimum:

- the job title
- the position in the company, including the job title of the person to whom the employee will report and the titles of those who will report to them, if any
- the location of the job
- a summary of the general nature and objectives of the job
- a list of the main duties or tasks of the employee.

A typical job advert might say: 'Sales Assistant required reporting to the Sales Manager and responsible for one Junior Sales Assistant in our Norwich shop. Responsibilities include dealing with customers, sales, handling payments and display. You will also offer advice to customers on stock availability and promotions.'

It is important to set minimum requirement levels; if all the candidates fall below these, do not recruit – wait a short while and re-advertise. The minimum requirements should be all the essential qualities you listed on the form above – if they really are essential no-one should be recruited without them! Never lower your standards just to have another pair of hands as it invariably causes problems further down the line and is, at the very least, unfair to the new team member.

ADVERTISING AND INTERVIEWING

Ensure your job advert is clear and concise; it helps to have it checked by others to save any potential confusion or embarrassment. You also need to know your legal responsibilities under the Equality Act so you don't unwittingly discriminate in the recruitment process on the basis of age, gender, disability, race or religion. If you want an experienced sales assistant that is fine to say, but you are not allowed to state an age. You'll find useful summaries of the laws covering equality and discrimination during the recruitment process on the Business Link website: www.businesslink.gov.uk.

There are a number of places to recruit and ways to advertise a vacancy, including:

- team member recommendations
- trade press
- local press
- websites such as Totaljobs (www.totaljobs.com) or Fish4Jobs (www.fish4.co.uk)
- national press
- recruitment agencies
- word of mouth
- job centres
- colleges and universities (particularly if you are looking for recent graduates with particular qualifications).

Choosing the best method will depend on the skillset you are recruiting for and the associated cost implications. If you are recruiting for a locally based junior position it's unlikely you will need a national press advert or the help of a recruitment company (which will take a percentage of the salary of the successful candidate). In this case, word of mouth, local press or job centre advertising and possibly your local college would be the most appropriate methods. However, if you were recruiting for a senior position you may consider trade press, as it's specific to your business and gets out to those you may want to 'poach' without you doing anything unethical. Also, for this type of role you may consider an agency (and its fees) to be worth it as they will have screened and interviewed their clients already and should only send you worthwhile candidates. The money saved in time and effort may well be worth the agency's commission. As with all things in business, have a plan, set a budget and don't rush your decision.

Managing the response is important too, as it can show your business in a good (or poor) light to prospective employees. Put one person in charge of telephone applications and send out standard application forms to all who apply via the phone, your website or other means, as this allows for easier comparison. When the responses are all in, match the application forms and CVs against your minimum requirements and divide them into three piles: 'interview', 'possible' and 'rejected'. Send positive and courteous letters to the rejected candidates immediately.

All business tasks need careful planning, implementation and evaluation, and interviews are no different. When thinking about who to invite to the interview, ensure it is only those applicants who meet your requirements, then draw up the final list. It is wise to assume a certain degree of CV creativity (ie lies), so look for any gaps in employment and/or inconsistencies that you may want to discuss over the telephone before offering an interview. The ability to measure candidates against set criteria and then against each other will help you get the best candidate, rather than relying on emotional judgements. A rating sheet against which you can measure each candidate and then all candidates against each other will give you a process that leaves little room for error, emotion or reliance on gut feelings. It will ultimately save you time, and time of course is money. It's easy to be taken in at an interview by a smiley face and a good reference, only to find three months later that the your new recruit has turned into a nightmare and the only reason they had a good reference was that their previous employer wanted to get rid of them!

Arrange interviews by telephone or letter and state if candidates are to undergo any practical tests. Decide which tests are to be carried out and who will manage this – where the tests will take place, what the feedback mechanisms will be, what other team members will be involved and so on. It's good practice to let the candidate know who will be conducting the interview, how long it will take and who they should ask for on arrival.

Plan where and when the interviews will take place, who will be involved, how the interviews will be structured and what you need to find out.

Prepare an interview sheet for each candidate, noting specific points from their CV to discuss, and then prepare an interview rating sheet with criteria highlighted based on the job description and person specification.

The interview process

Ensure that the interview room is quiet with no interruptions, that there are no unnecessary physical barriers between the candidate and the interviewer (s) and that the heating and lighting are appropriate. Ask members of the team to record their first impressions of the candidates as they arrive, and ask them to show the interviewees around. Don't offer biscuits or other food during the interview but do offer hot or cold drinks (for example tea, coffee, water).

Make sure you stick to the same format with each candidate and ask the same general questions. Have a copy of the candidate's CV handy, as well as a list of specific questions you want to ask. Make very brief notes during the interview (marks out of 10 and so on), which should be transferred onto the rating sheet immediately the candidate leaves, while he or she is fresh in your mind. Towards the end of the interview, allow time for the applicant to ask questions. Generally speaking you should never offer the job there and then. Instead, say when and how you will contact the candidate – by telephone, email or letter. This gives you time to reflect and minimises the risk of making an impetuous and ultimately regrettable decision.

INTERVIEW RATING SHEET

CANDIDATES NAME: _____ JOB: _____
INTERVIEW PANEL: _____ DATE: _____

INTERVIEW SKILL	RATING /10
First impressions	/10
CV suitability	/10
Experience to date	/10
Friendliness and professionalism	/10
Ability to answer questions	/10
Asked relevant questions	/10
Interpersonal skills	/10
Body language	/10
How well will integrate	/10
Main achievement	/10
TOTAL	**/100**

JOB DESCRIPTION	RATING /10
Essential	/10
Important	/10
Good to have	/10
TOTAL	**/30**
TOTAL SCORE	**/130**
PUT FORWARD FOR NEXT STAGE	Y: N:

When using this type of rating sheet:

- Enter the candidate's name, the vacancy, who is on the interview panel and the date. This is so you have all the information to refer to later in the recruitment process should you want to speak to someone else about their views on the candidate, and if you are recruiting for more than one vacancy.
- During the interview, score the candidate out of 10 against each of the criteria. Try to add the numbers you want to award the candidate at the time, as by the end of the interview you may have forgotten your earlier impressions.
  - First impressions – How much did you like what you saw?
  - CV suitability – How well did the candidate's CV match your requirements?

- Experience to date – How well did the candidate's experience match your requirements?
- Friendliness and professionalism – How well did the candidate's friendliness and professionalism match your requirements?
- Ability to answer questions – How well did the candidate's ability to answer your questions match your requirements?
- Asked relevant questions – How relevant were the questions the candidate asked?
- Interpersonal skills – How well did the candidate relate to you and others?
- Body language – What was the candidate's body language saying about him?
- How well will the candidate integrate?
- Main achievement – How relevant and of value was the candidate's main achievement?

- Total the score out of 100: add all the individual totals together and write the result at the bottom of the interview skill box.
- Score the individual out of 10 for how well they matched the job description characteristics you defined and considered to be 'essential', 'important' or 'good to have'. Some of this can be marked in pencil beforehand as you relate their CV to your requirements; however, some issues will require questioning to get all the information you need.
- Total out of 30 how the individual measured against the job description. When you have satisfied yourself that you have all the information you can determine about that candidate, add up their marks in the job description box.
- Add together all the totals from 'Interview skill' and 'Job description' and add to 'Total score' – to give a score out of 130.
- Decide whether you will put the individual forward to the next stage when you have interviewed all the candidates. Indicate this by ticking Y or N.

At this stage you'll be basing your decision purely on the figures on the score sheets. This takes away the risk of going with your gut instinct and appointing someone just because they were friendly and personable. The reason you spent time creating the 'essential', 'important' and 'good to have' lists was so you have something concrete to measure candidates against; to take some of the risk of making the wrong choice away. You may also want to create a separate set of questions, with marks allocated, about being a team player, or an example of something they have achieved at work, for instance. These numbers can then be added to the form. Only when all the 'essential' boxes have been ticked should you consider someone. The candidate should also have a very high number of the 'important' attributes and preferably a few of the 'good to have' ones too.

The next step is to thank the applicant for attending the interview. You should avoid rushing to offer a job there and then; however, if the candidate is to have a practical test at a separate time you can certainly arrange it at this point. When the candidate has gone, ask for feedback from your team as they may have seen something you missed, or the candidate may have said something important to them that may colour your judgement (for example, 'I only want a job for six months').

Making an offer

You should preferably make contact by phone (email or letter are also possible), informing the candidate if he or she has been successful or not – within a week, but before if possible. If a candidate is not successful, be kind, focus on any strengths he showed and stress that he only just missed out. If you really did like a candidate, but he missed out on a couple of essential or important issues, tell him so he has the opportunity to address them through personal development, and ask if you can keep his CV on file.

If there is more than one suitable candidate, contact them and invite them to attend a second interview. Preferably see the competing candidates on the same day or as close together as you can so you can compare them more easily. This is when you would talk more in depth about salary, commission, holiday pay and so on, and ask them if they have any questions. The questions they ask can also tell you a great deal – if they are all about money and holidays and nothing about training and career progression, you might think again.

When you have chosen your preferred candidate, make contact and say you want to offer the position subject to taking up references – this is known as a conditional offer. He or she may decline at this stage, so contact your first-choice candidate before you notify the second choice that he or she has not been successful. Once you have received the references and any necessary paperwork (for example, qualification certificates, or proof of eligibility to work in the UK) you should make a formal unconditional offer. It's usual at this stage to send a contract of employment stating everything discussed – salary, holidays, job title, roles and responsibilities, starting date, probationary period (normally three months), what will be provided by you and so on. If you do not provide this level of detail now, you will need to give your new employee a written statement of the main terms and conditions of the contract of employment within two months of the start date. You should ask for and receive a written acceptance of your unconditional offer – once it has been accepted, a contract of employment exists between you and the candidate and neither party has the right to withdraw without agreement. Because of this, it is important that you have taken up any references and made any necessary background checks before you make an unconditional offer, to ensure that the candidate is really suitable.

CASE STUDY 5

Monty and his brother Nass have been running an off-licence for two years. They think it is now a good time to open a second branch. Each brother will run one branch, so they need to recruit two assistants. They decide to advertise both jobs together and interview all the applicants jointly so that they can be sure to select the best candidates.

They write a job description and a person specification.
Job description:
- To achieve sales budgets
- Responsibility for store layout
- Responsibility for promotions and presentation
- Strict compliance with legislation and company policies
- Implement 'challenge 25' policy
- Responsibility for accurate pricing and labelling
- Ensure excellent housekeeping standards maintained
- Receiving deliveries
- Maintain records of 'refused sales'
- Carry out cash handling procedures

Person specification:
- Over 18 in order to meet legislation on age-related sales
- Retail experience
- Good communication skills
- Adaptable to change
- Knowledge of products an advantage
- Self-motivated
- Responsible and co-operative
- Team player

They create an interview rating sheet so that they can score the individual applicants objectively and select the two candidates with the highest overall scores.

OVER TO YOU

Create an interview rating sheet for your own business. You are looking for an assistant – what questions would you want answered by prospective applicants?

INTEGRATING A NEW MEMBER INTO THE TEAM

When a new member joins a team and/or an old one leaves there is a change in the dynamics between all the team members. Various stages of team building are gone through:

- Forming – When the new members get to know each other.
- Storming – When there may be some concerns or issues that need to be faced.
- Norming – When issues have been dealt with and everyone is settling down in their role.
- Performing – When everyone pulls together as a team.

The quicker the stages are passed through, the better it is for your business – it is most productive when the team reaches the performing stage. There is an additional stage called 'mourning', which is when a team member leaves, after which the remaining team go through the stages again as they adapt to their new roles.

When new people join the team they can feel like the odd one out; they are joining an already established group of people who know each other well. It's extremely valuable to give a new employee relevant information not just about the company but about the roles and responsibilities of their colleagues before they arrive, so they get a feel for the business and where everyone fits in. It also helps with the team bonding process if you can give your existing team members relevant information about their new colleague's role and experience, so they understand how he'll fit in. Be careful not to give out the new employee's personal information to the team though, as the Data Protection Act applies. To find out more about the implications of the Data Protection Act, visit: www.businesslink.gov.uk.

You looked at the benefits of mentoring earlier in this chapter; now is a good time to put someone in charge of mentoring the new colleague through the induction process. This will be the person the new team member can go to for answers to any questions, concerns or problems that may arise. Sharing of information and assimilating new members into the team should be seen as part of the whole recruitment process, and as much time and effort should be put into assimilation as into advertising and interviewing candidates – the quicker assimilation takes place, the quicker the reformed team will begin to perform.

WHERE TO GO FOR MORE INFORMATION

For a small business, finding and recruiting the right staff as you grow is crucial to your success. The following links will help you master the basics and provide up-to-date references:

- Employment law for small businesses:
  - www.businesslink.gov.uk.
  - Acas Helpline: 08457 47 47 47.
- Recruiting advice:
  - www.businesslink.gov.uk.
  - www.smallbusiness.co.uk.
- Help with contracts of employment: www.businesslink.gov.uk.
- Advice on growing your business: online.businesslink.gov.uk.

If you feel you need professional recruitment assistance, the 'voice' of the recruitment industry and the membership organisation for recruitment companies is the Recruitment & Employment Confederation. There is a directory of members on their website: www.rec.uk.com.

The Chartered Institute of Personnel and Development (CIPD) is a good resource for all issues relating to human resources including coaching and mentoring: www.cipd.co.uk. CIPD also delivers training and arranges networking events, recruitment fairs and conferences.

You may also find the following links helpful:

- Making the most of your team's skills: visit www.businesslink.gov.uk and search for 'Making the most of your team's skills'.
- Help and support for managers: visit www.businesslink.gov.uk and search for 'Help and support for managers'.

It's certainly worth considering training in leadership and management. The Institute of Leadership & Management (ILM) is the leader in the field, providing resources, courses and a membership scheme: www.i-l-m.com.

Should you wish to formalise your CPD, the CPD Certification Service can help and acts as a point of contact for those seeking to obtain certified CPD material. Visit: www.cpduk.co.uk.

Finally, the Forum of Private Business aims to give advice and protection to small businesses on a wide range of issues; you can join as an introductory member free of charge at: www.fpb.org/.

CONCLUSION

In this chapter you have seen that your team is an integral part of your business and your long-term vision. Putting into place plans and actions to motivate, empower and encourage your team members will bring you great business benefits, not just in terms of a dedicated and happy team but also because they are unlikely to be won over, or poached, by your competition. If working with you is absolutely wonderful, it is a high-risk strategy for a team member to leave, as the chances of getting the same or better is doubtful. However, if working with you is dreadful there is little risk for them in leaving – almost anything will better than what they have. You need to make sure you are viewed as wonderful – view things through the eyes of these 'internal customers' and communicate your messages in ways they understand.

CHAPTER 6
MANAGING YOUR TIME AND KEEPING MOTIVATED

INTRODUCTION

The owners of small businesses that grow into larger units are most often the busiest of all the team, as they may continue to try to do everything themselves, just as they did when they first started out. They do this for a number of reasons: they are the closest to their core business, have initiated it and been responsible for its growth and success – in essence it is their 'baby'. They have always done it; they don't believe anyone can do the tasks better, or even as well, as they can; they know more than anyone else so can carry out the tasks more quickly. Delegation is often hard for small business owners. Consequently they don't have much – or even any – time left for planning. Behaving like a 'busy fool' is not an effective or efficient use of the business owner's time.

To avoid being the busy fool you need to realise that your time is something you can't buy more of, so you'll need to use it wisely. In this chapter you'll be looking at how you spend your time, why you should consider delegation and how that delegation process should be implemented. Time is also a cost, so it's important you take into account the time a task will take, plus how long it will be before you are ready to start another one. In your business you're the team leader, you're the one motivating others and leading by example, but you also have to develop the skills to motivate yourself, and this chapter also investigates that side of things.

PLANNING YOUR WORK TIME

You can never buy more time, however wealthy you are, so you need to use your time wisely and to the greatest benefit of your business.

The example below shows that planning how you spend your time is the key to time management:

Get a bucket, enough big rocks to fill it, some pebbles, some sand and water.
Put the big rocks in the bucket until you can't get any more in – is it full? No.
Put the pebbles in around the big rocks – is it full? No.
Put the sand in and give it a shake – is it full? No.
Put the water in. Now it's full.

The point: Unless you put the big rocks in first, you won't get them in at all.

What this means: Plan enough time for the big issues (the rocks) before you add anything else, otherwise the 'sand' and 'water' – the small issues – will fill up your days and you won't fit the big issues in. A big issue doesn't necessarily have to be a work task – it could be your child's sports day, or a holiday.

KEY TO SUCCESS

You, just like everyone else in your business, are a resource. Ensure you plan to use all your resources wisely.

FIRST THINGS FIRST

Before you can save time or decide how to better spend your time, you have to know how you currently spend it. Only when you have produced a time log can the process of understanding how your time is spent, and how to use it more effectively, be carried out.

Creating a time log (see page 206) is a process whereby your working day is broken down into small sections, usually of 15–30 minutes' duration. Everything is added to the time log, even going to the toilet and having a break; nothing must be left out. A time log must be truthful, as it's the first stage in managing your time more effectively and efficiently.

When the first day's time log has been completed the process is repeated daily for at least two weeks, preferably four weeks. You can then analyse the logs to look for trends or patterns in your behaviour. Analysis of your time logs will flag up not only what you do and when, but enable you to analyse which activities are important, non-important, urgent and non-urgent, which allows you to prioritise. This process also allows you to see how your time is split in percentage terms, so, for example, if a lot of time is spent discussing future plans but not much time is spent in the implementation of those plans, then you need to change your behaviour.

TIME LOG

		MONDAY	TUESDAY	WEDNESDAY	THURSDAY	FRIDAY	SATURDAY	SUNDAY
AM	8.30							
	9.00							
	9.30							
	10.00							
	10.30							
	11.00							
	11.30							
	12.00							
LUNCH	12.00							
	13.00							
PM	13.30							
	14.00							
	14.30							
	15.00							
	15.30							
	16.00							
	16.30							
	17.00							
	17.30							
	18.00							
	18.30							
	19.00							
	19.30							
	20.00							
	20.30							
	21.00							
	21.30							
	22.00							

⤷ OVER TO YOU

Complete the time log above for at least two weeks. Log every activity in 15–30-minute sections for every day of your working week. What patterns can you spot about how you allocate your time? Are there certain times of day that are more productive for you than others? When is the best time for you to tackle important business decisions?

What you want to achieve is that your main efforts are spent on the most urgent activities – which may or not be important but certainly need to be carried out promptly – followed closely by important activities that are fairly urgent, then activities that are important but not urgent. Last on anyone's list of activities should be those that are neither important nor urgent.

Urgency and importance

A vital management skill is being able to understand the difference between 'urgent' and 'important'. Going back to the bucket analogy, the big rocks are the urgent and important issues. Sometimes the urgent issues just seem to come out of the blue – a fire, a faulty product/piece of equipment or poor workmanship that has an immediate safety implication – and dealing with them is often referred to as 'firefighting'. They may not always be important, but they need dealing with now and are therefore urgent!

Important issues are central to your business and certainly need dealing with, but may not be urgent – for example, organising the next sales team meeting agenda is important but is not more urgent than putting out a fire.

Urgent	Important
Three members of staff ring in sick – organise replacements	Organise sales promotion
Frozen/chilled stock delivery – put into appropriate storage	Complete staff rota
Till breakdown – organise a repair or replacement and put into operation contingency plan	Order Christmas stock
Display window broken – organise boarding up and replacement	Organise team meetings
Customer complaint – deal with immediately	Ensure sufficient change available

Urgent vs Important

Having a form (see page 208) into which activities can be placed gives you an immediate overview of the priorities of each task. Prioritising activities is the second step to effective and efficient time management, after completion of the time log.

First, you need to decide which things on your to-do list are important. Once you have done that, you then need to decide how urgent they are. Important and urgent tasks are placed in box 1, important but non-urgent tasks in box 2 and so on. Obviously, tasks that are both important and urgent should be your top priority; the important but non-urgent tasks will need to be carried out and must be scheduled to be dealt with as soon as the important and urgent tasks have been completed. Non-important and urgent tasks (those that have associated time issues, such as ensuring the post goes out in time) go in box 3, but these could be delegated to a member of your team (see the section on delegation on page 213). You need to take a long hard look at any task in box 4 – these are both non-important and non-urgent, so ask yourself if they need doing at all, or if you need to be doing them.

The following websites may help you to decide which boxes your tasks should go in:

- www.mindtools.com
- ni.comindwork.com.

ACTIVITY PRIORITISING FORM

	URGENT	NON-URGENT
IMPORTANT		
NON-IMPORTANT		

OVER TO YOU

Take a look at the activities that you did yesterday and decide how urgent and important each was. Put them into the four sections in the activity prioritising form. Is this how you would have prioritised them at the time?

Planning how you spend your time is as important as planning how you spend money, your business growth or your marketing activity. Part of planning your time is creating a list of things that need to be done, and in the next section you'll look at the ways of doing this.

LISTS AND PLANS

For the same reason that you make a shopping list, you should make to-do lists on a weekly and daily basis – if you don't write things down, you're likely to forget them.

However, is one list enough? Consider making the following:

- A daily essential list – This is a list of the day's important and urgent issues. There should only be a few items – aim for no more than five or six tasks, depending on their complexity.
- A general list – For the less important issues.
- A list of items that you do not want to do now but that you don't want to forget about.
- A list of things you are waiting for people to get back to you on.

When you make a list you are emptying your head of the things that are going round and round in it, and this should help you to relax. You may find it beneficial to keep a pen and paper by your bed, so if you wake in the night with an idea or concern you can scribble down your thoughts without worrying that you'll forget about it and spend all night awake.

When creating your to-do lists, you'll need to consider how long it will take you to carry out each task. It's not enough to just put down the name of the task – you need to allow for the time it takes to carry it out too.

For complex tasks or jobs – those that take a long time and are quite involved – there are a couple of project planning tools that are helpful, as they allow you to visually track what needs to be done, when it should be done and how long it should take, bearing in mind the other things that need to be done at the same time. Critical path analysis (CPA) and Gantt charts are popular planning tools; examples of both are shown below.

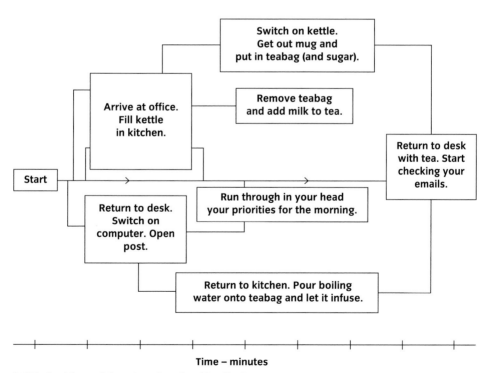

A CPA chart for arriving at work and making the tea

	8.00	8.01	8.02	8.03	8.04	8.05	8.06	8.07	Minutes
Arrive at office. Fill kettle in kitchen.	■								1
Switch on kettle. Get out mug and put in teabag (and sugar).		■	■	■					3
Return to desk. Switch on computer. Open post.			■	■					2
Sort post into priority piles while computer is starting up.				■					1
Return to kitchen. Pour boiling water onto teabag and let it infuse.					■	■			2
Run through in your head your priorities for the morning.						■			1
Remove teabag and add milk to tea.							■		1
Return to desk with tea. Start checking your emails.								■	

A Gantt chart for arriving at work and making the tea

Activities can be broken down into tasks, some of which need to be done one after another, and others that can be done at the same time. Using the above tools helps you to see what should be done and when. These processes also help you see where to allocate team members, and are a vital part of calculating your costs for any task.

For further information on these two project management tools, visit:
- www.ganttchart.com
- www.mindtools.com.

Time-wasting statistics
A survey by Proudfoot Consulting (Guardian, 22 Oct 2007) covering 2500 businesses in 38 countries over four years indicated that wasted time costs UK businesses £80 billion per year.

The causes of wasted time were highlighted as:
- inadequate workforce supervision (31 per cent)
- poor management planning (30 per cent)
- poor communication (18 per cent)
- IT problems, low morale and a lack or mismatch of skills (21 per cent).

What is time-wasting costing your business?

As the survey results demonstrate, wasting time costs money. So far you've looked at your time expenditure, but you may also consider time logs and their analysis for each of your team members – now if you already have a team, or in the future if you don't yet. Perhaps this is something to add to your to-do list?

STAFF SCHEDULING

A critical area of planning is staff scheduling. You will need to ensure that the business is staffed efficiently, so that customers are not kept waiting and all other tasks are carried out in a timely manner. On the other hand, you will need to keep within the budget available. Weekly and daily rotas should be completed, showing what hours staff are working each day and what tasks they have planned to carry out.

Weekly rotas should be completed as far in advance as possible, so that staff know when they are required to work and can give the maximum notice if they are on holiday or otherwise unavailable to work their scheduled hours. Daily rotas should be completed a week in advance. When drawing up rotas you need to take into account:

- The Working Time Regulations (details of these can be found in Chapter 9).
- The staff's contracted hours – Scheduling staff to work more hours can incur overtime payments.
- Staff holidays.
- Staff skills – You will need the correct mix of skills available among the staff scheduled to work to cover the tasks to be carried out.
- Level of supervision – You will need at least one responsible person available at all times.
- Security – You will need enough staff at all times to ensure the safety of the staff, the premises and the stock.
- Sales patterns – Some days of the week will be busier than others, and some periods of the year will be busier due to the season or promotions.

There will be situations which arise that you haven't been able to take into account when setting your rotas. Staff sickness, delayed deliveries, severe weather conditions or unusual trading patterns will have to be coped with as they arise.

All of the above relate to a small and medium enterprise (SME) that is perhaps larger than the average small business, which usually consists of one to three people.

Andrea is the supervisor in a convenience store and has created the staff rota for Tuesday as below.

	8-9	9-10	10-11	11-12	12-1	1-2	2-3	3-4	4-5	5-6
Andrea	S	S	S	S	L	S	S	S		
Brian					S	T	L	T	S	S
Christine		T	T	T	T					
David							SR	D	T	R
Eric			SR	SR	T	T				
Francis							T	SR	SR	R

S = Supervisor, T = Till, SR = Stock replenishment, D = Delivery, R = Recovery, L = Lunch

At 8.30am on Tuesday, Christine rings Andrea to tell her that she will not be able to come into work as she is unwell. Andrea looks at the rota to see how she can cover Christine's hours on the till at the least extra cost. She decides to call Eric and ask him if he can come in early, so that from 9.00am–12.00pm Andrea and Eric can staff the shop between them. If the shop is not too busy at 1.00pm she will let Eric go home early.

OVER TO YOU

Create a weekly rota based on the daily rota above. Create weekly and daily rotas for your own business taking into account the points described above.

As you can now see, planning work time is a crucial skill when running your own business. Planning will help ensure that the things that need to be done get done, in an organised way. It will help prevent you wasting your time doing things you don't need to be doing. Wasted time costs money, so you must ensure you make the most of this valuable resource and avoid duplication. To help you stay focused on the important issues in your business you need to delegate the less important tasks to others, and the next section looks at this in detail.

DELEGATION

Delegation is the act of empowering someone else to act for you – in other words, giving another person the skills to do some of what you do and ultimately giving him the authority and responsibility for it too. Lots of business owners have difficulty with delegation as it involves giving away an element of control, but without it the business can't grow – one person can't do everything (even the one-man/small partnership can delegate some tasks, for example accounting/bookkeeping to an outside person/company). Delegation is also a team-motivating factor – you would only train and up-skill someone if you believed in him, saw a future with him in it and trusted him, so by delegating you are actually saying that he is important to you. Delegation is normally thought of as being within the business, but you could also delegate bookkeeping, payroll or human resources to an external company.

WHAT CAN YOU DELEGATE?

The starting point for delegation is to carry out further analysis of your time log, but this time it's to see how wisely you are using your time. Ask yourself: 'Am I doing things that others could, or should, be doing?'

OVER TO YOU

Get three different-coloured highlighter pens. Using the first colour, highlight activities on your time log that others can do without training – that they could do now. Then, with your second colour, highlight activities that others could do with training. Finally with your third colour, highlight activities that only you can, or should, do.

When you have completed this activity, add the activities to the chart below, with timescales for others to take over.

DELEGATION ACTION PLANNER

ACTIVITES THAT CAN BE DELEGATED <u>WITHOUT</u> TRAINING

ACTIVITY	TO WHOM	WHEN
*	*	*
*	*	*
*	*	*
*	*	*
*	*	*
*	*	*

ACTIVITES THAT CAN BE DELEGATED <u>WITH</u> TRAINING

ACTIVITY	TO WHOM	WHEN
*	*	*
*	*	*
*	*	*
*	*	*
*	*	*
*	*	*

You now need to follow the three steps below:

1 See what percentage of your time is spent doing activities that others could do now. You also need to think about what else you could be doing with that time if it were freed up and how much more you could earn in that time, and then work out what it is actually costing you to do those activities yourself. The next question is: which members of your team have the time and skills to take on these activities immediately, without the need for training? When you have carried out this analysis you can give these activities to the team members best suited to carry them out. However, if you give them a task, you need to ask yourself what they will not be able to do if they are doing the delegated tasks. The issue of time being a valuable resource is relevant to them as well as you.

2 Then do the same again to find out what percentage of your time is spent doing activities that others could do if they had training. And again, what it is costing your business for you to be carrying them out. This is not as straightforward, the training requirement will take time, and will involve training costs. There may not be the direct cost of paying for training, as it may be internally delivered, but there will still be a cost in the time it takes them to learn and the time it takes you, or another team member, to train them. There are also other considerations, such as what skills are required for these activities to be delegated, and if other team members take on your activities, what will be the implications for what they normally do – do any of their activities need to be delegated, too?

3 The remaining activities are those that only you can or should do. However, if you are the only one who can do an activity, you may need to consider up-skilling others. Also, if you believe you are the only one who should do an activity, you need to reflect on your management style and check that you're not being too much of a control freak!

The final consideration is what you are going to do with the time you have saved – will your time be spent doing an additional activity or will it be spent planning? Most small business owners don't have enough time to plan, so ensure you make the most of any freed-up time in this way.

MANAGING DELEGATION

Delegation is an important part of any team leader's role as it motivates and improves the team as a whole, as well as individual team members. Delegation is a process that has to be gone through when an activity, task or project is taken over by one person from another, from the delegator to the delegatee. Sometimes the delegator retains responsibility for the activity, task or project even though someone else actually carries it out – on other occasions, total responsibility is delegated.

 CASE STUDY 2

Michael had his own car valeting business with three vans; his customers were mainly business owners from the nearby business park and they had 'executive' cars. He wanted to create a website, because he believed it would give a better impression of the scale of his business to his executive customers. He found someone to design his website and do all the hosting and email management, but the designer, who knew nothing about car valeting, said from the very beginning 'You must supply me with the copy to go on the site as I don't know your business and you need to make sure it's right', and this was agreed. After a few meetings and a few drafts, the final website design was decided on and the various heading and images added. The designer had used dummy text to see how it would look as he laid out the design. Michael promised to get the copy to him so it could be added ready for final approval at the next meeting. Michael was away at a trade exhibition, so delegated the task of submitting the rough draft of text to Tony, his second-in-command. Michael trusted that Tony would be able to get all the facts over, although he knew his spelling and grammar wasn't very good, but that it didn't matter as it was just the draft.

Continued

While at the exhibition, Michael met one of his customers, who said he could have a section on his website but needed the link as soon as possible. Michael rang Tony and asked him to hurry up with the copy for the site as he had an opportunity to be part of something big and the task was now urgent. Tony said he'd do it and would forward the draft copy to Michael for approval, which was agreed.

However, someone from the customer's website department rang Michael's office and said they needed the website details immediately. Worried he'd otherwise be letting Michael down, Tony forwarded the web address he had to send the draft copy to. Unknown to Tony, this was the administration address for the site, which the designer was using to complete all the behind-the-scenes work while waiting for final approval, and he didn't know the customer's site was going live that day. Tony didn't know this was a different website address as he hadn't been involved in any of the meetings.

Michael came back from the exhibition to find that the unfinished version of his company website was now live with lots of errors, bad grammar, wrong spellings and dummy text! His customer was angry as it made his website look bad and therefore his business. Michael was furious with Tony and blamed him for losing a customer and giving approval for the website to go live, which he didn't have the authority to do. Tony blamed Michael for not giving him all the relevant information or agreeing clearly what he could and couldn't do; their relationship suffered as a result.

What do you think? Was it Tony's fault? Was it Michael's? It is hard to accept, but most mistakes can be traced back to poor management – you. This mistake can most definitely be laid at Michael's door, although he refused to see it, saying 'Tony should have known'. But how could Tony have known when he hadn't been involved in the whole process and had responsibility for only a small part? Tony acted as he did because he thought he was being helpful; he also felt it would help cement the relationship with their best customer. You must ensure that anyone you delegate anything to is clear where their responsibilities begin and end; if it includes total or part responsibility and if they have ultimate authority. Don't assume they know, as they won't unless you tell them.

In retail, dealing with customer complaints may be delegated to a senior salesperson. If they are given the authority to decide on the action that is to be taken without referring to the owner or manager, both the activity and the responsibility have been delegated. If they have to seek permission to satisfy the customer's requirements, only the activity has been delegated. If you have delegated responsibility, it is important that you support the decision that is taken, and do not override it.

The process of delegation must be clear to all the team members so they are aware that a change in a member's job role is happening and can give help and support if required, or even stay out of the way during the learning process.

Delegation should take place in stages:
- Stage 1: The team member observes the activity to be delegated, makes notes and so on.
- The team member carries out the activity under your close supervision, with immediate corrections from you.
- After the activity has finished, you give comprehensive feedback.
- Stage 2: The team member carries out the activity under your close supervision but without immediate corrections.
- After the activity has finished, you give comprehensive feedback.
- Stage 3: The team member carries out the activity under your distant supervision without immediate corrections.
- After the activity has finished, you give comprehensive feedback.
- Stage 4: The team member carries out the activity without supervision.
- After the activity has finished, you discuss with the team member the delegation process – if you are both happy, continue on to the final stages; if not, repeat until you both are.
- Final stage: The team member has ownership of the activity and authority.
- You inform the rest of the team of the change.

Delegation is not just from you to your senior team members but from them to others and so on down the line; in that way, everyone gets up-skilled.

Benefits to team members	Benefits to you	Benefits to the business
Feelings of importance	More time to plan	Motivated team members
Feelings of security	More time to earn	In-business progression route
Feelings of belonging		
Feeling of being good at what they do		
Recognition within the team		

Benefits of delegation

	ACTIVITY						
	Stock ordering	Stock rotation	Stock display	Banking	Meeting-with sales representatives	Team CPD	Socials
Team member:							
Ann	Yes	Yes	Yes	Yes	Yes	Yes	Yes
David	Yes WT	Yes	Yes	No	Yes WT	Yes WT	Yes
Michael	Yes WT	Yes WT	Yes	No	Yes WT	Yes WT	Yes WT
Damien	Yes WT	Yes WT	Yes	No	Yes WT	No	Yes WT
Sandy	No	Yes WT	Yes WT	No	No	No	No
Zoe	No	Yes WT	Yes WT	No	No	No	No

Key:
Yes = can do immediately
Yes WT = can do with training
No = can't do even with training

Example of task/team skills analysis

A junior sales assistant may benefit from being delegated the task of helping customers to find the stock they are looking for. This will help them to learn skills in customer service, product knowledge and selling.

Delegation goals

Any activity that is to be delegated should be SMART:

- **S** is the Specific activity to be delegated.
- **M** is how you can Measure whether the delegation has been successful or not.
- **A** is how Achievable the delegation is, bearing in mind the complexity of the activity or task.
- **R** is how Relevant this activity is to the delegator and the business in general; in other words, how much of a difference will it make?
- **T** is for the Timescale involved in another person taking over that specific activity or task.

You can use a chart such as the one below to record these SMART goals:

- List the specific activity to be delegated.
- List what measurement of success you will put in place to know whether the delegation has been successful.
- Give each activity an achievability rating of 1–5, 1 being extremely unrealistic and 5 being highly realistic.
- Give each activity a relevancy rating of 1–5, 1 being very irrelevant and 5 being highly relevant. Activities should be delegated only if they're relevant to the overall objectives of the business, otherwise they're an expensive waste of time and could harm team morale.

- List the timescale allowed for the delegation process to be completed. How long should the total process of delegation take? This needs to be appropriate to the amount of work to be undertaken. If the delegation is from one person to another of equal skill in that area then it may be only minutes, as the process is more to do with paperwork and organisation. However, if there is a training requirement then it could take days, weeks or months.
- Add the costs for this delegation. No process, delegation or otherwise, should proceed without it being fully costed. What are the training implications and are they internally or externally delivered? If internal, will any work be postponed or cancelled? How many man-hours will it cost? Two team members for two 8-hour days = 16 hours @ £20 per hour = £320. Do you require any training aids or materials? Will they be free or will you have to pay? If training is external, what is the cost of the course? What travel, food and hotel costs are there? How long will the delegatee be away? What is the cost in postponed or cancelled work?
- Add the date by which the delegation process is to be completed. There should be a timescale agreed for when responsibility is handed over. Also, those booking work in need to know who is doing what jobs and when; if promotional communications are to be created they need to be planned too.
- The delegatee will often make comments that need to be noted during your discussions. These are likely to crop up due to a particular concern or difficulty with an activity or task that needs to be highlighted separately. For example, if you are delegating a customer-facing responsibility, the delegatee might say 'I really need to know the features and benefits of Product X as I don't feel that I can answer customers' questions about it.'

DELEGATION SMART GOALS

SPECIFIC ACTIVITY	MEASUREMENT OF SUCCESS	ACHIEVEABLE 1 - 5	RELEVANT 1 - 5	TIMED	COST	DATE	COMMENTS

You should always look back to these SMART goals at the end of the delegation process to analyse how well it went:
- What went well and how do you know? What didn't go well and how do you know?
- What would you change for next time?
- How did the delegation to team members not requiring training go?

- How did the delegation to team members who did require training go?
- Were there any positive or negative changes to team dynamics?
- Do you have more time as a result of the delegation? (If yes, what are you doing with it? If no, why not?)
- Are you earning more money?
- Are you planning more delegation?

Delegation is important – it prevents you from being bogged down with minor things so you can get on with the major aspects of moving your business forward. However, one concern is that there might be duplication of effort, which is time-consuming and costly.

PREVENTING DUPLICATION OF EFFORT

Wasting time is one of the biggest causes of concern for business owners. Activities such as time logs and subsequent prioritisation and delegation are helpful in ensuring that you and your team members make your time count. But another big cause of time wasting is duplication of effort, and this happens all too frequently in businesses of all sizes.

In most businesses there are people with different job roles, but the nature of small businesses is that everyone mucks in to some extent and pulls together to help each other out. Although team spirit is commendable, if roles and activities are being carried out in an unstructured manner it can cause mayhem, with many people carrying out the same task or activity. A classic case is when two people place the same order with a supplier, each believing that they are being helpful to the other.

You (or the person you have delegated this task to) have to take charge of the process of who does what, who checks it and who needs to be kept in the know. This is a management-led process known as DCK (for Doer, Checker and Knower), and can be recorded on a DCK sheet. This basic process should list all the activities that are undertaken in your business, and then next to each team member's name the words 'doer', 'checker' or 'knower':

- Doer – This is the person who actually carries out the activity, task or action, and it is his or her responsibility alone; no one else should do it.
- Checker – This is the person who the doer goes to when the activity, task or action has been completed, to check the standard of work and to sign it off as done. The checker will also be the person the doer goes to if he needs any help or support in carrying out the activity, task or action. The checker is most likely to be a past doer of that activity, task or action who therefore has the necessary experience and knowledge.

- Knower – This person is generally, although not always, in a supervisory or management role and therefore has ultimate responsibility and authority for all activities and actions. His role is mainly to be aware of everything that is going on, although not necessarily in detail. He often liaises with checkers to know what is going on and for any specific feedback regarding an activity, task or action.

Each team member will have a copy of the DCK sheet so will be clear about the activities he or she is involved in and what their role is – doer, checker or knower. When implemented and reviewed quarterly, this type of information will save duplication of effort, which in turn will save time and prevent confusion. Saved time = saved money = more profit.

How to fill in the DCK sheet:
- Add the date.
- In the first column, list the activities.
- In the second column, list the DCK roles for yourself across all activities.
- In the third column, list the DCK roles for the supervisor across all activities.
- In the fourth column, list the DCK roles for the junior member of staff across all activities.

Activities	You	Supervisor	Junior	Date
Welcoming customers	Knower	Doer, Checker	Doer	
Dealing with customer complaints	Checker, Knower	Doer		
Serving customers	Knower	Doer, Checker	Doer	
Cash Handling	Knower	Doer, Checker	Doer	
Product displays	Knower	Knower, Doer, Checker	Doer	
Mentoring	Doer, Checker, Knower	Doer		
Dealing with suppliers	Doer, Checker, Knower	Doer		
Planning promotions	Doer, Checker, Knower	Doer		
Managing the business	Doer			
Cleaning and general upkeep	Knower	Checker	Doer	

DCK sheet

This form needs to be completed whenever there are any changes and at least once every quarter, which will fit in with your appraisal meetings.

Confused communications are the main cause of problems within any team. The ongoing use of this form will help ensure that everyone knows what they are supposed to be doing, who needs to check these tasks and who needs to know about it. The clearer all communications are within teams, the better team members perform.

The keys to delegation are: don't try to do everything yourself, learn to let go, and trust others to both do and check things for you, even though you will always be the ultimate knower of all things. You can never grow your business if you do everything yourself; if you do try, not only are you setting yourself up for failure but you will put yourself through a tremendous amount of stress and, as you'll see in the next section, that can be damaging to your health and that of your business.

MANAGING STRESS

Stress can be positive or negative. Negative stress is the type that can make you, or your team members, ill. As the owner of a small business you need to do all you can to ensure there is as little negative stress as possible. But not all stress is bad; winning the Olympic 100 metres race is stressful, waiting for exam results is stressful, waiting to hear if you've won a contract is also stressful… These are examples of positive stress where something good is achieved; it makes people perform and feel better. We often refer to this sort of short-term stress as feeling nervous or having butterflies – it's not harmful. However, stress that affects our bodies negatively can lead to long-term health problems and/or behavioural or performance problems. You need to be aware of what causes stress in your workplace and do what you can to minimise its risks.

As a business owner you have a legal duty under the Health and Safety at Work Act 1974 to ensure that your workplace is as stress-free as possible. Statistics on stress from the UK Health and Safety Executive (HSE) show that:

■ In the UK over 13 million working days are lost every year because of stress. Stress is believed to trigger 70 per cent of visits to doctors and 85 per cent of serious illnesses, and the number of people suffering from work-related stress isn't reducing.
■ HSE statistics suggest that stress-related costs to UK employers are in the region of £700m every year.

It makes sound business sense to prevent negative stress and to deal with it effectively as soon as possible should it start to become an issue, as it is a cause of litigation for employers, with significant financial costs relating to damages, as well as negative publicity. Dealing with claims takes a lot of time and involves considerable costs, particularly if you require external legal advice or representation. Apart from not wanting your team to suffer any ill effects through negative stress, these are significant financial reasons for you to reduce the number of **stressors** and manage their effects at work.

RECOGNISING THE CAUSES AND SIGNS OF STRESS

Stressors may be external or internal:

- External stressors – These are external to your body, such as the physical environment you find yourself in; it may be too hot or too cold, for example. Or they may involve working conditions and abusive relationships, such as bullying by colleagues or team leaders.
- Internal stressors – These are physical things to do with your mind or body – ailments such as infection or inflammation, or psychological problems such as worrying about something, which could be a home- or work-related issue.

Stressors can be short-term (acute) or long-term (chronic):

- Short-term stress – This is when you react to an immediate threat. You have a surge of adrenaline that gives your muscles strength, also known as the 'fight or flight' response. This goes back to primitive times when we needed to either run away very fast from a danger or stand and fight. Our brains still react in the same way to a perceived threat, which in the modern world might be the risk of getting stuck in a lift, feeling as though you are about to be attacked in the street and so on. As the name suggests, this kind of stress doesn't last long and has no long-term negative effects.
- Long-term stress – This is caused by factors that can cause ongoing health problems; the stressors are not violent or threatening but of a chronic nature. The fight or flight response doesn't kick in as it's not relevant – there's no immediate danger. These stressors are ongoing and include pressure of work, home and work relationship issues, and money worries.

Stressors in the working environment are mainly long-term, but may also be short-term. During the appraisal interviews is a good time to uncover sources of stress among the team members within your business.

Examples of long-term stressors at work include:

- being the subject of bullying or harassment
- spending time away from home and family
- feeling unimportant
- lack of financial security
- lack of job security
- lack of, or inadequate, resolution of concerns
- lack of reward for efforts
- customer complaints
- aggressive customers
- pressure of specific time-based tasks
- poor communication across the team and with team leaders
- unfair and long working hours on an ongoing basis.

The following list shows some classic signs of being stressed but any behaviour that is different from normal will need investigating:

- alcohol or drug abuse
- emotional outbursts
- loss of appetite
- development of nervous tics or habits
- fall-off in achievement
- reduction in concentration and memory
- disturbed sleep patterns
- violent/angry/antisocial behaviour.

STRESS REDUCTION TECHNIQUES

This section describes some general techniques to help you and your team reduce the effects of stress. It's important to realise that these techniques won't change the stressor itself but may help to alter the reaction to it. After all, you may have little or no control over the stressor, but you do have control over how you react to it.

- If possible, try to remove yourself from the stressor – perhaps go for a walk, preferably in the fresh air.
- On an ongoing basis, try to change your working habits, to remove yourself from your stressors or at least to limit their effects.
- Laughing, if at all possible, is a great way to reduce stress as it immediately produces feel-good hormones (endorphins) in the brain; it distracts you and defuses the feelings of stress. Perhaps keep something that makes you laugh handy – a silly email or a holiday photo, for instance.
- Find a 'stress buddy' – someone to go to when you feel stressed. Perhaps they can make you laugh! You will have heard the phrase 'a problem shared is a problem halved'... well, it's true.
- Drinking can help. Not caffeine- or sugar-based drinks, and definitely not alcohol, but water is good. The act of getting the water is also a distraction as it makes you leave your office or work area, walk around and communicate with others.
- Try taking a complete break to allow your brain to switch off; this is best done in the form of a power nap. These are something that we generally don't do in the UK once we have grown up, but in other countries power naps are perfectly normal and acceptable (as in a siesta). They can last 10–30 minutes.
- Any relaxation technique, such as deep breathing and self-hypnosis, can also help.

Gently getting rid of the effects of stress, rather than allowing them to build up and then erupt like a volcano, is preferable. People get rid of stress in different ways: some scream, dance wildly (until they laugh), some cry. It doesn't matter how you get rid of the effects, it's the act of getting rid of them that's important. Crying is particularly helpful to some people – and shouldn't be discouraged. If you have the space available, you could consider creating a private space where members of your team can go to let off steam.

As a business owner, you'll need to uncover the stressors for each member of your team and, where possible, either remove the stressor, remove the team member from it or, if either is impossible, help the team member to deal with it. Also, you cannot and must not overlook your own health and wellbeing! You need to accept that you have stressors too and the first step in dealing with yours is to recognise them.

Make a list of your stressors, why they stress you, and then see what you can do to minimise their effects.

When you do feel stressed, or even when you are just down, you need not just to deal with those stressors but you also need to develop the skills of mentally getting yourself back on track.

SELF-MOTIVATION

What – or who – motivates you?

You are a great team leader – you inspire, lead and motivate your team – but who motivates you? You may have a great support network around you – colleagues at work, friends and family at home, perhaps even an ex-employer or lecturer who acts as your mentor – but there is really only one main motivator in your business life and that person is you.

People who are unable to motivate themselves must be content with mediocrity, no matter how impressive their other talents. – Andrew Carnegie

DEALING WITH DEMOTIVATION

When do you feel demotivated? People normally feel demotivated either before or during a task, activity or project. If you feel demotivated beforehand, you need to ask yourself what it is about the task you feel uncomfortable about. Are you concerned the goal is not achievable? That it's not relevant? That it will cause disruption? That it's going to cost too much? That you can't 'see' the end result? You need to be clear exactly what it is you want to achieve and why, because if you don't know, it's difficult to be enthusiastic and motivated by it. Just like an athlete, you need a goal; you need to have the finishing line in your sights so you have something to aim for.

If you're demotivated during the task, activity or project and the goal is appropriate and relevant but just difficult, try breaking it down into smaller, bite-sized goals and allow yourself to celebrate each one as you achieve it. It helps to focus on the benefits that achieving the ultimate goal will bring. It may also be helpful to see if there are any other ways of achieving a goal.

Demotivation and confusion can occur when a more important goal has come along in the time since you set the current one, so the current one is not your priority any more. If this happens you must reprioritise – deal with the more important goal first. See page 207 for more about classifying activities into 'urgent', 'important', 'non-urgent' and 'non-important' categories.

In the short term you may find you are more likely to be motivated or demotivated at certain times of the day, so arrange planning meetings and any team motivation activities accordingly. Likewise, in the longer term, you need to note when in the duration of achieving a goal you are most likely to be motivated or demotivated.

OVER TO YOU

Make a note of when your motivation starts to lag in both the short and long term and see what the trends are. You may find it helpful to refer back to the activity log that you completed earlier in the chapter.

Understanding what you want, what you need, what you like, what you don't like, what you are trying to achieve and what excites you in business will help you motivate yourself. However, one of the biggest causes of demotivation for you and your team is change – the management of change is crucial to keeping everyone motivated.

Harry has owned a traditional bookshop for 17 years. Recently, sales have been down and Harry has noticed that the staff morale has been poor. By listening to his staff, he realises that they are worried that recent advances in technology, such as the Kindle and other e-book readers, will threaten their jobs.

Harry realises that this reduction in staff morale could have a knock-on effect on levels of customer service, leading to further reductions in sales and ultimately to the loss of his experienced staff before the business collapses.

Harry has always used material benefits as staff motivators, offering bonuses for increased sales, increases in wages or promotion to keep his staff happy. He realises that he is not in a position to use these methods in this situation, so he looks for a motivator which will be both cost-effective and help to overcome the difficulties the business finds itself in.

He decides to hold a staff meeting at which he will lay out the facts about the situation. He feels this will defuse any rumours that exaggerate the seriousness of the situation and make the team feel that they are trusted with the information. At the meeting, he will suggest that the way forward is to diversify, but tell the staff that he has not decided what diversification will be most effective. He will ask the team to go away and think about it for a week, after which they will hold another meeting to formulate a plan going forward. He believes this will motivate the staff as they will feel involved in the continuing success of the business.

MANAGING CHANGE AND SOLVING PROBLEMS

It is not the strongest species that survive, nor the most intelligent, but the ones who are most responsive to change. – Charles Darwin

Change is part of business and indeed life; it will always happen and you can't alter that. What you can adjust is the level of concern it causes you and your team. Managing change is important; any change can cause demotivation – and demotivation, as shown in the previous section, can have a negative impact on your team and your bottom line.

DECIDING ON CHANGES

It may be there are lots of things that need to be dealt with through change – whenever this is the case you should prioritise by making a simple list of 'urgent' and 'important' issues as looked at earlier in the chapter. Anything urgent normally needs to be done immediately. Of the important issues, ask yourself which have the most potential for damage if not dealt with quickly. Other criteria might involve ranking changes in order of cost, or customer relationships, or – arguably more important – your own health and wellbeing. The key is, when you've made your decision on the criteria you are going to use to decide on changes, you must stick to them.

Decision-making techniques

Even an 'easy' decision should be made based on research, understanding of the issues, appreciation of the implications and it being the right thing to do. These things might seem intuitive, but in practice you should be using a logical decision-making process that helps you see the main issues clearly.

Think about choosing a meal in a restaurant. Just like making a business decision, it's a process based on a number of factors: what you like to eat, what you feel like eating at that moment in time, whether you are trying to lose weight, what else you ate that day, perhaps how tight your clothes are, whether you should avoid garlic if you have a meeting the following morning, and so on.

When making business decisions there are six steps in the decision-making process:

1 The general environment and atmosphere must be suitable for change – constructive, not destructive.
2 There should be alternative decisions to evaluate and compare; it's never good to view a decision in isolation.
3 Time should be spent researching and evaluating the alternatives.
4 When you have fully evaluated all alternatives, choose the best one.
5 Don't rush into making a decision, but don't waste time either. Decisions have to be made.
6 When you have made your decision, ensure that all the people involved are made aware of it and of any repercussions, and then implement the decision.

THE CHANGE PROCESS

When implementing change you must make sure that you and your senior team members are committed to it and that commitment is communicated for everyone else to see. The ability to take the whole team with you on the journey towards change is vital. The concept of internal marketing was discussed in Chapter 5; managing change is a classic case of internal marketing being used to achieve team ownership of the change, which will, in turn, benefit everyone. The change need not be massive in order to cause concern, and what does cause concern differs from person to person. The things you need to manage are their expectations of how the change will affect them – what they think they'll lose as a result of the change and any general fears they may have.

As well as the rest of the team, you should also include customers and suppliers when considering the implications and management of change. As part of your planning, you'll need to put in place all the resources required to make change happen, such as human resources and time. Lastly, just as important is to let everyone know what is happening before it actually happens so they feel in control of the process rather than the change being in control of them.

Early communication regarding the change should be to everyone at the same time – this prevents 'Chinese whispers' and office gossip. Be honest about the reason for the change, what form the change will take, the effects on the business and team members, and what the outcome of the change will be. Bear in mind that you may need to hold one-to-one meetings to uncover, and allay, specific fears. A big change, such as relocation, will have a massive impact on team members and their families. Their choice could be seen as choosing between a rock and a hard place – to relocate and uproot their family in order to to keep their job, or to stay where they are with redundancy money but possibly no job to go to. Always see things from your team's perspective; a great move for your business might not be a great move for them. Small changes can also cause upset, such as taking away parking spaces or redesigning the layout of the office. If the change does involve a perceived loss (of a parking space for example) try to replace it with something else. Again, think like your team – if they aren't especially well paid they might rely on outward signs of success like parking spaces to prove their worth. Losing this might be very difficult for them, as well as having financial implications (as they'll have to pay parking charges).

Leadership is getting others to do what you want them to do because they want to do it. – US President Dwight D. Eisenhower

As with any business decision, change needs to be planned for, with a budget, timescale and SMART objectives. If the change involves the structure of the team, they may go through a period of mourning as the team dynamics alter, before they start the forming, storming, norming and performing stages all over again.

How to spot problems

You may first notice there are problems following a change if the behaviour of your team members alters. Behavioural change can be slow and by the time you notice it, most if not all of your team members may have got themselves well and truly wound up. Keep an eye out for changes in behaviour and pay particular attention to the feelings forms if you use them as part of your team meetings. Any change can cause distress, which may manifest itself in a number of ways. Although not a complete list, the following are some indications that someone may be feeling upset or under pressure:

- demotivation
- signs of stress
- different behaviour
- not wanting to be involved in any way with the change
- being either withdrawn or loud.

Having a set change implementation process ensures that you make decisions based on information and evaluation and don't rely too much on gut feelings. However, there are many variables which will affect this process; some, such as those relating to customers or suppliers, may not be under your control. If you embrace the six steps you will make better decisions, and if you communicate these to your colleagues in a positive way, you will bring them along with you.

The next section looks at how to implement solutions to problems to make dealing with them as stress-free as possible.

SOLVING PROBLEMS

Once you have spotted an issue, a concern or a problem, you must act as soon as possible. It's rare for them to get better by being left, although knee-jerk reactions should also be avoided.

As with other issues to do with running your business, you should make a plan before acting. The following is a guide to the process to help keep you on track.

Analysis stage

The problem

What is the problem?

What areas of the business could it affect?

On a scale of 1–10 how much disruption is it causing?

And to which areas of your business?

Research

Have you had the same or a similar problem before?

If so, how did you deal with it before?

Is this problem specific to your business or is it a trade-wide issue?

How have other businesses dealt with it?

Planning stage

Solutions

What is the least expensive solution in terms of resources (time and money)?

What is the least expensive solution in terms of human resources?

Who has the most knowledge about this problem?

Who is the best person to manage the solution?

What is to be achieved in SMART terms?

Who is in charge and who is in the team?

Have you defined what their roles and responsibilities are?

Prepare a selection of plans covering the different solutions that you've identified.

Prepare internal marketing communications.

If applicable, prepare external marketing communications.

Making choices and decisions

Which is the most likely choice to have the least impact on customers?

Which is the most likely choice to have the least impact on suppliers?

Which choice is your team most likely to support?

Which is most likely to succeed on a scale of 1–10?

What are the key points that need to be addressed along the way?

Implementation stage

Doing

Is everyone involved achieving what they should?

Are all resources achieving what they should?

Are key performance indicators being met?

What are the issues/queries?

Measure against SMART objectives detailed in the planning stage.

Control stage

Checking and evaluation

Was the outcome achieved?

Was it on time and on budget?

What worked and why?

What didn't work and why?

What would you do differently?

What would you do the same?

Problem-solving processes

OVER TO YOU

Give one example of a problem in your business and take it through the process above.

This guide will make you think about a problem and the plan for solving it in a logical way. In other words, you'll do your research and analyse that research, then look at a variety of possible solutions and analyse those options across a number of factors. Then you choose which is best. Having made your decision you then need to implement your choice – you do it! You will follow a project plan like those you looked at earlier in this chapter (the CPA or Gantt charts), which will help you keep on track. In any plan there are important milestones along the way that you must achieve on time and in budget; these are often called key performance indicators (KPIs). Think of them as flags on a golf course showing where the holes are when they too far away to be seen. Part of creating your plan is to put in place KPIs that will show you if you are – or aren't – on track and allow you to make changes. After the implementation stage comes evaluation, which is covered in the next section.

EVALUATING CHANGE

There are different ways to evaluate the success, or otherwise, of managing change. The most obvious is to set SMART objectives at the beginning so you have something tangible to measure against at the end. If there is nothing to measure against, you'll never know if anything has worked and why. You'd never say about going out on a Saturday night that you just want to have a nice time, as that doesn't mean anything. You need to quantify what you consider a nice time to consist of, then you have an objective to measure against.

You can evaluate success based on financial or non-financial criteria.

Financial success:
- higher profit
- higher turnover
- less money tied up in stock/resources
- more time.

Non-financial success:
- increased customer satisfaction levels
- increased word-of-mouth recommendations
- increased market share
- more motivated team

- less stress
- more storage space.

You will recognise by now that everything needs to be planned for. Nothing should be done in the heat of the moment. There is an old saying, 'Act in haste, repent at leisure', and that holds very true. You need to view everything you do – whether it's to do with implementing change, dealing with stress or dealing with problems – as a learning process. Ask yourself every time you are in the middle of implementing something:

- What is going well and why?
- What isn't going as well as planned and why?
- What should I change, how should I change it, what will that change achieve and how will I know whether it has been achieved?

Ask the same type of questions after completion:

- What went well and why?
- What didn't go as well as planned and why?
- What would I do differently next time and why?

If the change hasn't achieved what you wanted it to, then you have to take a long hard look at the situation. You can't go back to how it was before because that didn't work, and the change you made isn't right either. So once again, as so often in business, you need to take a step back and look at the situation without emotion. This review needs time; if you rush into it thinking that any action is better than none it will probably not be the right action. Try to analyse what is wrong by adding the opinions of those around you, including customers and suppliers, to your own understanding of the situation. Then work out what you ultimately want to achieve – the outcome you need – and work back to how you can best achieve it – the solution. When you have the solution you can then put the people in place to manage it, although as a small business owner it may fall on your shoulders to manage the whole thing. Remember, you need to implement this new change in the same planned and measured way as the previous one. Only then will you be able to review whether it has made the difference that you need.

You will make mistakes – all entrepreneurs do – but if you learn from them, rather than getting stressed by them, they become learning opportunities, through which you can get better and your business can get stronger.

WHERE TO GO FOR MORE INFORMATION

The following sources of information will help you to manage your time and stay motivated:

- Further information on delegation for owners and directors can be found on the Business Link website: www.businesslink.gov.uk.
- Additional information on time management for front-line managers can also be found on the Business Link website: visit www.businesslink.gov.uk and search for 'Time management'.
- A free trial version of time management software, which may give you some ideas, is available at: www.qbissystem.co.uk.
- Institute of Leadership & Management (ILM) courses in time management can be viewed at: www.i-l-m.com.
- The Health and Safety Executive has an Infoline on stress in the workplace, call: 0845 345 0055.
- The Health for Work Adviceline for Small Business is another useful number to have: 0800 0 77 88 44.
- The Business Link website has a section on how to manage stress in the workplace, which makes useful reading: www.businesslink.gov.uk.
- Another useful source of information for dealing with stress and other health issues in the workplace is the Health and Safety Executive: www.hse.gov.uk. For details of courses and training, visit www.workplacehealthconnect.co.uk.
- Some information on the benefits of and research into power napping can be found at: ririanproject.com.

A useful quiz on your ability to self-motivate can be found at: www.mindtools.com.

CONCLUSION

In this chapter you will have worked through how you spend your time and how much of it you can free up through delegation. As a business owner you must learn to let go, and allow your team to take authority and responsibility for tasks through empowering them to do more and be better, as it's the only way your business can grow. You have read in previous chapters how important it is to look after your team and keep them motivated; it's just as important to make sure their working environment is as stress-free as possible and that you put in place ways of reducing and combating the negative effects of stress. Lastly, you need to have a means of keeping yourself motivated; this is something you can do yourself or, more often, it's through a support network. The passion for your business keeps you motivated, and revisiting why you started it, what you might do if you ended the business (as most business owners would not want to be doing anything else!) and reflecting on your successes – and how you can build on these – will help to keep you motivated. You are the one your team, your customers and your suppliers look to, and they will follow your lead. If you're demotivated, they will be too.

CHAPTER 7
BUSINESS ADMINISTRATION

INTRODUCTION

No matter how good you are at what you do, you'll still have to deal with administration. This is the management of the affairs of the business, including all the paperwork, payroll procedures, communications and support services. No matter what kind of retail business you're operating, there are always likely to be invoices to send out, bank accounts to keep track of, letters to post, telephones to answer and health and safety issues to deal with. You may choose to do this yourself or employ someone else to do it if this is more practical or cost effective. Either way, if it's your business, it's your responsibility. This chapter covers the key forms needed to start up and operate a business; the records you need to keep and how to keep them; how to communicate effectively; and how to choose and use **ICT** and other technology support services such as PDQ machines for processing credit and debit card payments, and Electronic Point of Sale (EPOS) systems.

KEY FORMS FOR RUNNING A BUSINESS

Whether you're operating as a sole trader, a partnership or a private company, you'll have to let HM Revenue & Customs (HMRC) know that you are starting a business and complete the relevant forms. There are other forms that you will need to complete on an ongoing basis, many of which have deadlines and carry penalties if not submitted on time.

FORMS TO REGISTER WITH HMRC

This section builds on what you learnt in Chapter 1 by looking at the specifics of what you have to do when setting up a business. The type of forms you need when starting a business vary according to the legal structure you have chosen (see Chapter 1, pages 32–36). If you are setting up as a sole trader or a partnership you must notify HMRC that you are in business within three months of the end of the month in which you begin to be self-employed. To register as a sole trader you must complete HMRC form CWF1 'Registering for Self Assessment and National Insurance contributions if you are a self-employed sole trader'. The form can be downloaded from www.hmrc.gov.uk and on completion sent to:

> HMRC
> National Insurance Contributions and Employer Office
> Self-Employment and Self Assessment Registrations
> Benton Park View
> Newcastle-upon-Tyne
> NE98 1ZZ

The information you will need to complete the form is:
- your title, first name and surname
- your date of birth
- your National Insurance number
- when you started working for yourself
- the sort of work you do
- your home address
- whether you are a UK resident.

HMRC offers free advice and guidance about tax matters and often run complementary local workshops aimed at new business start-ups.

To register an ordinary partnership you must complete HMRC form SA400 'Registering a partnership for Self Assessment'. The form can be downloaded from www.hmrc.gov.uk and on completion sent to the address given above.

The information you will need to complete the form is:

- the name of the partnership
- the address and phone number of the partnership
- the trading name and address, if different
- the name and address of the nominated partner (the partner who will deal with HMRC)
- the nature of the business
- when the business started
- the type of partnership
- the partnership's accounting date
- the **Unique Taxpayer Reference** of the nominated partner.

Limited Partnerships and Limited Liability Partnerships that weren't registered with Companies House before 25 October 2010 do not have to complete form SA400. Limited Liability Partnerships register with Companies House on form LLIN01.

Each partner must complete HMRC form SA401 'Registering a partner for Self Assessment and Class 2 NICs' which can be downloaded from www.hmrc.gov.uk and on completion sent to the address given on page 236.

The information you will need to complete the form is:

- your title, surname and first name
- your address and phone number
- your date of birth
- your National Insurance number
- whether you are a UK resident
- whether you have entered the UK from a non-EU country in the past 12 months
- your Unique Taxpayer Reference if already registered
- whether you are the nominated partner
- when self-employment began
- the name and address of the partnership
- the nature of the business
- when you joined the partnership
- the Unique Taxpayer Reference of the partnership if already registered
- the Company Registration Number if a Limited Liability Partnership or Limited Partnership registered after 25 October 2010
- whether you are entitled to a share of the partnership's profits, losses and other income
- whether you engage in **sharefishing**.

FORMS TO REGISTER WITH COMPANIES HOUSE

If you are starting a limited company, it will need to be registered with Companies House before it starts trading. This can be done in three ways. The first of these is to use the Business Link/Companies House web incorporation service. You will need to register at www.businesslink.gov.uk with your email address and a password of your choice. You will then need the following information to complete the form:

- the company name and address
- details of directors and secretary (optional)
- details of each shareholder and the value of their shares
- payment details – there is a fee for this service payable to Companies House.

The second way is to use a Formation Agent to complete the formalities for you. A list of Formation Agents can be found at www.companieshouse.gov.uk.

The third way is by submitting details on paper to Companies House. You need to fill in a form IN01, which can be downloaded from www.companieshouse.gov.uk and on completion should be sent to one of the following addresses.

For companies situated in England and Wales the form should be sent to:

> The Registrar of Companies
> Companies House
> Crown Way
> Cardiff
> CF14 3UZ

For companies situated in Scotland the form should be sent to:

> The Registrar of Companies
> Companies House
> Fourth Floor
> Edinburgh Quay 2
> 139 Fountainbridge
> Edinburgh
> EH3 9FF

For companies situated in Northern Ireland the form should be sent to:

> The Registrar of Companies
> Companies House
> Second Floor
> The Linenhall
> 32–38 Linenhall Street
> Belfast
> BT2 8BG

The information you will need to complete the form is:
- the name of the company
- the type of company
- the **registered office** address
- the type of Articles of Association
- the name and address of the company secretary
- the names and addresses of the directors
- the date of birth, nationality and occupation of each director
- a **statement of capital**
- the names and addresses of the shareholders
- payment details – there is a fee for this service payable to Companies House.

You will also need a **Memorandum of Association** (with or without share capital) and **Articles of Association**. Standard versions of these can be downloaded from www.companieshouse.gov.uk.

When you register with Companies House, HMRC is informed, and will send you an introductory pack that contains form CT41G. This will tell you which HMRC office will deal with your company, and the company's Unique Taxpayer Reference. When the company starts any business activity, you must complete the form and send it to the HMRC office you've been assigned.

The information you will need to complete the form is:
- the date the first **accounting period** began
- the company name
- a shortened version of your company name if it is over 56 characters, otherwise HMRC will shorten it
- the company's registration number
- the company's registered office address
- the company's principal place of business
- the nature of the business
- the date to which accounts are to be prepared

JARGON BUSTER

The **registered office** is the address that Companies House will use to send letters and documents to. It needn't be the address you are actually trading from; it could be your accountant's address, for example.

JARGON BUSTER

A **statement of capital** is an explanation of the type of shares issued, the rights that come with the differing types, and the currency and denomination of the shares.

JARGON BUSTER

A **Memorandum of Association** is a statement that people wish to form a company, have agreed to become members and take at least one share each.

JARGON BUSTER

Articles of Association set out the rules for the running of a company's internal affairs.

JARGON BUSTER

The **accounting period** is the period of time for which the company's books are balanced and financial statements prepared.

- if the company has taken over another business, the details of this
- if operating **PAYE**, the start date
- the parent company, if any
- the name and home address, National Insurance number and Unique Taxpayer Reference of each director
- details of any agent dealing with Corporation Tax
- details of PAYE tax office
- whether the company is a charity.

CASE STUDY 1

Ravi Duplaga is a qualified pharmacist working for a major high street chain of pharmacies. As a result of an inheritance, he is now able to realise his ambition and purchase the freehold of a local shop which has become vacant. He is going to open an independent pharmacy, and needs to decide whether to operate as a sole trader, a partnership or a limited company.

He considers operating as a sole trader, as this would give him control of the business, but decides that the financial risk is too great as his family home and assets would have to be used as security for any loans.

He considers operating as a partnership, as this would share the financial responsibility, but decides that the loss of control combined with the fact that his home is still at risk rule out this option.

He decides that the best option is a private limited company, as he can retain control of the business as he will be the only director, while the company will be a separate legal entity, meaning any debts incurred by the company will be the responsibility of the company, not of Ravi personally.

APPOINTING AN ACCOUNTANT, TAX AGENT OR ADVISOR

Whether you are setting up as a sole trader, partnership or a limited company, you may want to appoint an accountant, tax agent or advisor to deal with HMRC on your behalf. A good accountant who has experience of retail business can advise on the best type of business to set up and act as a business advisor. They can be crucial in the development of a new business by advising on how to save costs, when to register for VAT, how to recognise indicators of poor performance etc. The cost of an accountant should be considered.

If you appoint an accountant, tax agent or advisor you will need to complete form 64-8, which authorises HMRC to communicate with your agent; this can be downloaded from http://www.hmrc.gov.uk. The form covers authorisation for individual tax affairs (partnerships, trusts, tax credits and individuals under PAYE) and business taxes (VAT, PAYE for employers and Corporation Tax). On completion, the form should be sent to:

> HMRC
> Central Agent Authorisation Team
> Longbenton
> Newcastle-upon-Tyne
> NE98 1ZZ

The information you will need to complete the form is:
- your name
- the business name
- the agent's business name
- the business address
- the agent's business address
- your National Insurance number
- your Unique Taxpayer Reference
- the company's registration number
- the company's Unique Taxpayer Reference
- the VAT registration number.

REGISTERING FOR VAT

You may have to register for VAT if your sales are expected to be over the VAT threshold (currently a turnover of £73,000, but check the HMRC website for updates: www.hmrc.gov.uk). You may choose to register voluntarily if your sales are below the threshold in order to be able to reclaim the VAT paid on purchases and expenses. Who you sell goods to and where you buy goods from will be part of the decision-making process you will have to make to decide this. For example, registering voluntarily for VAT may not be an advantage if your business is mostly service-based and the amount of goods you are buying in is small. Also, other countries may have higher VAT costs than the UK and if you buy goods regularly from these countries you will have to do your sums to decide whether voluntary declaration is wise. For example, VAT charged on goods from Denmark is currently 25 per cent. An accountant will be able to project figures based on your future business plans and be able to advise you. If you need to register for VAT, you should use form VAT 1 to apply for registration. You can complete this form online through HMRC Online Services (online.hmrc.gov.uk), or you can download the form, print it out and send it back by post.

If you send your registration form by post, send it to:

> HM Revenue & Customs
> Deansgate
> 62–70 Tettenhall Road
> Wolverhampton
> WV1 4TZ

If you are registering a partnership for VAT, you will also have to complete form VAT 2 to tell HMRC who the partners are, and send this with form VAT 1.

Claiming VAT for a new business can be quite complicated and an accountant could help guide you through these processes if you decide to register for VAT.

OVER TO YOU

Make a list of all the forms that you need for your business or the business you are planning to start. List where you will get them from and when you will need them. Make a list of the people who could help you in these processes, for example an accountant, a friend who may be in business and have experience.

VAT returns

Once the business is trading, there will be forms that you need to complete to meet the requirements of HMRC. If you have registered for VAT you will need to complete a VAT return every three months. This will be sent to you automatically in time for you to complete it and return it by the due date, which is one month after the end of the VAT quarter.

VAT returns must be completed online. For information on signing up and to register to complete them online, go to www.hmrc.gov.uk. Select 'VAT'. Click on 'Register for VAT' and on the page that appears, click on 'Register' under 'New user'. On the next page that appears, click on 'Sign up for HMRC online services'. If you're a sole trader click on 'Individual' on the following page; if you're a partnership or a limited company click on 'Organisation'. You will then be asked to select the services you wish to use. Click on 'VAT (submit return or change details)'. To register you will need the following information:

- your VAT registration number
- your business postcode
- the date of registration for VAT
- the final month of your last VAT return
- the amount of VAT paid or reclaimed on your last VAT return.

You'll need to have the following information for the three months covered by the VAT return:

- the amount of VAT included in your sales
- the amount of VAT paid on business purchases
- the amount of your sales not including VAT
- the amount of your business purchases not including VAT.

If you make business purchases from other countries in the European Union, VAT may have to be accounted for on the VAT return. It is probably best to employ the services of an accountant to complete VAT returns in this case.

Notification of any changes in your business circumstances, including change of address, must be sent to:

HM Revenue and Customs
Imperial House
77 Victoria Street
Grimsby
Lincolnshire
DN31 1DB

You can also notify HMRC of changes online at www.hmrc.gov.uk. Select 'VAT', then 'Changing or cancelling your VAT registration'.

OVER TO YOU

Think about whether you should register voluntarily for VAT if you are trading below the threshold. Look at the benefits and drawbacks of registering and speak to the VAT National Advice Service on 0845 010 9000. Think about whether there might be a 'perception benefit' – customers and potential customers may perceive you as being bigger or more successful if you are registered for VAT. However, whether this is seen as a benefit or not will depend if they are VAT payers themselves.

TAX RETURNS

Sole traders and partners will receive a tax return covering the tax year which runs from 6 April to 5 April. Partnerships will also receive a partnership tax return. These can be completed on paper and returned to the address given on the form by 31 October, or completed online at www.hmrc.gov.uk by 31 January the following year. Enclosed with the paper return sent to you by HMRC is a guide to completing it. If you need help completing the returns, there is a phone number on the return, or alternatively you can call the Self Assessment Helpline: 0845 9000 444.

If you don't send the return by these dates there are penalties. In the tax year 2012–13 these start at £100, and if the return is more than three months late, there's a penalty of £10 per day up to a maximum of £900. If the return is more than six months late, there's a further penalty of 5 per cent of the tax due or £300 – whichever is higher. If the return is more than 12 months late, there's yet another penalty of 5 per cent of the tax due or £300 – again, whichever is higher.

Limited companies must complete annual company tax returns online. Follow the same procedure as for completing VAT returns (see page 242), but click on 'Corporation Tax (CT)' instead of 'VAT (submit return or change details)'. You will need the following information to register:
- Corporation Tax reference
- Companies House registration number
- registered office postcode.

If you file your company tax return late, you will be charged a flat-rate penalty, which in 2012–13 is £100, and if the return is more than three months late, a further penalty of £100 applies. If your company tax return is late for three or more accounting periods in a row, the initial flat-rate penalty increases to £500 with a further £500 if you file your return more than three months late. If you don't file your company tax return by the later of 12 months from the end of your Corporation Tax accounting period or your filing deadline, HMRC may charge you further penalties on top of the flat-rate penalty, calculated as follows:
- where a return is filed 18 – 24 months after the end of your company's accounting period – 10 per cent of any unpaid Corporation Tax
- where a return is still not filed 24 months after the end of your accounting period – a further 10 per cent of any unpaid Corporation Tax.

You may find completing tax returns a complicated and time-consuming process, but failure to complete them properly can lead to severe problems. For this reason you may want to think about using an accountant, certainly in your first years of trading.

KEY TO SUCCESS

Knowing what forms have to be completed and where to get them, and getting them filled in and returned on time will save you an awful lot of hassle and a lot of money. Weigh up whether you have time or want to do this yourself or engage the services of an accountant for an agreed fee.

OVER TO YOU

Talk to any friends or family members who have businesses and ask them if they use an accountant or agent to help with their tax affairs. Find out what costs would be involved. Make a list of the advantages and disadvantages. Make a decision on which direction to take.

The tax forms shown are examples to give you an idea of what the forms look like. Make sure you always use the latest, up to date version. These forms can be obtained using the information given in the text.

Now you have started filling in forms, you are a businessperson, operating a business. You'll find that from this moment on, you'll start to amass information and documentation that you need to complete and to store in such a way that you can find it again when you need it.

FILING INFORMATION

Filing is one of the most critical skills in operating a business, but is often seen as a task to be delegated to the most junior member of staff. Delegation of this responsibility must follow the steps you learnt about in Chapter 6 or it can lead to major problems, with important documentation being 'lost' – and therefore unavailable when it is most needed – because it has been misfiled.

BASIC FILING PRINCIPLES

Setting up an efficient filing system, whether you're filing paper documents or storing electronic files, will save time and make your business much more efficient. Deciding on the filing method to use will depend on the type of information to be stored. Paper files can be stored in a number of different ways:

- Alphabetically – Files of customers' names, suppliers' names, staff files and so on are stored in alphabetical order. Usually, people's names are filed by their family name, company names ignore 'The', and files starting with the same letter are filed in order of the second letter (Ma, Me, Mi...).
- Numerically – Orders, invoices, account numbers and suchlike are stored in ascending order. Avoid giving customers or suppliers account numbers and filing them numerically if this requires you to look up their account number in an alphabetical list in order to find them.
- Alphanumerically – Some files will have names containing both letters and numbers – vehicle registration numbers, National Insurance numbers or purchase order numbers for example. These are normally filed alphabetically and then numerically where the letters are the same.

KEY TO SUCCESS

Setting up an efficient filing system and making sure everybody knows how to use it is a very good place to start, but keeping the filing up to date is the real key. Hunting through the filing tray for important documents that have not yet been filed is a very frustrating activity.

- Chronologically – Some information will need to be kept in date order. This may be monthly, quarterly, annually or even daily. It is usually best to keep the most recent information at the front, although outstanding invoices may be best filed with the oldest at the front. Information within individual files that are stored alphabetically or numerically is normally filed with the most recent at the front.
- Geographically – In some circumstances information may be filed geographically. For example, sales information may be kept by region or travel and accommodation information may be ordered by county.

ELECTRONIC FILING SYSTEMS

If you set up your filing electronically, remember that there will still be paper documents that have to be stored. Customers may send orders, and suppliers will send delivery notes and invoices. Electronic files will not require filing cabinets but will need be stored on hard drives, CD-ROMs, DVDs or memory sticks. The computer will sort the files alphabetically, numerically, alphanumerically, chronologically or by type, according to the instructions you give it. The important thing is to have a consistent method of naming files, as the computer will use the file name when sorting.

Don't start file names with 'draft' or 'letter to' or you will never find them again. Make sure that file names:
- are short and to the point
- contain at least two digits, if using numbers; remember that 07 will appear before 54, while 7 would appear after it
- that contain dates include the date styled in the order YYYYMMDD, not DDMMYYYY, to maintain chronological order. For example, 13101951 will appear before 18091948; 19480918 will appear before 19511013
- use the family name first, as with paper files.

Files can be grouped into folders and directories so that all the information on a particular subject can be kept together; files within folders and directories will be sorted in the same way as above.

If you give a file a name that already exists, the computer will ask you if you want to overwrite the existing file. This will prompt you to give the new file a different name. If you don't, the original file will be lost forever, which could be a disaster if the information is vital. It's good practice to back up electronic files onto a flash drive/'memory stick' or external hard drive so that you have a second copy in case of corruption or loss of the original files. One method commonly used is the grandfather–father–son system. Files are backed up daily onto disk and once a week a full back-up to another disk is performed. The disk containing the last weekly back-up in the month is permanently stored in a secure location, while the daily and weekly disks can be reused. The secure location should be off-site or in a fireproof container.

STORING FILES

One of the decisions you will need to make is how much space you need to keep all the files. How many filing cabinets will paper files fill? How much memory will electronic files fill – do you need external hard drives, flash drives or CD-ROMs? Make a policy decision on how long to keep files. Some files have to be kept for a set time for legal reasons. Examples of these are shown in the table below.

Accounting records	3 years for private companies, 6 years for Public Limited Companies
Income tax and NI returns	3 years from the end of the financial year
Wage/salary records	6 years
Statutory sick pay and statutory maternity pay records	3 years from the end of the tax year
National minimum wage records	3 years
Records relating to working time	2 years
Retirement benefits schemes records	6 years from the end of the scheme year
Accident book, accident records and reports	3 years after the last entry

How long to keep files

Files that do not have a set time should be kept long enough to be available should they be required for purposes such as industrial tribunals. For information on this, go to the website of the Chartered Institute of Personnel and Development, www.cipd.co.uk.

Files may well contain confidential information or information that you don't want competitors or members of staff to see. In this case, use lockable filing cabinets and password-protect your computer or individual files. Shred paper files before sending them for recycling and make sure all information is removed from any computer or storage device before disposing of it.

OVER TO YOU

Make a policy on how long information such as recruitment, personnel, training and pension records will be kept, then set up a system for archiving, and eventually destroying, information.

BUSINESS COMMUNICATION

As a business you will need to communicate regularly with customers, suppliers, professionals such as solicitors and accountants, and government departments such as the Tax Office. You may also need to prepare reports, either for customers or for internal use, or for quotations and estimates.

BUSINESS LETTERS AND EMAILS

Writing a business letter is different from writing a personal letter. The person you're writing to is likely to be busy and may well skim through the letter, looking for the important information – the point you are making and what response is required. You need to find a third way between the formal language required for writing a contract and the kind of informal language often used in emails: too formal and you may put off the reader; too informal and you may look unprofessional. Often such a letter will be the first impression your customer or supplier gets of your business, so your first one should be professional. Use letter-headed paper and remember to **proofread** the letter before sending it, as errors will create a poor impression; you may wish to get someone else to proofread it too, as it's easy to miss things in your own writing. As your correspondence progresses, letters may get steadily more informal.

Business letters should have correct spelling and grammar; they should be clear so that they cannot be misunderstood, concise without being blunt or abrupt, and coherent so there is a logical flow. There is an accepted format for writing business letters: they should be fully blocked with open punctuation, which means that all parts start at the left-hand margin and punctuation is used only where it is necessary for grammatical accuracy and ease of understanding.

Business letters should be written on paper headed with the business name, address and contact details. The format of business letters is as follows:
- date
- name and address of the recipient
- 'Dear Sir or Madam' or 'Dear Mr/Mrs/Miss/Ms...'
- opening remarks
- main message
- actions or results
- closing remarks
- 'Yours faithfully' or 'Yours sincerely'.

? JARGON BUSTER

To **proofread** means to check text carefully for correct spelling, punctuation, layout and grammar.

The following is an example of a poorly written business letter in response to the cancellation of an order:

Hoopers Plumbing and Electrical Ltd

45 Albion Street, Westwick, Sussex WW2 3WW
01234 567234 | hoopers@theend.com

26 May 2011

Wilson and May
The Street
Westwick
Sussex
WW5 7WW

Dear Sirs

We note you cancelled your order. This was particularly disappointing as we had had to order the parts from Sweden and we will not be able to return these for refund so we will have to hold onto them in the hope that someone else orders them in the future.

If you decide to place an order in the future with us we would appreciate it if you would only do so if you intend not to cancel it at such a late stage.

Yours faithfully

B Hooper
Managing Director

An example of a poorly written business letter

A better way of responding to the situation would be:

Hoopers Plumbing and Electrical Ltd

45 Albion Street, Westwick, Sussex WW2 3WW
01234 567234 | hoopers@theend.com

26 May 2011

Wilson and May
The Street
Westwick
Sussex
WW5 7WW

Dear Sirs

I am writing to acknowledge receipt of your letter of 23 May 2011 in which you explain your reasons for cancelling your purchase (order number PO000567).

I am sorry that on this occasion we were unable to meet your requirements within the specified timescale and have passed on your comments to our suppliers in order to ensure that a similar problem does not happen again.

I trust that you will bear us in mind when you have further requirements that we may be able to supply. If we can be of any assistance in the future please do not hesitate to contact us.

Yours faithfully

B Hooper
Managing Director

An example of a better business letter

A word about email

A communication of this type would not be an appropriate use of email. Email has lots of uses in business, and can often use a much more informal tone than letters. It's particularly effective for internal communication with colleagues, especially when more information is needed than can be given over the phone or where documents need to be attached, either for reference or for editing. Purchase orders and invoices can be sent by email to save time and cost, as can newsletters and advertising. The tone of an email needs to be carefully considered; while generally less formal than a letter, you still need to consider the recipient and pitch the email at the correct level. Emails are also generally shorter than letters, as much of the standard format (address, date and so on) can be left out.

**OVER
TO YOU**

Take a look at www.4hb.com, www.writing-business-letters.com or www.samples-help.org.uk for sample business letters. If you have already written similar letters, compare them with the samples; if you haven't written this sort of letter, have a go at writing some now.

QUOTATIONS AND ESTIMATES

You will have to give customers prices for your products and services. Many businesses, such as hairdressers and retailers, use a price list that remains the same for every customer. Other businesses, such as mechanics, plumbers, and painters and decorators, have to provide prices for the specific products or services required. This is usually done with an estimate or a quotation.

A quotation is a fixed-price offer that can't be changed once accepted by the customer, even if you have to carry out much more work than you expected. Specify in the quotation exactly what is covered and that any change to this will be subject to additional charges. If this is likely to be the case, it makes more sense to give an estimate. An estimate is an educated guess at what a job may cost, but it isn't binding. It will prevent your customer from being surprised by the costs involved in a job but allows some leeway.

To work out a quotation or estimate, you need to know your fixed and variable costs (see Chapter 1). These include the cost per hour of manual labour and the cost of the materials. Your quotation or estimate is then calculated according to what you think the job will involve.

You should provide all your quotations and estimates in writing and include a detailed breakdown. This will help to avoid any disputes about what work is included in your overall price. You should state clearly whether it is a quotation or an estimate. You may wish to set an expiry date, after which time your quotation or estimate is no longer valid.

Preparing a written quotation or estimate

Both written quotations and estimates must show your full business contact details and should include:

- a breakdown of what is included and what is not
- a schedule when the work will be done or products delivered
- terms and conditions
- the period the quotation is valid for
- the overall price
- payment terms
- whether VAT is included or not.

Quotations commit you to the price you specify, so use them only when:

- the job has clear requirements in terms of time, labour and materials
- the cost to you of labour and materials is unlikely to change
- you are sure the job won't turn out more complicated than you thought.

Get written confirmation from your customer that they accept the price and the work included before you carry out the work or provide goods or services. You could simply add a line at the bottom of the quotation for the customer to sign. If the job changes after you start, agree a revised quotation with the customer before you finish the job. When giving an estimate remember to include a disclaimer stating that the price is subject to change, and agree in advance how you will charge for any changes in requirements or unforeseen complications in the work.

When you start to work or supply goods or services, keep comprehensive records of any additional costs so that you can present these to the customer when providing your final invoice.

If you need to forward quotations or estimates to prospective customers by email, send them as attachments (not in the body of the email) and create them as **PDF files** so they can't be altered. PDF files can be created using free software downloads from Adobe (www. adobe.com).

KEY TO SUCCESS

Being clear about the differences between quotations and estimates will avoid a situation where a customer insists on paying the estimated price, believing it to be a quotation. Well-written quotations and estimates will encourage customers to give you their business.

JARGON BUSTER

PDF files can be opened by anyone on a computer using a program called Adobe Reader, but they cannot be edited, so the details can't be changed.

REPORTS

Informal reports can be presented in the form of a letter, but formal reports such as business plans and those produced by surveyors and engineers for their clients should follow a set structure. Produce a draft report first and check that it contains all of the required information and that the conclusions and recommendations are supported by that information. The final report should include:

- the title of the report
- the executive summary, which gives a brief overview of the report for people who don't need to understand the detail
- an introduction, which gives the background
- the **methodology**, where you explain how you collected the information
- the main body of the report, which contains your findings and the information you have gathered
- the conclusion, which analyses the findings and states what you think they mean
- the recommendations, which state the actions you feel should be taken as a result of the conclusion
- acknowledgements of any outside sources that have contributed to the report
- a **bibliography** of source material stating the author and the date published for each
- **appendices**, which provide detailed or statistical information that would confuse the reader if the full detail were given in the main body.

CHOOSING AND USING ICT

The function of ICT is for capturing, processing, storing and distributing information or data. You need to make sure that the ICT system you choose supports your business and adds value to it. You must have a clear understanding of your business to ensure that you will get the most out of any ICT investment.

Your objectives may be to:

- improve customer service
- communicate with customers and suppliers more effectively
- cut your costs
- increase staff productivity
- respond to change more quickly
- improve the way you manage, share and use knowledge in your business.

You also need to consider what you do and how you do it. Take into account:

- the structure of the organisation
- individual responsibilities
- markets
- products
- key customers
- key suppliers.

Also look at ways in which the business is likely to change due to:
- legislation and regulation
- technology
- customers
- suppliers.

It is important to understand how these changes will impact on the business and how ICT will help you adapt to these changes.

 CASE STUDY 2

James Daniels runs an electrical store. He has been in business as a sole trader for 15 years and has always spent Sunday afternoons doing his paperwork, sending out invoices, estimates and quotes, and preparing to bank the cheques that he has received during the week. Once a quarter, he has filled in his VAT return and sent it off with a cheque, and once a year, he has filled in his Self Assessment tax return.

James reads in the notes that come with his VAT return that all VAT-registered businesses will have to submit their VAT returns online and pay electronically by April 2012. He decides that this will be a good opportunity to bring in accounting software so that he can do his books electronically and produce his VAT returns and tax returns automatically.

James contacts a friend who is an ICT specialist and asks her advice on the best software package to buy in his circumstances. She suggests an off-the-shelf package and helps him learn how to use it. At first, James finds it takes him longer to do his paperwork using the new system but, after a while, he gets used to it and finds that he can now save himself a couple of hours on a Sunday.

To make the most of your investment in ICT:
- Focus on the business benefits, not the technology. If you want to make your business more productive, all you need to know is whether ICT will achieve this; you don't need to know the technical specifications.

- Only approve projects that support your business objectives.
- Make sure your planned improvements are measurable.
- Budget for future spending on maintenance, replacement and upgrades so that you will have the money you need to improve your system or take advantage of new technology.
- Review performance regularly to make sure you are getting the benefits that you planned.
- Give ongoing support to staff in using the ICT systems so that problems are quickly resolved and any related performance issues are dealt with.

ICT SYSTEMS

Your ICT system will consist of hardware and software. Hardware includes PCs, servers, network equipment, scanners and printers, and will be more effective if you have the correct software. Decide whether you want:

- an off-the-shelf package that is **compatible** with any existing software or systems used by suppliers and customers
- a more complex package, in which case you need to prioritise your requirements into 'must haves', 'advantageous' and 'nice to haves'
- a **bespoke** system, in which case you may require professional advice.

? JARGON BUSTER

Compatible means 'will work alongside'.

? JARGON BUSTER

Bespoke means something that is made to the buyer's specification.

↳ OVER TO YOU

Think about the ICT system you already have. Is it delivering the benefits you expected? If you don't have an ICT system yet, what would you like, what would it cost and would it deliver increased profits? Talk to the people who actually use similar systems and get their opinions on how they could be improved.

To produce a set of requirements, look at what you need the system to do, not how it will do it. These are known as functional requirements. Next, look at the things that are important but not related directly to the business function, such as how quickly the application works. These are non-functional requirements. Talk to the staff who will be using the package – they will have the best idea of which functions are 'must haves' and which are 'nice to have'.

To find the best packages and suppliers, do research on the internet and in the trade press and magazines. Put together a specification of your requirements and send it to a number of different suppliers asking for quotations. A typical specification for an accounting software package might look like the following.

Must haves	Nice to haves
Ability to produce invoices and statements	Ability to produce letters following up overdue invoices
Ability to update sales ledger, purchase ledger and nominal ledger	Ability to produce management information
Ability to calculate current bank balance	Ability to reconcile bank balance
Ability to control company credit card account	Ability to print cheques automatically
Ability to control petty cash account	Ability to carry out BACS transfers

Specifications for accounting software

Don't worry about any technical terms in the example that you don't understand – bookkeeping and finance are covered in Chapter 8.

OVER TO YOU

Write down your top three 'must haves' for an ICT system. Get your team to do the same and compare lists – it may surprise you! Which of these must haves do you think would have the biggest effect on the way your business works?

When you have the information on the prices and packages available, reject any package that does not meet all your must-have criteria and select the package that has the most advantageous and nice-to-have criteria at an affordable price. Remember to include the cost of upgrades, warranties and future technical support in the overall costs.

THE BENEFITS OF USING ICT

Even the simplest technology can improve productivity and efficiency. For instance:

- accounting software can make your bookkeeping faster and more accurate
- word processing software speeds up the production and improves the quality of documents
- email improves and speeds up communication
- database software allows you to keep and manipulate information
- spreadsheet software speeds up calculations and improves their accuracy
- **intranet** software makes company information available to all staff instantly
- **extranet** software makes company information available to selected customers and suppliers instantly
- systems integration software links your systems to suppliers and customers to speed up the supply chain.

? JARGON BUSTER

An **intranet** is a company's internal website.

? JARGON BUSTER

An **extranet** is when the intranet is shared with selected external businesses.

The key to making the best use of your ICT budget is choosing the software most appropriate to your business and its present development.

Technology can bring tremendous benefits to your business. Improving communication with customers and suppliers could save time, money and energy. Involving customers in designing and choosing the products and services you supply will give you the opportunity to make sure that you are meeting their needs.

For example, simply improving your phone system can improve efficiency. Customers can contact the correct member of staff directly if they have their own direct line phone numbers and voicemail accounts. Upgrading your internet connection to a faster speed makes electronic communication with customers and suppliers faster and more reliable. Giving team members who work away from the office business mobile phones and access to your ICT system will make them more efficient.

Another example of technology which benefits the retail industry in particular is the PDQ machine. This is a device used to process credit and debit card transactions. The customer places their card in the machine and follows prompts which appear on the screen requesting them to enter their personal identification number (PIN) for the card. The transaction then takes place automatically, transferring the money into your bank account. Technology is moving so fast that trials are taking place on systems using mobile telephones as payment devices without the need for a plastic card.

Using standard documents such as purchase orders and invoices that can be sent and received electronically will also save time and money. Customer service can be improved by using information more effectively, for instance, the tracking of an order or a complaint so that the customer does not have to supply the same information repeatedly. Mobile computing solutions can improve efficiency, for example, by connecting the sales staff to your network through laptops and mobile phones so that orders can be placed directly, or enabling reports to be generated by staff while they are out of the office.

Marketing by email and on the internet allows you to target potential customers more easily and is faster and cheaper than direct mail. **Search engines** and **social media** also offer cost-effective ways of reaching customers.

? JARGON BUSTER

Search engines are designed to search for information on the World Wide Web. The best known is Google.

? JARGON BUSTER

Social media are internet-based tools for sharing and discussing information. The best known are Twitter, YouTube and Facebook.

Monitoring changes in the market by using online questionnaires to gather feedback from your customers, researching the internet to find new products, finding out what your competitors are doing and looking at market research available online will all help you to exploit new opportunities.

📄 **CASE STUDY 3**

Partiger's Health Foods is owned and run by Liz Partiger. Traditionally, the company has used a simple cash register to accept payments and the ordering system consists of a weekly walk around the shop and the stock room, making a note of products that are low on stock and then telephoning suppliers with orders.

Liz is approached by a representative of a company that provides Electronic Point of Sale (EPOS) systems, who tells her that she can lease or buy equipment which will increase the company's margins by 3 per cent. The representative leaves Liz with some information for her to consider.

Liz goes through the information to decide whether this system would be suitable for her business. She sees the benefits as follows:

- it will eliminate the need to physically check stock weekly, as the system will provide instant information on the stock levels of every individual product
- it will reduce the number of occasions when products become out of stock, losing sales, as the system will automatically flag up when minimum stock levels are reached
- if linked to suppliers' systems, orders can be automatically generated.

Additionally, the system can be programmed to automatically calculate discounts, operate promotions and recognise offers such as 'buy one get one free' (BOGOF) or 'buy one get one half price'. It can also print shelf-edge labels and barcode labels, and provide management information for use in completing VAT returns and analysing sales.

HOME WORKING

One of the benefits of a good ICT system that can be accessed remotely is that it can give you the flexibility to allow home working. Establishing a virtual workforce where people work from home can save costs in providing premises and allow staff to make better use of their time, as they do not need to travel to and from the office. A virtual workplace is not located in any one place. Workplaces are connected by the internet, allowing employees to work together regardless of where they are, which decreases unnecessary costs. The benefits include:

- individuals can work anywhere at any time
- convenience to the employee and the customers
- decreased costs and increased efficiency
- reduction in business travel, saving time and money
- projects can be completed more quickly and efficiently
- training can be delivered to all employees at the same time
- employees' work/life balance can improve.

The challenges include:

- the need to ensure that all employees have access to the company server and databases remotely
- the need to ensure that databases are up to date at all times
- lack of human contact could reduce team spirit, trust and productivity.

Many of these challenges can be overcome by effective team leadership.

One issue that arises in home working is the question of who is responsible for providing the equipment used in the home. The usual situation is that employees have the equipment provided at the employer's expense, while self-employed people providing consultancy, for instance, pay for their own equipment.

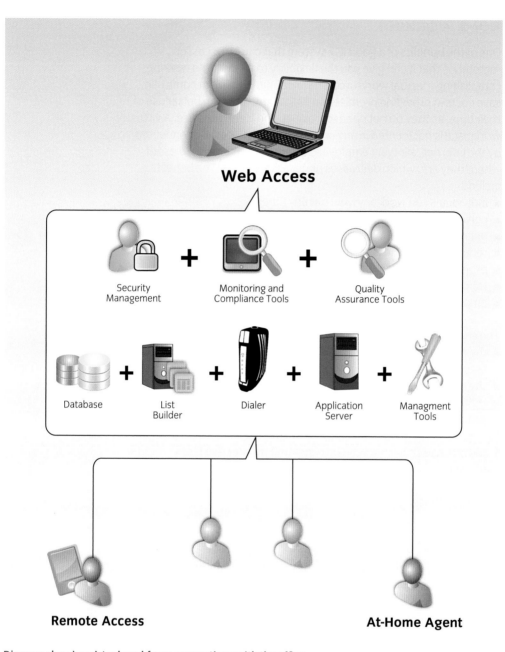

Web Access

Security Management + Monitoring and Compliance Tools + Quality Assurance Tools

Database + List Builder + Dialer + Application Server + Managment Tools

Remote Access

At-Home Agent

Diagram showing virtual workforce connections with the office

E-COMMERCE

Perhaps the greatest benefit of ICT comes from the possibility of e-commerce. This allows you to sell your goods and services online and receive payment electronically direct to your bank account. It is important to plan the development of your e-commerce system. Get the best available design for your website right from the start. Customers will want the website to be user-friendly, so the overall look and feel of the site is important. There are also regulations to consider when trading over the internet. The E-commerce Regulations 2002 are intended to ensure that electronic contracts are binding and enforceable, and under the Equality Act websites must be accessible for disabled people. If you store details about customers and suppliers on your system you must comply with the Data Protection Act. This is looked at in more detail in Chapter 9.

To sell directly through a website, it will need to give information on the products and services available, and be able to process orders and accept payment electronically. There are three different methods for accepting payment electronically. You should choose the one that best suits your type of business:

■ Internet merchant account (IMA) – This is most suitable if you already take debit and credit card payments and expect a fairly high number of online sales, most of which are simple and low-risk. Payment will come direct from your customer to your bank account, arriving after 3–4 working days. You can apply directly for an IMA from a high street bank or other financial institution that processes debit and credit cards.

■ Payment-processing company – This is most suitable if you do not already take debit and credit card payments and expect a small number of online transactions. Payment will go from your customer to the payment-processing company, which will forward it to your bank account, but this may take up to 60 working days. These are generally more expensive than IMAs but applications to open accounts are much simpler and can be processed much more quickly. Details of payment-processing companies can be found on the Electronic Payments website, www.electronic-payments.co.uk.

■ Online shopping mall – This is most suitable if your business is small, you do not already take debit or credit card payments and you have very limited ICT skills. There are higher transaction fees and fixed costs than in the other methods but an online shopping mall allows you to establish a web presence with minimal difficulty. Payment will go from your customer to the mall, which will deduct its charges before passing the money on to you. There will probably be a joining fee, monthly or annual fees and a percentage charge made on each transaction.

Information on accepting online payments can be found by going to www.businesslink.gov.uk and selecting 'IT & e-commerce' and then following the links.

You will probably need to employ the services of a specialist website designer to set up your online shop and once your business is online you will need to drive traffic to the site. This can be done through **search engine optimisation (SEO)** and **pay-per-click (PPC) advertising**. The relative costs of this form of advertising need to be taken into account, as would any other form of advertising.

INVESTING IN ICT

Your investment in ICT is likely to be a significant part of your business costs, so it is important to measure the benefits achieved in financial terms. Identify the total cost of the system, including training and technical support, and consider how much the system will save you and how much profit the new business opportunities will bring. Use measurable benchmarks such as an increased response to marketing, a reduction in staff costs or time saved in carrying out accounting functions. Set a date for a formal review of the system and assess whether the objectives you set when you implemented the system have been met and, if not, what needs to be done.

As the business grows, you will probably want to consider whether to employ an ICT expert, in which case you may have to recruit someone if there is no-one already on the staff with the necessary expertise. Alternatively, you could use a specialist ICT support company, especially if there is not going to be enough work for an employee.

You may want to investigate the advantages of improving or increasing the capacity of your ICT system. You may want to go through the same research process that you used when purchasing your original system, or you may feel that you have a good relationship with your ICT supplier and want to use them again. Either way, use specialist advice to help you decide the best way to achieve your new objectives. Don't assume that every new software package or new piece of hardware on the market will deliver benefits to your business. Do look at buying hardware that can be added to at a later date rather than needing to be replaced.

You also need to make sure that the content of your website is accurate and updated regularly, and that all of your systems are protected from **hackers**, **viruses** and fraudsters by using security software. Identify the threats that your system is exposed to and look for effective information security measures. Ask your ICT specialist to check that your security meets the British Standard BS ISO/IEC 27001.

Look on the internet for useful websites on the subject of choosing and using ICT systems. You might try www.ictknowledgebase. org.uk. Using the list you produced when you asked your staff for their top three must haves, price up a system that would satisfy everybody's wish list. Now price up a system that satisfies the minimum requirements. Compare the prices of the two systems.

WHERE TO GO FOR MORE INFORMATION

The following sources will be helpful in getting to grips with business administration:

- Sector Skills Councils/standard setting bodies:
  - Council for Administration, www.cfa.uk.com.
  - Skillsmart Retail, www.skillsmartretail.com.
- Government bodies:
  - HMRC, www.hmrc.gov.uk, for all information relating to tax matters.
  - Business Link, www.businesslink.gov.uk, for lots of useful information, from starting businesses, finding finance and grants, and running the business right through to selling the business. In particular, search for 'e-learning' and then select 'starting up' to find pages with useful information on starting a business, including the most appropriate structure for your business.
  - Companies House, www.companieshouse.gov.uk, for information on every company registered in the UK.
- The Chartered Institute of Personnel and Development, www.cipd. co.uk, for information on employment and training.
- Which?, www.which.co.uk, for information and reviews on all sorts of products you may need to buy, as well as consumer rights advice.
- Trade magazines
  - *Which?*
  - *Computer Shopper*
  - *Computeractive*
  - *PC Answers.*

KEY TO
SUCCESS

Remember you are investing in ICT to increase the profits your business makes, not as a vanity project, so choose the system that will give you the best return on your investment. Time spent researching and investing in an ICT system will pay dividends in smoother working and more time later on.

CONCLUSION

You should now understand the key forms needed to get a business up and running, where to get them and when to fill them in. Remember that, if administration is not your strong point, there are professionals who can help you with this part of your business. Don't ignore the taxman and hope he will go away – he won't. Keeping accurate records and storing them where you can put your hands on them will help you to deal with any enquiries you may get, and knowing how to communicate effectively will make dealing with customers, suppliers and officials less taxing.

Most businesses will rely on ICT to some extent, so knowing how to choose and use it will enable you to make the best use of technology that will take your business forward.

CHAPTER 8
BOOKKEEPING AND FINANCE

INTRODUCTION

This chapter continues the administration theme and looks at the importance of understanding financial information, sources of finance, accounting, purchasing and business viability. Owners/ managers of small businesses must understand the way their business works in financial terms; failure to grasp the basics will greatly reduce the chance of the business surviving the difficult early years. Even if you engage an accountant it is important to have an understanding of the importance of getting to grips with business finances and of how having some financial savvy can help your business grow.

According to Warwick Business School, only 19 per cent of businesses survive to their fifth birthday. This is not just because of poor finances – often small businesses are started by entrepreneurial types and after five years they are bored and move onto something else! Five years is also the most common term for which one might take a lease, and this has a relevance to bear on this figure too. However, it is a fact these days that businesses with poor financial strategies or a lack of cash flow are unlikely to last more than three years. The Society of Insolvency Practitioners discovered that 22 per cent of business failures in 2010 were caused by weak management. In a small business, the owner/manager is likely to have a hands-on role in dealing with the accounts. Understanding that businesses don't always fail because of a short-term lack of profitability, but because they run out of cash, is vital to understanding financial information.

UNDERSTANDING FINANCIAL INFORMATION

This section builds on the finance concepts that you learnt in Chapters 1 and 7. Drawing on your work on creating a business plan, it looks at the options for getting finance into your business in the first place. It also introduces the key measurements and budgeting tools that you'll need to understand to keep track of the financial health of your business.

SOURCES OF BUSINESS FINANCE

Whether you're starting up a new retail business or growing an existing one, the chances are that at some point you'll need money. This money is called business finance – and there are various ways of getting it, with different advantages and disadvantages. The most appropriate sources of business finance will depend on what the money is needed for:

- starting up a new business
- dealing with a shortage of cash
- buying capital equipment
- buying new premises
- buying or taking over another business
- paying off debts.

Certain sources of finance will be appropriate for some businesses but not for others. For example, the sources of finance for starting a mobile car valeting business will be different from building a car showroom complete with offices.

There are a number of things to consider when sourcing business finance. First, do you need the money for a short period of time (to pay a supplier's bill, to buy stock for a seasonal promotion or to pay for a marketing campaign, for instance) or a long period of time (perhaps to build premises, refit the shop or make alterations to the building)?

Short-term finance
This refers to money that you need for a short period of time – normally less than a year. It's usually used for the day-to-day running of your business.

Some examples of short-term finance include:
- Bank overdraft – This is where your bank allows you to spend an agreed amount of money over the amount that you actually have in your account, which they then charge you interest on, so you have money for an agreed short period of time. This can be arranged quickly but the interest rate can be quite high.

- Trade credit – This is where your suppliers give you longer to pay their bills and so help fund your business for a while by not asking for payment. This is a cost-free option but it may flag up to a supplier that you find paying bills difficult, and this may not be a good basis for long-term business.
- Leasing – If you need to buy equipment and don't have the money, you may be able to get it via a leasing company, which buys it and allows you to use it while you pay for it over an agreed period of time. You pay the company back at an agreed rate of interest, at agreed intervals. At the end of the leasing agreement, when all monies have been paid to the leasing company, the ownership of the equipment passes to you. The cost of leasing is spread over time, which is good, but it can be costly in terms of interest.
- Credit cards – A company credit card is a popular way of getting finance and, when paid off every month, or as quickly as possible, is a good way of managing money. The interest levels are high if your payment is over a longer period of time, so this is normally used only for small amounts of money for the short term. However, when banks and other finance methods are not available, entrepreneurs have been known to 'max out' their cards – borrowing as much as possible across all of them.
- Bank loans – These may be short- or long-term depending on what you have agreed with your bank manager. You'll have to pay interest, which can vary and be expensive.

Long-term finance
This refers to money that you need for much longer than a year – probably many years. It's usually used for major expansion plans of an existing business, or a start-up that requires a lot of investment.

Some examples of long-term finance include:
- Bank loans – See above.
- Private capital – for example family savings.
- Share capital – Shares are part ownership of a limited company or Private Limited Company. Shares are sold from limited companies only with the agreement of the shareholders, but anyone can buy shares in a Private Limited Company. Shares are sold to raise money but at the expense of losing some control of the business.
- Asset sales – This is selling something you have of value to fund the business. This could be a tangible item such as a piece of equipment or it could be an idea (intellectual property). The downside is that you could be selling the very thing that your business is based on.

- Venture capital – Venture capitalists are wealthy people in their own right who invest in businesses that they believe will give them a good return on their investment. They take a stake in the company in return for their investment of money and expertise. They expect to get that investment back in a percentage of the profit. For example, for a 20 per cent stake in the company they will want a set percentage of the profits. That percentage of profits may be 20 per cent too, but is likely to be more. The exact deal is a discussion point when negotiating with a venture capitalist. If the venture capitalist has a larger stake than you, you may lose control of the business – this risk has to be weighed up against the experience and orders such a person can bring to the business. You need to decide if it's better to keep a lesser percentage of a lot more money than having all the profits of next to nothing.
- Retained profit – This is not taking out the profits in terms of salary or drawings but keeping it in the business (retaining it) and using it for growth – commonly known as 'ploughing it back in'. For example, if at the end of the year and after paying all business expenses, salaries and suppliers you have £4500 clear profit left over, you have the option of taking it out or leaving it in the company (retaining it) where it will be highlighted in your profit and loss account.
- Owners' capital – This is where you put your own money into the business. You then have total control over the payback timescale and any interest you decide to pay yourself. You need to weigh up whether you might get a better return elsewhere, and essentially, if you can afford to lose the money if the business fails.
- Government, local authority or EU grants – There may be funding grants available from various sources but to get them you will have to meet stiff criteria and usually show how you will benefit the community in some way.
- Lottery funding – If you're involved in the arts or sports you may be able to get funding grants from the National Lottery; as with all grants, there are tough criteria to meet.

As the lists above demonstrate, there are pros and cons to most sources of business finance. You and your financial advisors will need to investigate all the sources on offer and their cost implications. Remember: 'If it sounds too good to be true, it normally is'; read the small print and take advice.

Don Avery is going to open a butcher's shop in a row of local shops. He has a certain amount of capital which he has saved over the years, but knows he will need more finance to start the business and as working capital. Having investigated sources of finance, he has identified four which he thinks are the most applicable to his situation.

The sources he has identified are:
- A bank loan
- A bank overdraft
- Leasing the equipment he needs
- Government/local council/EU grants.

Don decides that he should research these sources in the following order: first he will look for any available grants, as this may provide low-cost finance. He will then look at leasing equipment, so that he will have information on the costs involved which he can compare with the costs of buying the equipment with a bank loan. When he approaches his bank he will be able to discuss the costs and loans and overdrafts from a position of knowing the costs of alternative finance.

Don searches on the internet for business grants and finds the Business Link website www.businesslink.gov.uk. He looks at the 'Finance and grants' section of the site, goes to 'Finance options and selects 'Grants and government support' where he can search for available support. He inputs 'butchery equipment' and finds a range of suppliers who can supply the equipment he needs on lease or to buy outright. He contacts a number of suppliers and gets the full details.

Armed with this information and his business plan, he makes an appointment with his business manager at the bank and discusses with her the best way to finance the opening of the business. He is seeking a bank loan to finance the start-up investment required and an overdraft facility so that he has access to further capital on demand in case of cash flow issues.

KEY MEASURES OF FINANCIAL HEALTH

There are three essential measurement reports that allow you to see how well, or otherwise, your business is doing. A thorough understanding of your cashflow, balance sheet and profit and loss is vital – this section gives you an overview of what these are and what information they tell you. Later in this chapter, you'll see when each is produced in the accounting process, and how they are used in context.

Cashflow

Cashflow is, as the name suggests, the flow of money that comes into your business in terms of sales (often called turnover) and the money that goes out of it in terms of costs –salaries, equipment, stock and so on.

If the money flowing out of the business goes out more quickly, or is more, than the money flowing in, then the business can face a situation where there isn't enough money to pay bills. When people talk of a cashflow problem, this is exactly what they mean.

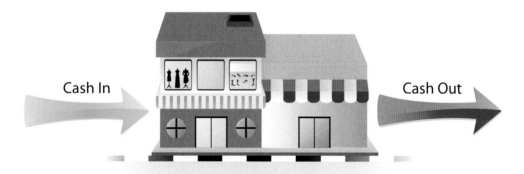

Cash In

Cash Out

This simple diagram explains the concept of cashflow

Examples of situations that can cause cashflow problems include:
- The need to buy large volumes of stock prior to a seasonal event such as Christmas for which the income will not be made until during the event.
- The need to pay a large quarterly rent bill, which may follow a slow trading period or coincide with the need to buy stock.
- The need to pay staff sickness or holiday pay while also having to pay temporary staff or overtime to existing staff to cover.

Balance sheet

The balance sheet is like a snapshot that shows you where the money is in your business. The term comes from itemising where the money that's in your business came from and where it is now – these two aspects should balance each other just like a set of scales. For example, if you spend £10 on an item then you have £10 going out of the business – which shows on the left scale. Then you might have the item valued at £10 on the other scale, so there is a balance.

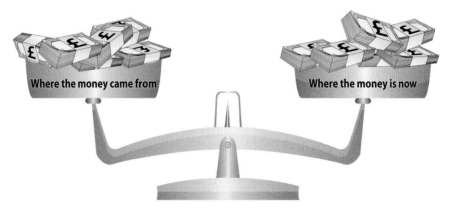

The balance sheet shows where money came from and where it is now – and these aspects should balance like a set of scales

For things to balance, if money goes out of the business on the left, there must be a corresponding amount or item to that same value on the right.

Profit and loss

The last of the three measurement reports is the profit and loss statement or, as it's more often shortened to, the P&L. The P&L is a summary of your business transactions for a set period of time, normally 12 months, and shows how it is performing – are you making profits or making a loss?

Sales	**180,000**
Cost of sales	
Stock	48,759
Delivery	2,000
	50,759
Gross profit	**129,241**
Variable costs	
Packaging	582
Training	2,500
Sales promotions	750
Advertising	1,200
Website servicing	110
Finance charges	200
	5,342
Fixed costs	
Wages and salaries	51,376
Rent and rates	18,000
Vehicles	7,400
Administration	4,000
Website hosting	600
Accountant's fees	300
Legal fees	100
	81,776
Total costs	**87,118**
Net Profit	**42,123**

An example of a profit and loss statement

Setting and monitoring your budget

You have seen this word – budget – used many times in this book, so you'll know by now that a budget is the amount of money that you have planned to spend in order to carry out a particular activity or task.

However, in financial planning, the budget is the total amount of money you plan to spend over all your business expenses and activities for the whole financial year, and is divided into the different sales areas. Also included are the total amounts of sales you intend to make across those different sales areas. The information is actually the same as that in the above P&L – the difference is how you use it. The budget should be laid out over 12 months so you have the ability to see at a glance what is happening to sales and costs and to change or adapt these figures. Adding an 'Actual' column and a 'Variance' column allows you to see, per month, whether the actual sales and costs are what you predicted – and if not, how they varied (by more than or less than you predicted) and by how much. A quick look at the layout of this type of information will immediately tell you whether you are on track or not to meet your financial targets at the end of the year.

January	Projected	Actual	Variance
Sales	18,000	15,000	−3,000
Cost of sales			
Stock	5,000	4,200	−800
Delivery	200	160	−40
	5,200	**4,360**	**−840**
Gross profit	**12,800**	**10,640**	**−2,160**
Variable costs			
Wages and salaries	4,500	4,281	−219
Packaging	60	45	−15
Training	20	20	0
Light and heating	180	180	0
Sales promotions	60	60	0
Advertising	100	100	0
Website servicing	10	10	0
Finance charges	20	20	0
	4,950	**4,716**	**−234**
Fixed costs			
Rent and rates	1,500	1,500	0
Vehicles	650	650	0
Administration	350	350	0
Website hosting	50	50	0
Accountant's fees	0	0	0
Legal fees	0	0	0
	2,550	**2,550**	**0**
Total costs	**7,500**	**7,266**	**−234**
Net Profit	**5,300**	**3,374**	**−1,926**

Example of a monthly budget of costs and sales, with projected, actual and variance

In this example there are no figures in the 'Variance' column of the 'Fixed costs' section, unlike the 'Variable costs/direct expenses' section, where the 'Variance' column does show the difference between what was planned and what actually was spent. However, it is unlikely for there to be a variance in fixed costs, as these costs by definition stay the same regardless of sales activity. However if you have asked your accountant to do extra work, or the landlord has put up your rent, this will show here.

For more information on budgets, visit www.businesslink.gov.uk.

Once you have written your annual budget for the following year, that's not the end of it – it's not a document that stays stagnant. You will need to monitor it and make alterations according to what actually happens in your business, showing, for example, if the sales and costs are more or less than you'd planned. The annual budget is divided into 12 months – breaking it down in this way makes it easier for you to see whether you're on target or not and if any alterations need to be made. You may need to reduce your costs if sales are down, or increase your marketing spend to boost sales and cover your costs. Writing your budget requires serious thought, so allow at least a few days to get your thoughts down on paper. Walk away, think about it, return, make adjustments; walk away, return, make more adjustments… and then, when you are sure you have thought of every single possible cost and every feasible sale, ask the opinions of others in the business before you complete it. It's far better to have a collaborative approach with budgets, which will gain your team's support and give them ownership of the budget, than to be dictatorial.

Budgets are important. Think about your home budget: when there is not enough money in your wallet or purse to pay the bills you need to cut your costs or get more money in, and when there is more money you can save or spend it; it's the same in business. Each week check your costs – money going out, and sales – money coming in, against the budget, and adjust as necessary to keep your business on track. Your accountant (if you have one) can help you set this up, but you need to put the information in yourself, as only then will you have a handle on where your business is at any time.

Whatever the source of the finance that comes into your business, and however you plan to use it, you will need to be able to access and manage it. In the next section you'll find out about business bank accounts and how they help you manage your finances.

Examples of the three reports described can be downloaded from the Business Link website at: online.businesslink.gov.uk/Starting_a_Business_files/Profit_loss_cashflow_sales_v2.xls.

Matt and Jamie Christian own a toy shop. At the beginning of their financial year they have agreed a budget which shows their planned sales, fixed costs and variable costs. After three months of the year their management information shows that sales are 15 per cent above budget, fixed costs are on budget and variable costs are 7 per cent above budget.

Matt is very excited by these figures and suggests that sales could be increased even further if they stayed open later on Thursday and Saturday evenings when the local department stores open late. He points out that sales have increased by 15 per cent at a cost of only 7 per cent, which means more profit.

Jamie points out that the reason costs have increased by only 7 percent is that the increased sales have been achieved without incurring any extra costs other than the cost of buying stock. If they increase the opening hours, it is likely that they will incur additional costs for staff, light and heat, sales promotions and advertising. They may also need additional storage space if sales increase further.

The brothers agree that they should create a revised budget projecting these increased costs so that they can see how many additional sales would be needed to justify the extra expense.

SETTING UP A BUSINESS ACCOUNT

You'll need to have bank accounts for your business that are separate from your personal bank accounts. It is very unwise to attempt to operate any business, however small, through your personal bank account, as this makes assessing the financial health of the business very difficult.

? JARGON BUSTER

BACS is an acronym for Bankers' Automated Clearing Services, which is a UK scheme for the electronic processing of financial transactions. In simple terms, it's a means of transferring money from one bank account to another electronically.

You may decide to open your business accounts with the same bank that you have your personal account with. Staff there may be more helpful because they know your financial history. It is worth looking at what other banks can offer, though, as their services and the fees charged may differ greatly. On business bank accounts, banks will charge for:

- Direct Debits paid out of the account
- cheques drawn on the account
- **BACS** payments from the account
- BACS payments into the account
- cheques deposited into the account
- cash deposited into the account
- exchanging notes for coins.

Some banks will offer a charge-free period to attract new business accounts. This should be explored – some banks offer up to 24 months' free banking, which may be very useful. And some banks will have more information and support for new businesses than others.

CHOOSING A BANK

Compare at least three banks before making a decision. You may want to take into consideration the bank's ethical or religious attitude; some banks have investment policies that consider human rights, environmental responsibility and fair trade issues. Some banks provide Sharia compliant lending (consistent with the principles of Islamic law).

When comparing banks you need to consider:
- whether the bank has a small-business team
- the services offered, for example fast-track counter services for business customers, and their cost
- what charges there are for writing letters
- what charges there are for exceeding your **overdraft limit**
- whether there are local branches
- whether there are special offers for new businesses
- whether there are telephone or internet banking facilities available
- whether there will be a dedicated business manager for your account.

Be careful when comparing charges as different banks charge in different ways, and these can be difficult to compare. The best value will depend on the needs of your business. Some bank accounts charge per transaction, while others operate a fixed monthly fee. If you have lots of transactions, the fixed fee may be more cost-effective. Some accounts charge for Direct Debits and standing orders, while others include this in the fixed fee. All of these factors need to be considered.

Choosing a bank should be a decision taken with the longer term in mind. A bank may offer free banking for a short period to new customers, but will this be the bank that can give you the best advice and service as your business grows? It is not always the best idea to stay with the same bank forever; some banks will offer special deals to new customers, so review your decision at least once a year.

? JARGON BUSTER

The **overdraft limit** is the amount your bank has agreed that your account is allowed to go overdrawn, or 'into the red', before additional charges are made.

KEY TO SUCCESS

Many businesses, even the largest, operate on an overdraft. This allows the business to use all of its capital to operate, rather than keeping it in the bank where it will earn a poor return. The key, however, is to operate within your agreed overdraft limit. If you think you are going to exceed the limit, negotiate a new limit with your bank – don't just let the size of the overdraft grow.

OVER TO YOU

Research three banks to compare the factors mentioned above. If you already have a business bank account, compare your present bank with three others. Are you getting the best deal available? Fill in the table below.

	Bank 1	Bank 2	Bank 3
Small business team?			
Local branches?			
Free banking period?			
Telephone banking?			
Internet banking?			
Business manager?			
Charge per transaction?			
Charge for Direct Debits/standing orders?			
Charge for BACS?			
Monthly fee?			

TYPES OF ACCOUNT

? JARGON BUSTER

The **credit balance** is the amount of your money in your bank account. It's the opposite of an overdraft.

Once you have chosen the bank that offers the best deal, you'll need to look at the types of account you need to open. There are a number of different types of bank account available. You may need more than one of the following if you are to operate your business effectively:

- Current account – This is used for day-to-day payments and receipts. Some banks pay interest on **credit balances**.
- Instant access deposit account – This is used for cash that's not needed immediately but needs to be available when required. Interest will be higher than for a current account but less than for a term deposit account.

? JARGON BUSTER

Exporting is selling products or services in foreign countries.

- Term deposit account – This is used for cash that's not likely to be needed at short notice.
- Foreign currency account – This is used if you're **exporting** or **importing** and need to receive or pay in a foreign currency.
- Loan account – If you will need to borrow money from the bank that you will not pay back in a short time, a loan account will cost less in interest than an overdraft on your current account.
- Merchant or commercial account – This is used to accept debit and credit card transactions.

? JARGON BUSTER

Importing is buying products or services from foreign countries.

If the bank you choose to open your account with doesn't offer all of the types of account you need, or different banks have the best deals on different accounts, it's possible to have accounts with more than one bank. However, you may be able to negotiate a better deal with a bank if you agree to have all your accounts with it.

Online banking

All major banks offer online access to the types of account listed, which can help you manage your bank accounts more efficiently. Charges are often lower than for accounts operated through a branch, and online accounts may offer higher interest rates. Online banking allows you to:

■ check your balances
■ look at your statements
■ make payments
■ set up regular payments
■ order cheque books and paying-in books
■ transfer money between accounts.

The greatest benefit of online banking is that you have access to your balances at all times, wherever you are, if you have an internet – connection including on some mobile phones – so there is less chance of going overdrawn without realising it and incurring charges until your next monthly statement arrives.

OPENING THE ACCOUNTS

You'll need to have a meeting with the bank in order to open the accounts you have decided you want. To prepare for the meeting, you will need the following information:

■ the name and purpose of your business
■ if it is a new business, where the money has come from
■ a business plan
■ if it is a limited company, a certificate of incorporation
■ if it is an existing business and you are moving to a new bank, bank statements from your existing bank
■ copies of the bank's forms so you can consider its terms.

A bank statement

At the meeting, the bank will want to see:

■ A driving licence or passport for each person involved in managing the business. If it is a limited company, this will include all directors and the company secretary. Banks have to check the identity of people opening accounts under money laundering laws.

- A list of people who will be able to sign on the accounts and how many will be required to sign. It is a good idea if all cheques and payments have to be signed by at least two people.
- Sample signatures from everybody on the list.

You may want to take away the paperwork and consider it carefully in your own time, possibly discussing it with your partners or your financial advisor before signing on the dotted line.

BANK CHARGES

You'll receive a statement from your bank explaining the charges made to your account, usually monthly or quarterly. It is important that you check the statement to ensure that you understand what the charges are and that you have not incurred any unexpectedly. Query any unexpected charges – it may be possible to get them reversed.

Charges will be high if you don't keep to the agreements you made with the bank when you opened the accounts. Going overdrawn without permission will result in a high interest charge – as well as a fee for the bank writing to tell you that you have gone overdrawn without permission. If you write cheques without enough money in the bank to cover them, the bank may refuse to pay them, which will give you a bad reputation with your suppliers, and the bank will charge you again for writing to tell you that they have refused to pay the cheque.

If you operate a business that receives payments in cash, remember that the bank will charge you for giving them your money and for writing cheques, so try to pay your suppliers in cash if you can. This is probably only practical where relatively small amounts are concerned, and you will still need to record the transactions in your accounts.

Businesses that have to give customers change in cash, such as retailers, will be charged by the bank for depositing coins and for changing notes into coins.

AS YOUR BUSINESS GROWS...

You may need to change the arrangements and the type of accounts that you have with your bank as your business grows. Agree changes with your bank rather than exceeding your credit limit, which will result in extra charges and could get you a bad **credit rating**. Don't allow your current account to go overdrawn unless you have an agreed overdraft, and don't exceed your agreed overdraft without the bank's permission.

Aaa	smallest degree of risk
Aa	very low credit risk
A	low credit risk
Baa	moderate credit risk
Ba	questionable credit quality
B	generally poor credit quality
Caa	extremely poor credit quality
Ca	highly speculative
C	potential recovery values are low

A credit rating

Talk to your business manager regularly, and let him know if you plan any unusual transactions such as capital expenditure. If you need to negotiate new loans or increase your overdraft, the bank will want to see updated copies of your business plan. If you are having any financial difficulties, let your bank know as soon as possible, as it may be able to offer help or advice.

A meeting with the bank manager

If you have problems with the bank itself, take up your complaint with your business manager. If you are not happy with their response you may be able to contact the Financial Ombudsman. There are restrictions on the use of this service by businesses based on their annual turnover and the number of employees. Detailed information can be found at www.financial-ombudsman.org.uk.

ACCOUNTING

? JARGON BUSTER

Expenditure is all the spending, outgoings and expenses.

However large or small, every business has to keep financial records of all its income and **expenditure**. This is required by law so that tax returns and VAT returns can be checked for accuracy, but there are also business benefits. If you don't keep accurate and up-to-date records, you won't know how much tax you should be paying, how much your customers owe you or how much you owe to your suppliers. Without understanding the basics of accounting, you will not be able to make informed business decisions.

As suggested in Chapters 1 and 7, you may well want to use an accountant to produce your year-end accounts and complete your tax returns. If you're running a small business, it is probably cost-effective to complete the day-to-day books and records yourself and pass them on to the accountant at the end of the financial year. You may find it useful to take a course in bookkeeping, or encourage a member of your team to do so. Courses may be available from your local college or there are distance-learning packages available from organisations such as the Institute of Certified Bookkeepers or the International Association of Book-keepers.

If you run a small, simple business it is perfectly possible to complete all of the bookkeeping and accounting tasks manually. In a more complex business, or as your business grows larger, it is probably a good idea to invest in accounting software and/or employ the services of a qualified bookkeeper or accountant.

? JARGON BUSTER

Double entry is a bookkeeping system in which every transaction is entered as both a debit and a credit. This enables you to analyse your receipts and expenditure. Very simple businesses can use single entry bookkeeping, which simply records how much money has been received and how much has been spent. A disadvantage of single entry is that it is not self-balancing, so mathematical errors can go unnoticed.

A good quality accounting software package will produce a form of **double entry** accounts and the management information required to operate the business using information that only has to be entered once.

BASIC BOOKKEEPING

Every business will need to keep a basic set of financial records, including:

- a receipts book
- a purchases book
- a petty cash book.

These must include details of everything you have sold, everything you have purchased and every business expense you have paid for.

Receipts book

In the receipts book you record all of the income that you get from sales. The receipts book will need the following columns:

- Date – The date you received the money

- Received from – The customer's name if you make sales to individual customers, or 'Daily takings' if you are operating a business that makes lots of sales, such as a shop
- Cash
- Cheques
- BACS
- Banking – The date, deposit number and total deposited
- Debit cards
- Credit cards
- Total.

Each day, record the money you have received that day for sales. This may come through a till or in the post, or directly into the bank, for online payments.

Date	Received from	Cash	Cheques	Amount banked	Deposit number	BACS	Debit cards	Credit cards	Total
22.08.11	Tills	1237.50	472.67				612.34	432.27	
	Johnson					1200.00			
	Williams		600.00	2310.17	0124				4554.78
23.08.11	Tills	1469.20	155.00				331.24	189.20	
	Smith					184.50			
	Khan		122.45	1746.65	0125				2451.59

Receipts book

When you deposit the money into the bank, total up the 'Cash' and 'Cheques' columns. This total will be the amount that you are depositing in the bank. Enter the amount banked and the deposit number (from the paying-in slip). Total the 'Amount banked', 'BACS', 'Debit cards' and 'Credit cards' columns and enter in the 'Total' column. This is the value of the day's sales.

Purchases book

In the purchases book you record all the purchases you make and the expenses you pay for by cheque or BACS. The purchases book will need the following columns:
- Date – The date you wrote the cheque or raised the BACS payment
- Purchased from – Who the cheque or BACS payment is payable to
- The net value of the purchase
- The VAT included in the purchase
- Amount – The total amount of the purchase
- Cheque number.

Date	Supplier	Net	VAT	Amount	Cheque No.
22.08.11	Hollins	223.54	44.71	268.25	01253
22.08.11	British Gas	846.25	42.31	888.56	BACS
31.08.11	Petty cash	104.52	6.27	110.79	01257

Purchases book

Petty cash book

You will need a petty cash book in order to record all the small purchases that you make in cash, to avoid cluttering up the purchases book with every postage stamp and car park receipt. To start the petty cash system, cash a cheque or withdraw enough money from the bank to cover your day-to-day business expenses for a month. Enter this in your purchases book by writing 'Petty cash' in the 'Purchased from' column.

Many small business keep the cash in a petty cash tin. As you spend the cash, you will replace it with receipts, so the total amount of receipts and remaining money should always come back to the original amount of money. At the end of each month, add up the receipts and enter the total into the purchases book. You may either cash a cheque for this amount or withdraw further cash from the bank to top up the petty cash tin.

Checking your bank statement

When you get your bank statement, or at the end of the month if you are using online banking, tick off the deposits from your receipts book and the cheques from your purchases book against your bank statement. This will show you whether any deposits or cheques have not yet gone through your bank account or if any amounts have gone through that do not agree with your records. Any discrepancies may need following up.

Deposits of debit and credit card payments will appear on your Merchant account and will need reconciling separately.

This type of basic bookkeeping should only be used by very small businesses which do not need to analyse what they have spent their money on, as it will not provide the information you need to complete a VAT return or a full tax return. You will still need to keep all of your receipts and copies of sales and purchase invoices, as the Tax Office may want to inspect them.

DETAILED BOOKKEEPING

In addition to the records explained above, you will also need:
- a sales ledger

- a purchase ledger
- a wages book if you are employing staff.

All of these could be paper-based (for example loose leaves kept in files), or stored on a computer – either on simple spreadsheets or using accounting software.

Sales ledger

As you raise each **sales invoice**, record it on a spreadsheet. The spreadsheet will need the following columns:
- Date
- Customer's name
- Invoice number
- Total – The total amount of the sale, including VAT if applicable
- Net – The amount of the sale, excluding VAT
- VAT
- Paid – Record of when the payment is received

You can add extra columns to analyse the sales using any categories that you will find useful. For instance, a plumber may further break down sales into 'Materials' and 'Labour', or a photographer may want to analyse sales by 'Portraits', 'Passport photos', 'Weddings', 'Photojournalism' and so on. This information can then be used when making business decisions on how resources and time are best utilised.

On a regular basis you can look down the paid column and identify any outstanding invoices that need following up. At the end of the month, total the columns – this will tell you where your income is coming from.

Date	Customer name	Invoice No.	Total sale	Net sale	VAT	Paid

Sales ledger

Purchase ledger

As you receive each **purchase invoice**, you'll need to check that the products or services were ordered by you, have been received and that the prices on the invoice are correct. Most businesses will issue purchase orders when making purchases. The purchase order number should be quoted on the purchase invoice, making these checks more straightforward.

? JARGON BUSTER

A **sales invoice** is a commercial document issued by a seller to a buyer, indicating the products, quantities and agreed prices for products or services the seller has provided to the buyer. An invoice indicates that the buyer must pay the seller, according to the payment terms. The buyer has a maximum number of days to pay for the goods.

? JARGON BUSTER

A **purchase invoice** is a sales invoice that you receive from a supplier from whom you have purchased products or services.

When you are satisfied that the purchase invoice is correct, record it on a spreadsheet. The spreadsheet will need the following columns:

- Date
- Purchased from
- Invoice number
- Total
- Net
- VAT (if applicable)
- Cheque number or BACS and the date when the invoice is paid.

Date	Purchased from	Invoice no.	Total purchase	Net purchase	VAT	Cheque no.

Purchase ledger

You can add extra columns to analyse the purchases as separate categories. In order to complete your tax return, purchases must be broken down into the following categories:

- Cost of sales – This usually means stock you have bought to re-sell.
- Construction industry subcontractor costs – Obviously this is only used in the construction industry.
- Other direct costs – Any other costs involved in buying or making stock to sell.
- Employee costs.
- Premises costs – Rent, business rates, water rates, light, heat, power, property insurance and security.
- Repairs – Maintenance of premises and machinery.
- General administrative expenses – Telephone, postage, stationery and general office expenses.
- Motor expenses – Motor insurance, servicing, repairs, road tax, fuel, car parking and vehicle hire.
- Travel and subsistence – Rail, air and taxi fares, hotels and similar costs.
- Advertising, promotion and entertainment – Mailshots, newspaper advertisements and so on.
- Legal and professional costs – Accountants, solicitors, surveyors, architects, stocktakers, plus professional indemnity insurance.
- Bad debts – Sales invoices included in your sales that you believe you are not going to get the money for.
- Interest and alternative finance payments – Interest on loans, including overdrafts.
- Other finance charges – Bank charges, credit card charges and interest on hire purchase or leases.

You will probably want fewer columns in your purchase ledger than these, as long as you or your accountant will be able to complete this information on your tax return. On the other hand, you may want separate columns for stationery, telephone and postage, for instance.

Remember, when you write a cheque for the petty cash at the end of the month, you will need to enter it on the purchase ledger as if it were a purchase invoice, broken down under the different headings, so that you can analyse what has been spent.

At the end of the month, total the columns – this will tell you where your money has been spent.

END-OF-YEAR ACCOUNTING

At the end of the financial year, if you have a limited company you will be required to produce a profit and loss account and a balance sheet. These will be needed in order to complete your company tax return, which is due within 12 months of your Corporation Tax accounting period. In practice, it is a really good idea to complete your profit and loss account and balance sheet as you go along – as soon as all of the necessary information is available. Even if your business is not a limited company you will find it useful to produce these documents. They will tell you the state of health of your business, allowing you to make decisions on whether any changes are necessary. They will also provide information on what the business owns and what it owes, which will help you decide whether you need a further injection of capital, and will provide evidence to present to the bank or prospective investors. They may also show that you have under-utilised capital that could be invested in growing the business.

Profit and loss account

As explained earlier, this is a summary of the income and expenditure of the business for a period, usually 12 months. By taking the total expenditure from the total income, you can calculate whether the business has made a profit or a loss. It is used to show you, shareholders, potential investors and HMRC how well the business is performing. If you're looking to borrow money for the business, most lenders will expect to see a profit and loss account, usually for the last three years.

Balance sheet

This is a financial statement of what the business owns, is owed and owes at a particular date. Limited companies and limited liability partnerships have to produce a balance sheet for:
- Companies House
- HMRC
- shareholders.

Other businesses may use a balance sheet to help them see how much the business is worth and to analyse and improve the management of the business. Balance sheets will be needed in discussions with potential lenders or investors and potential purchasers of the business should you be looking to sell it.

Business Name
Business address
Suburb

Balance Sheet
As of 31 December 2011

Assets			Liabilities		
Current Assets			**Current Liabilities**		
Cash On hand	£ 100		Trade Creditors	£ 25,130	
Cash at Bank	£ 4,706		Other Creditors	£ 3,000	
Trade Debtors	£ 32,532		Provision for Tax	£ 1,525	
Total Current Assets		£ 37,338	**Total Current Liabilities**		£ 29,665
Non-Current Assets			**Non-Current Liabilities**		
Shares in listed companies	£ 75,000		Bank Loans	£ 50,000	
Loan - Associated Entitiess	£ 5,000		Hire Purchase	£ 14,095	
Office Equipment	£ 3,500		**Total Non-current Liabilities**		£ 64,095
Total Non-Current Assets		£ 83,500	**Total Liabilities**		£ 93,750
Total Assets		£ 120,838	**Net Assets**		£ 27,088

A typical balance sheet

If you want to bid for large contracts, especially government contracts, the clients will probably want to see your accounts to satisfy themselves that you are in a position to complete the contract.

The profit and loss account and the balance sheet will be produced on request by the accounting software package if you are completing your accounts using a computer.

MANAGEMENT INFORMATION

In addition to contributing to the accounting information that you need to produce your annual accounts, the sales and purchase ledgers will provide you with management information on a monthly, quarterly, half-yearly or annual basis. They'll show where your income has come from and where your money has gone. This information needs to be compiled on a spreadsheet so that it can be compared with previous periods and the budget. This will identify trends that will enable you to make business decisions – perhaps to focus your attention on the most successful areas, in order to increase sales efforts there, or on the least successful areas, in order to decide whether these areas are worth carrying on with. It will also flag up any areas of concern regarding your expenditure so you can take action if particular areas are exceeding your budget.

	This month	Last month	+/-	Budget	+/-
Income	70,000	63,000	7,000	75,000	(5,000)
Expenditure	41,000	21,000	20,000	25,000	16,000
Income – expenditure	29,000	42,000	(13,000)	50,000	(21,000)

Management information table

A brief look at the table above would tell the owner of the business that:
- sales have increased, but not by as much as expected
- expenditure has increased, by much more than sales and much more than expected
- the surplus generated is much less than last month and than expected .

The business owner would want to look at expenditure in greater detail to identify where the increase has come from and whether action can be taken to reduce it. By now, it should be clear that if you are not accessing and using this type of financial information about the performance of your business, you are not in a position to make informed decisions about its future.

BUSINESS VIABILITY

As stated at the beginning of the book, you must make a profit otherwise your business will fail. To make a profit you must make sure that you maximise your sales and minimise your costs. In order to control your costs, you must first work out your costs accurately, as you did in Chapter 1 with fixed and variable costs.

Once you know what your costs are, you will be able to measure your profitability. As you saw at the beginning of this chapter, there are standard measures used for this:
- Gross profit – This is calculated as sales minus the direct cost of sales. The direct cost of sales includes the cost of the goods sold, whether purchased or produced.
- Net profit before tax – Overheads such as the staff, stationery, rent and insurance are deducted from the gross profit.
- Net profit after tax – Tax payments are deducted from the net profit before tax.

Sales	100,000
– Cost of sales	40,000
Gross profit	60,000
– Overheads	25,000
Net profit before tax	35,000
– Tax	7,000
Net profit after tax	28,000

Costs table

Without carrying out these calculations, you will not know whether your business is actually viable or if you are turning over a lot of money without making much profit. Remember the well-known business saying: 'Turnover for vanity, profit for sanity'.

CASHFLOW FORECASTING REVIEW

While the measures listed in the previous section tell you if you are making a worthwhile return on your investment and effort, forecasting your cashflow will tell you whether you will be able to continue operating the business, or whether you will run out of money – even though you may be making a profit.

It is important to make sure that you have enough money coming into the business to cover the costs you're incurring, and that it's coming in before your bills become due. To do this it is necessary to look at your current cash position and forecast when money will be received and when money will need to be paid out. How often you need to do this will depend on the type of business you're running. Most expenses will run on a cyclical basis – electricity bills will be quarterly, business rates will be annual or monthly, telephone bills will be monthly or quarterly. You can plan for these in your budget. The problem areas are items such as stock, where you may buy a large quantity in advance in order to get a good deal, but you will probably have to pay for the stock one month after receiving it. If the stock is sitting in the warehouse unsold, you may have a cashflow problem, even though you will be generating a good net profit.

A property developer has found a plot of land that he can buy very cheaply, and gets planning permission to build a block of apartments that he can sell at very high prices. His problem is that he has to pay for the land, buy the materials to build the apartments, pay a builder to build the apartments, pay the rent on his office, run his car, pay his business rates, pay his telephone bill, pay his electricity bills and pay his office staff for the period between buying the land and selling the apartments with no income from the sale of the apartments. This could be as long as a year, so he has to have either a large sum of money in the business to start with or access to loans that he can afford to pay the interest on that will carry him through until the apartments are sold.

BREAK-EVEN POINT

The break-even point of a business is the time when the costs involved in setting up the business and the costs involved in running the business up to that time become less than the income received. Every business has to spend money before it can generate any income; you may have to rent premises, buy stock, buy raw materials and so on, before you can make any sales at all. Only when all of these costs have been recovered have you reached the break-even point.

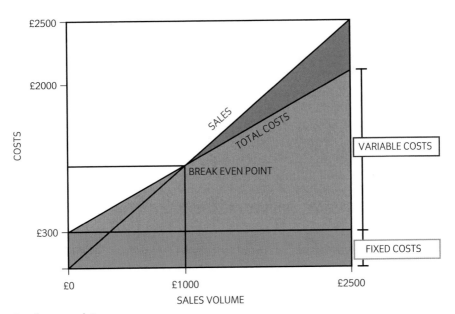

Break-even point

In the graph above, when sales volume reaches £1000, fixed costs plus variable costs also reach £1000. This is the break-even point. All sales above this point produce a profit; until this point is reached, the introduction of a new product costs the business money.

Each change you introduce to the business will have its own break-even point. If you introduce a new line of stock, buy new equipment to improve production or move into bigger premises to increase your sales, costs will be incurred that have to be covered by the increased sales before the break-even point is reached for that change.

Once you know the break-even point, you will be able to consider the length of time it will take to reach it. This will then influence your decision as to whether to go ahead with the proposed change. The acceptable length of time to reach the break-even point will vary according to the type and size of business; an oil exploration company deciding whether to drill for oil on a new site may find a break-even point 20 years in the future acceptable, while a cafe investing in a new coffee machine would be looking at a much shorter period.

When you have established the viability of your business, you will be able to consider areas that you can influence to improve your profits, for instance by developing a more efficient purchasing policy or by looking at your pricing strategy.

PURCHASING

One of the best ways to increase your profits is to buy more efficiently, whether in terms of stock for resale, raw materials for manufacturing or overheads such as rent, electricity, stationery or even fuel for the vehicles. Remember, however, that the lowest price is not necessarily the best value. Especially when buying stock or raw materials, quality may be as important as price.

MANAGING THE SUPPLIER RELATIONSHIP

Use the management information that you have produced to identify areas where you spend most money and concentrate on these when looking at reducing your costs. Talk to your existing suppliers and ask whether there are any reductions in price available, or if there is any discount for early payment. In times of low bank interest rates, it is worthwhile paying your bills early if you can get a 5 or 10 per cent discount.

Look at your management information and identify areas where you could reduce your costs by negotiating with your existing suppliers or looking for alternatives.

Having negotiated with your existing suppliers to find out what they can offer, consider changing to new suppliers. Look at how many suppliers you are buying from; buying the same or similar products from a number of suppliers is inefficient and reduces your chance of negotiating a good deal, but tying yourself to one or two suppliers puts you at risk if they have problems supplying. Look back at the work you did in Chapter 2 on rating your suppliers and analysing the level of risk each one represented to your business.

Buying from a carefully selected group of suppliers can mean:
- it is easier to control stock levels
- you will be a more important customer in their eyes
- you may be able to negotiate a better deal.

On the other hand, having too few suppliers can mean that they take your business for granted and their standards of customer service fall.

When looking for new suppliers, remember that there is more to consider than the quality of the products or services and the price. You should be looking for suppliers who can regularly provide:
- an efficient delivery service so that you can keep your stock levels as low as possible
- flexibility, with the ability to react to changes in your requirements
- acceptable quality at an acceptable price – the cheapest is not necessarily the best value
- good communication so that you are made aware of any problems they may have in supplying your needs, but also of any special deals they may have.

Choosing the right supplier
Selecting a supplier for simple requirements such as fuel for your vehicles or paper for the printer will be a relatively straightforward task. As long as you are satisfied that the supplier is reliable and convenient, the decision will probably be made on price.

When you are selecting a supplier for products or services that form a major part of your business, such as stock or raw materials, you may want to draw up a shortlist from all the suppliers you have identified. Eliminate any suppliers who are too far away to supply a reliable delivery service, too small to cope with your requirements, too large

KEY TO
SUCCESS

It's worth asking whether there is a better price available if you agree a long-term contract or an annual minimum spend, but don't tie yourself into a deal that either leaves you buying more than you need or not in a position to switch to a new supplier at a better price.

to be interested in supplying the quantities you are looking for and give you a good service, too expensive to meet your budget or whose products do not match your quality requirements.

When you have a manageable shortlist, check their financial security. The accounts of limited companies are available from Companies House and credit-check companies. You can get a credit score for your potential suppliers. A high credit score means they are financially more stable than if they have a low credit score. You will want to make sure your suppliers are unlikely to go out of business when you need them, so you may want to get a financial advisor to look over the figures. Provide each supplier on your shortlist with a clear brief, summarising your requirements and the level of business you are hoping to do with them. Ask them to provide details of what they can supply, prices, delivery details and so on. When you receive the details, compare them to find the best supplier or suppliers for your requirements. Before committing yourself, it may be useful to visit the suppliers' premises so you can satisfy yourself that they are able to meet their commitments.

NEGOTIATING THE BEST DEAL

Once you have identified your suppliers, you will want to negotiate terms and conditions and, if appropriate, draw up contracts. Agree **service levels** before you start buying so that both you and your supplier know what is expected. Make sure your supplier knows what the most important aspect of their performance is. Written contracts will help avoid disputes and settle any disagreements that arise.

Before you start negotiating, make a list of the factors that are important to you and decide which you are not prepared to compromise on. These might include:

- price
- delivery
- after-sales service
- quality
- payment terms
- value for money.

For instance, if you are purchasing stock for your high-end ceramic tiles store, you may be prepared to compromise on price and payment terms, but not on quality. If you are purchasing envelopes for a mailshot, you may be prepared to compromise on quality but not on price and delivery.

You have to realise that you are probably going to have to compromise in some way; you are unlikely to find what you are looking for at the highest possible quality and the lowest possible price. Try to have some idea of what the supplier is likely to offer so you can prepare your response in advance.

Think about your business. What factors from the list above are most important to you and which might you be prepared to compromise on? In the table below, list all the significant purchases that you have to make for your business and tick the factors that are important to you.

	Price	Delivery	After-sales service	Quality	Payment terms	Value for money

Knowing your supplier

Find out how important your business is likely to be to the supplier. You may get an impression of this from its financial information or by talking to other customers. If possible, talk to staff at the supplier and try to gauge how hard they are chasing your business. If they respond quickly to your requests for information, it may be that they are tremendously efficient, but it could also suggest that they are desperate for your business.

There are a number of factors that you can use to your advantage if you know about them in advance:
- If the supplier needs your business you will be able to negotiate a better deal.
- The more alternative suppliers you have identified, the better position you will be in to negotiate.
- If a supplier has spare capacity, you should be able to get a lower price as any business is better than none; however, if the supplier picks up other customers, their service level may fall.
- A supplier new to the market may be willing to do a deal in order to get established.
- The supplier may need early payment to help their cashflow; this should also help you get a lower price.
- A salesperson may have a target to meet and be prepared to offer a good deal in order to get the business at the right time.

Make sure you are talking to the person who has the authority to agree the deal. You could get a great offer from a junior member of staff only to find that he cannot actually sign the deal. Also make sure that, while you are getting the best possible deal for yourself, the supplier

KEY TO SUCCESS

The more you know about your own business and the more you know about your potential suppliers, the better the deal you will be able to negotiate.

JARGON BUSTER

Concessions are compromises made in order to come to an agreement.

should also feel that they have made a reasonable deal. Forcing suppliers into positions where they are making money for you at a cost to themselves can lead to their failure, leaving you without a supplier, or to their being made a better offer by one of your competitors and pulling out of the deal with you.

Negotiating

Give the supplier the impression that you are being positive without letting them know which areas you are prepared to compromise on. Try to make **concessions** only in response to concessions from the supplier. It should be up to the supplier to state their selling price and terms first, not up to you to say what you are prepared to pay. You can then negotiate the price downwards by offering concessions that you are prepared to make until you reach terms that you are happy with.

Don't allow the supplier to pressure you by using tactics such as deals that are only available if you sign that day or artificially high prices with large discounts available. Counter these tactics by explaining that you are looking for a sustainable price for a long-term relationship, not a special-offer, one-day-only deal.

A negotiation with a supplier

Agreeing terms

At the end of the negotiation you should have agreed details of the price, any discounts for bulk orders, delivery times and payment terms. You now need to get these in writing to avoid any possibility of misunderstanding. Remember that verbal agreements are legally binding but are notoriously difficult to enforce. If the purchase is for a substantial amount, it is essential that you draw up a contract with the supplier. You will want to make sure that this includes:

- details of price, delivery and payment terms
- the level of after-sales service provided
- any penalties for late delivery or failure to meet quality standards.

The supplier will probably want to include clauses that say:
- that the goods are the property of the supplier until they are paid for
- that the seller's liability is limited to the **purchaser's statutory rights**.

If you are drawing up a contract for the supplier to sign, you may want to enlist the help of a solicitor for the first one. If you are signing a contract drawn up by the supplier, you may also want your solicitor to look over the terms and conditions before you sign it.

Your aim should be to have a contract that gives responsibility for any problems to the supplier. Make sure the contract has an exit procedure built in so you can withdraw if you are unhappy with the supplier's performance.

? **JARGON BUSTER**

The **purchaser's statutory rights** are the rights provided by legislation, such as the Sale and Supply of Goods and Services Act 1982.

STOCK MANAGEMENT

You will come across the term 'inventory' when looking at stock management. In this context, inventory means the total stock, or amount of products for sale that your company holds. One of the critical areas of purchasing is managing the level of inventory that you are carrying. If you have too much stock of a particular line, you will be using up space that could be better used to hold other lines of stock. You will also be tying up money that you could be using to negotiate better deals with, or, if you are operating the business on credit, that you could be using to reduce your debts. The best way to manage inventory is to establish a maximum and a minimum level of stock for each line that you carry.

Setting maximum and minimum stock levels is an art that comes with experience, but it is based on a science. The basic calculations are:
- Maximum stock level should be no higher than the amount of stock you can sell during its shelf life, that is, before it becomes obsolete, goes past its sell-by date or goes out of fashion.
- Minimum stock level should be no lower than the amount you expect to sell in a day multiplied by the number of days before an order for replacement stock can be received.

The art comes in knowing your business so you can adjust maximum and minimum levels to meet the circumstances. An example of this would be seasonality – there may be times of the year when your maximum and minimum stock levels will be higher or lower. Retailers will increase their maximum stock in accordance with the time of year; for instance, stocks of chocolates will increase prior to Valentine's Day, Mother's Day, Easter and Christmas. Similarly, the minimum stock levels will be adjusted as the number sold per day will increase.

You should not be so rigid in your stock management that you miss an opportunity to purchase a stock line at a really advantageous price because it would exceed your maximum stock level. In this case, you may be able to arrange a delivery schedule that will enable you to cope with the volume. One example of such a delivery schedule is known as 'just in time' (JIT), where deliveries are made as the stock is required. An advantage of this method is that there is less stock on hand, saving space and improving your cashflow; a disadvantage is the risk of disruption to supply, leaving you without stock when you need it.

Managing the supply chain is important so that you receive the right stock at the right place and at the right time. If you are to react to changing customer demands you will need accurate and efficient supply chain data management. You will need to liaise with manufacturers, suppliers and logistics companies to get the stock you need delivered to you when you need it. You should consider whether your best option is direct delivery from the manufacturer/grower or the use of warehousing facilities.

You may order stock using the EPOS system (see Chapter 7), which automatically generates orders to replace stock sold, through checking stock on a regular basis and creating orders to bring stock levels back to the maximum or, if you have a very small business, through ordering stock as and when you see a need. If you use EPOS systems or regular stock checks, you will need to physically count the stock – even electronic systems can contain errors over a period of time if products are incorrectly bar coded, errors in delivery are not corrected, damages are not dealt with correctly or shoplifting has taken place.

Stocktaking is carried out to correct the stock records and to identify errors so that action can be taken to prevent them recurring. When errors are identified you should count the physical stock again to make sure the count was accurate, check the goods received documentation for errors and then the shrinkage records. Make sure you reset the stock records so that errors are not carried forward from one count to the next. You may need to give staff extra training or look at security measures to prevent future errors.

Shrinkage is the reduction in the value of stock caused by theft and error. We have dealt with errors in the previous paragraph. Theft cost UK retailers almost £3 billion in the 12 months to 30 June 2011. Of this 55 per cent was theft by customers and 45 per cent was staff theft. UK retailers spent £1 billion on security in an attempt to reduce their losses. This included the employment of security staff, electronic tagging of stock, CCTV, staff badges, entry codes to keep unauthorised people out of stock rooms and office areas, and searching staff on leaving the premises.

OVER TO YOU

Think about setting maximum and minimum stock levels for each line of stock in your business. Consider the space required, the initial outlay and the shelf life of the stock.

Research potential suppliers, looking at delivery schedules that enable you to manage your maximum and minimum inventory levels.

CASE STUDY 4

Bill Eddington and his wife Jenny run a shop selling budget housewares in the town centre. There is no formal method of stock management. Bill also operates a cleaning business and is responsible for the buying while Jenny runs the shop. They employ two assistants working on the till and filling the shelves. While they have always been happy enough that the shelves are full and the customers served, they have never seen the need for stock management.

Bill comes back from a visit to their suppliers and tells Jenny he has ordered 10 pallets of a branded washing powder, because it is bankrupt stock and he has been able to buy it at such a low cost that they will be able to sell it at well below supermarket prices and still make a good margin.

Bill and Jenny go into the stockroom to decide where to store the washing powder and realise that there is nowhere near enough space. Bill notices a whole pallet of saucepans which he bought 12 months ago, and asks why they are still there. Jenny says that they sell maybe one or two a week, and they will go eventually.

Bill realises that the stockroom is full of stock that has been bought at different times and that no-one has any idea how much stock there is, how long it has been there and how well it is selling. This means that Bill could well be buying stock based solely on its price when there is already plenty of the same item in the stockroom.

Continued

Bill and Jenny realise that they need a strategy to clear the existing backlog of stock and then to control the future flow of stock. The first thing they do is a complete stocktake so they know what they have got. They then agree to hold a major sales promotion, discounting the stock that is slow-moving so that they can clear space in the stockroom and raise some capital.

They set up a stock management system on a spreadsheet on which they record the amount of stock on hand at the stocktake. They have columns on the spreadsheet for stock received and for regular weekly stock checks. The spreadsheet will calculate the number of items sold. This will give Bill the information he needs to make sensible buying decisions and allow Jenny to identify slow-moving stock that may need discounting.

SETTING PRICES

One of the most difficult decisions you will have to make when starting up a new business or introducing new products or services to your existing business is the prices that you are going to charge. Obviously you will want to charge as high a price as possible in order to maximise your profit, without pricing yourself out of the market by making your product or service too expensive for your customers.

METHODS OF SETTING PRICES

There are two methods used by most businesses to price their products and services:

- **Cost-plus pricing** – This uses the cost of buying the product or service and adds a percentage to calculate the selling price. This method works best for businesses that deal in high volumes or where competition for customers is based mainly on price. If you use this method, it is important that you take into account the fixed costs of running the business, not just the cost price of the product or service. An example of this would be low-cost food retailing.
- **Value-based pricing** – This is calculated from the price you believe customers will be willing to pay for your product or service. This works best in businesses that have a clear advantage over their competitors, whether through branding, exclusivity or reputation. If you use this method you will risk discouraging customers who think your prices are too high and encouraging competitors who will see an opportunity to undercut your prices for similar products or services. An example of this would be high-end fashion.

Think about a product or service that you sell. If you price it using cost-plus pricing and value-based pricing, does the sale price come out the same?

Pricing services is often more difficult than pricing products, as what you are selling is your expertise rather than simply your time. Solving someone's problem quickly and effectively is worth more to the customer than spending a long time working on the problem without fixing it. You need to fix a price point that enables you to make a reasonable profit – carry out market research into your competitors to see how you can deliver a higher level of service than them at a similar price.

PRICING STRATEGY

Having set your prices using either of the two methods described above, you may find when you start selling your products or services that you have got them wrong. If you have used value-based pricing and you cannot keep up with demand, you have underpriced your product or service; if sales are well below expectations, you may have overpriced them. If you have used cost-plus pricing, you will have estimated your unit sales in order to take into account your fixed costs. For example, if your fixed costs are £1000 and your variable costs are £25 per unit, your calculation would be as follows:

- If you sell 10 units, fixed costs + variable cost = £1250 or £125 per unit.
- If you sell 100 units, fixed costs + variable cost = £3500 or £35 per unit.

In order to set a price that gives you a profit, you need to estimate what your unit sales are going to be, or you won't know whether to sell at £150 per unit or £50 per unit. If your sales are below your estimate, your profit will be reduced and may even disappear entirely.

Before you change your prices, either increasing or decreasing them, you need to look at the impact the change will have on your profitability. Consider the effect the price change will have on the volume of sales and the profit per sale.

Increasing prices

This may have the effect of reducing your sales volume while increasing your profitability, but you will need to be careful about where your price sits in comparison with your competitors'. There are different ways of increasing prices:

- You can explain to your customers that the benefits your product or service provides in comparison with those of your competitors justify the higher price.
- You can introduce new products or services while making your existing products or services obsolete.
- You can lower the specification of your products or services and so lower your costs, and keep prices the same.

Explaining why you are increasing prices can help to maintain a good relationship with your customers. Trying to hide a price increase can damage your relationship when the customers notice.

Reducing prices

Often your customers will be buying from you because of the quality of the products or services you provide, and the price will only be part of the buying decision, so reducing prices to increase sales volume should not be your first reaction. Unless you are being undercut by a competitor offering something similar at a lower price, reducing your prices may have the effect of giving potential customers the impression that you are providing poor quality.

? JARGON BUSTER

Stock-turn is your annual turnover divided by your average stock holding. The higher your stock-turn, the lower the cost of your stock holding.

One form of price reduction that may work is discounting. The cost of discounts can often be recovered through lower costs. For example, in the retail sector, discounting may be used to clear old stock, or to encourage bulk or repeat orders by offering a discount for quantity. Clearing old stock improves cashflow and frees up resources; these can then be used to purchase newer stock, which can be sold at a higher price. Bulk or repeat orders can allow you to purchase stock in larger quantities yourself, which may enable you to negotiate better prices, and improves your **stock-turn**, again freeing up resources.

Be careful, however, not to discount too much or too often, or customers will come to see the discounted price as normal and will view a return to full price as a price increase.

↳ OVER TO YOU

Think about your pricing strategy. Are your margins (the profits on a sale as a percentage of the selling price) enough to give your business long-term profitability? Are your prices correct for your target market? Do you know what your competitors are charging? Discuss your pricing with members of your staff who are involved in bringing in business; do they think you are charging too much – or too little?

PRICING TACTICS

There are a number of tactics that you can use to attract more customers and maximise profits. These include:

- **Skimming** – If the product or service you provide is unique or exclusive, for example designer fashion, you can charge a much higher price for it. This only works if you are sure that competitors cannot provide the product or service to your customers at a lower price.
- **Penetration** – If you want to gain market share and create a loyal customer base, you can charge a lower price for your product or service, which you can then increase once you have become a major player in the market. This is known as penetration and is the opposite of skimming. An example would be a new shop making opening offers to attract custom.
- **Loss-leading** – If you sell a range of products or services, it may be worth offering some at a price which makes very little, or even no, profit in order to encourage customers who may purchase other products or services, which you can price to make higher profits. Supermarkets, for example, might sell bread at below cost price to encourage customers who they hope will then do all of their weekly shop.
- **Psychological pricing** – Where your products or services are sold to customers whose main reason for choosing them is price, offering prices of £9.99 or £99.00 will appear to be cheaper than offering the same products or services at £10.00 or £100.00, while the difference in your profit will be insignificant.
- **Captive product** – This is where a product is sold cheaply because once the customer has bought the product they have no choice about the consumables they buy, which will be sold at a high margin. An example would be where an inkjet printer is sold cheaply because the ink cartridges can be bought only from the manufacturer at a high price.
- **Bundling** – This is where several products are sold as a package deal. Examples are software bundles where related games or other software are sold as a single package.
- **Optional extras** – These are similar to captive product, but the customer has a choice whether to purchase the extras. An example would be a new bed, where the basic price is low but there is a range of optional extras such as mattresses, headboards and bed linen available.
- **Economy** – By driving down the costs in the business, products and services can be sold at a low price. An example would be a budget supermarket which displays stock in the cartons in which it has been delivered .
- **Premium** – This is used where the product or service is unique or seen as a luxury brand and customers are prepared to pay extra for the perception of being special. An example would be designer fashion.

KEY TO SUCCESS

Getting your prices right is one of the most important factors in running a profitable business. Don't forget: anyone can give their products and services away, but it takes skill and judgement to be able to sell them.

- **Value** – This is where a separate range of lower-priced products is sold alongside more expensive ones to attract customers who are looking for value for money. An example is supermarket own brands.
- **Promotions** – This is where prices are reduced for a period of time, usually to introduce a new product or service or to clear ends of lines. An example would be the 'buy one get one free' (BOGOF) offers in supermarkets.

PAYROLL

Your payroll is a list of your employees, the amounts that you pay them and the deductions you make from their pay. Employees' pay will include:

- basic wage or salary
- any overtime worked
- any commission or bonuses earned
- holiday pay
- statutory sick pay
- statutory maternity pay
- statutory paternity pay
- statutory adoption pay.

Deductions may be required by law. These include:

- Income Tax
- National Insurance contributions
- student loan deductions
- attachment of earnings orders.

Other deductions may be voluntary. These include:

- pension contributions
- charity contributions
- purchase of shares in the business under a share incentive plan
- trade union subscriptions
- social club membership fees
- hospital fund contributions
- repayments of advances
- contributions towards clothing or equipment
- private use of a company car or van
- contributions towards private medical insurance
- contributions towards meals provided.

One-off deductions may include:

- a charge for damaging company property, for instance damage to a company car that was the employee's fault
- a charge for non-return of company property on termination of employment
- recovery of holiday pay if the employee has been paid more than he or she is entitled to when terminating his or her employment

- recovery of payment for notice period if the notice period is not worked
- recovery of stock or till shortages where the employee is considered to be responsible.

It is unlikely that any small business owner will be making all of the above deductions, but it is important to remember that it is unlawful to make deductions from your employees' pay except in the following circumstances:

- you are required to do so by law
- the deduction is clearly stated in the contract of employment
- you have the employee's written authority to do so.

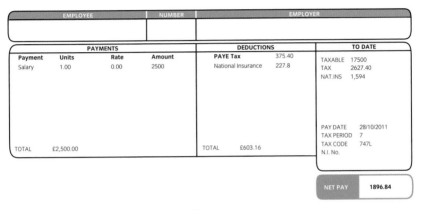

PAYMENTS				DEDUCTIONS		TO DATE	
Payment	Units	Rate	Amount	PAYE Tax	375.40	TAXABLE	17500
Salary	1.00	0.00	2500	National Insurance	227.8	TAX	2627.40
						NAT.INS	1,594
						PAY DATE	28/10/2011
						TAX PERIOD	7
						TAX CODE	747L
TOTAL	£2,500.00			TOTAL	£603.16	N.I. No.	

EMPLOYEE	NUMBER	EMPLOYER

NET PAY 1896.84

An illustration of a payslip showing deductions

OPERATING YOUR PAYROLL

There are three ways in which companies operate their payroll. Small businesses may use a manual system, using calculators and tables to work out pay and deductions and updating paper records for each employee. When you register as an employer with HMRC it will send you a New Employer Pack, which contains:

- details of Pay As You Earn (PAYE) and National Insurance contributions (NICs) rates and help books explaining how to use them
- calculators and tables for working out PAYE and NICs
- form P11 Deductions Working Sheet, which you can use to record details of employees' pay and deductions.

As almost all businesses now have to complete their annual returns to HMRC online, it may be a good idea to start your payroll using computer software. This can be done using commercial payroll software or using free software from HMRC.

Commercial payroll software will require you to enter each employee's details initially, and will then:

- calculate income tax, NICs and student loan deductions

- calculate the employer's NICs
- calculate the final pay of leavers, taking into account outstanding holiday pay and so on
- produce payslips
- keep records of pay and deductions.

At the end of the tax year, the software will produce the figures you need for your annual returns. If tax rates or NICs change during the tax year following a Budget, the software provider should send updates so that the software continues to make the correct calculations.

Free HMRC software doesn't offer a complete payroll system but does work out employees' deductions. The P11 calculator meets the requirement to file in-year starter and leaver forms and the employer annual return online. If you have nine employees or fewer on 5 April, the P11 calculator will also use the figures from your payroll records to complete your annual return automatically and connect you to HMRC and file your return online. This can be found by going to www.hmrc.gov.uk, and following the links to download the P11 calculator.

Other basic PAYE tools can be downloaded from HMRC, including:
- a database to record your employees' details
- calculators that work out statutory payments and the like
- interactive forms such as P11D working sheets.

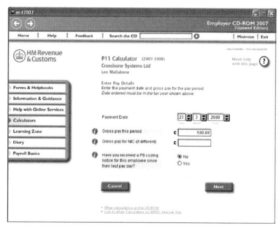

A screenshot of a P11 calculator

There is also a 'learning zone', which includes interactive material on how to use the PAYE tools.

A shortcut for downloading all of these PAYE tools is available by going to www.businesslink.gov.uk. Enter 'HMRC PAYE tools' in the search box and select 'Using HMRC's basic PAYE tools'. Scroll down to and select 'Downloading basic PAYE tools' and then choose the appropriate download for your computer.

Outsourcing your payroll

The third way to operate your payroll is to outsource it, either to an accountant or to a payroll agency. If you are using an accountant to complete your annual accounts, ask them if they provide a payroll service. They will already be familiar with your business and you may get a better rate for the payroll as part of a complete service.

Whether you use an accountant or a payroll agency, you will need to consider whether you want them to provide you with weekly/monthly payslips from which you will pay your employees and you will complete your payroll records yourself, or whether you want them to operate the whole of your payroll.

When choosing a supplier for your payroll service, consider:

- the charge for setting up the system
- the charge for running the system
- any additional fees for non-standard payments or deductions
- the provider's experience with your size and type of business
- whether the provider could cope with the growth of your business
- whether the software used is HMRC accredited, compatible with your software and allows for easy online filing of returns.

Remember, it is still your responsibility to check that the calculations have been made correctly, that your employees have been accurately paid and that your online returns are correct.

OVER TO YOU

Think about whether to operate your payroll yourself, either manually or using software, or to outsource it. Remember to take into account the cost of your time.

WHERE TO GO FOR MORE INFORMATION

The following sources will be helpful in getting to grips with bookkeeping and finance:

- Government bodies:
  - Financial Ombudsman Service www.financial-ombudsman .org.uk – An independent service for settling disputes between businesses providing financial services and their customers.
  - Business Link www.businesslink.gov.uk – For useful information about banking services and accounting practices.
  - Chambers of Commerce www.britishchambers.org.uk – Includes a link to your local Chamber of Commerce, which provides critical business advice, services and skills development.

- National Federation of Enterprise Agencies www.nationalenterprisenetwork.org – This organisation supports start-up and existing businesses.
- Credit check companies:
  - Experian www.experian.co.uk – Gives you access to your credit report and those of other businesses. Also has a video on cashflow.
  - Equifax www.equifax.co.uk – Gives you access to your credit report and those of other businesses.
- Business mentoring scheme www.mentorsme.co.uk – A new business mentoring scheme set up by Barclays, HSBC, RBS, Lloyds Banking Group and Santander.
- Bookkeeping membership organisations:
  - Institute of Certified Bookkeepers www.bookkeepers.org.uk – The largest bookkeeping institute in the world, providing professional qualifications and representing bookkeepers at all levels.
  - International Association of Book-keepers (IAB) www.iab.org.uk – The leading UK and international professional body for those providing bookkeeping and accounting services to small businesses.
  - Association of Accounting Technicians (AAT) www.aat.org.uk – UK qualification and membership body for accounting staff.

CONCLUSION

The information in this chapter should help you understand basic financial information, including how to set up and operate your bookkeeping systems, your payroll and your business bank accounts. Whether you choose to operate your accounting systems yourself, employ somebody to operate them within the business or outsource them to a professional, it is important that you understand the basics in order to keep a watchful eye on the business. You have also seen the importance of understanding management information and using it. This will help to make sure that your purchasing strategy and pricing strategy are set up in such a way that you can maximise profit while controlling your cashflow so that your business survives and grows. Remember those figures from the introduction to this chapter? You want to make sure that you are using all the tools and information you have to ensure that you are in the 19 per cent of new businesses that achieve long-term success.

CHAPTER 9
RIGHTS AND RESPONSIBILITIES

The very nature of this subject can make it seem a little dry – some would even say boring – but, as with administration and bookkeeping, it is vital to the success, or otherwise, of your business. Both you and your employees have rights and responsibilities that you need to be aware of. This chapter will cover five areas, giving you clear points of reference, basic information on each area and up-to-date links to full information. These areas are:

- health and safety
- employment law
- contract law/sale of goods
- insurance
- business-related taxes.

HEALTH AND SAFETY

Both you and your employees have the right to work in a safe environment. It also makes sound business sense to provide an environment in which people will be comfortable, as they will work far more effectively. The rights and responsibilities associated with the working environment are covered by legislation.

HEALTH AND SAFETY AT WORK ETC ACT (HASAWA) 1974

The main piece of legislation is the HASAWA. It says that employers must:

- provide a safe work area
- ensure safe systems of work
- ensure safe handling, storage and transport of stock
- train and supervise staff in health and safety matters
- maintain safe entries and exits
- provide adequate temperature, lighting, seating and so on
- ensure that visitors are informed of any hazards.

The Act also says that employees must:

- use equipment safely and correctly
- report potential risks
- help to identify training needs
- work in a safe and sensible way.

Failing to comply with this Act may result in legal action by the Health and Safety Executive (HSE).

Workplace (Health, Safety and Welfare) Regulations 1992

The HASAWA allows the Government to make regulations and apply directives from the European Union. The most important set of regulations is the Workplace (Health, Safety and Welfare) Regulations 1992. These cover the health and safety of everyone in the workplace, including visitors and customers, and the welfare of everyone at work, including people with disabilities.

Requirements to ensure people's health include:

- adequate ventilation without draughts
- temperatures that provide **thermal comfort**
- assessment of the risk to health of working in hot or cold environments
- adequate lighting to enable people to work and move about safely
- effective cleaning and removal of waste
- enough free space to move about with ease
- seating suitable for the people using it and the work they do.

There are different rules for different sized businesses, so check for the rules that apply to your own business. Your local council will also provide free advice and may even offer a free health and safety check.

? JARGON BUSTER

Thermal comfort is the temperature at which someone feels comfortable enough to carry out work, taking into account the humidity and sources of heat, clothing and the physical demands of the work.

Requirements to ensure people's safety include:

- maintenance of the workplace, equipment and systems
- stairs, ladders, doorways and so on should be wide and high enough to allow people and vehicles to move safely
- protection from the risk of falling into dangerous substances
- protection against walking into transparent doors or windows
- the design of windows, skylights and ventilators to enable them to be opened and cleaned safely
- transparent viewing panels in doors and gates on main traffic routes
- emergency stop controls on escalators and moving walkways.

Requirements to ensure people's welfare include:

- toilets and washing facilities with running water, soap and clean towels or dryers
- an adequate supply of high-quality drinking water
- facilities for changing and safe storage of clothing
- suitable rest facilities where workers can have their breaks and eat if they wish to.

Health and safety signs

Identifying and managing risk

Another set of regulations under the HASAWA is the Management of Health and Safety at Work (MHSW) Regulations 1999. These require all employers to carry out a risk assessment and to:

- review risk assessments and adapt to any significant changes
- improve safety procedures whenever possible
- know the hazards and risks in their workplace
- organise work, as this reduces the chance of accidents
- train staff to avoid hazardous situations.

The assessment must:

- identify hazards
- identify who might be harmed and how
- evaluate the risks from the identified hazards
- record the findings of the assessment
- provide for review and revision of the assessment
- state the period of time the assessment remains valid.

The Regulations require preventive and protective measures to:

- avoid risks
- evaluate risks that cannot be avoided
- combat risks at source
- adapt work to the individual
- adapt to technical progress
- replace the dangerous with the non-dangerous or the less dangerous
- develop an overall policy
- give appropriate instructions to employees.

Specific risk assessments must be carried out where younger employees or new and expectant mothers are employed.

If your business uses substances that are hazardous to health, for instance bleach, ammonia, acid and so on, the Control of Substances Hazardous to Health (COSHH) Regulations 2002 require you to:

- assess the risks from hazardous substances
- decide how to prevent or at least reduce those risks
- monitor the exposure to the risks
- ensure employees are properly informed, trained and supervised.

Retailers have additional risks to take into account as their premises are open to the public, often including children. All of the usual risks such as trailing wires, sharp edges, blocked aisles and inaccessible fire exits are made worse by the presence of the public, who will not have been trained in health and safety in your premises.

Specific stock such as knives and fireworks, and hazardous substances such as bleach, paint, cleaning fluids and solvents must also be stored in such a way that they do not pose a risk to the public or staff.

DISABILITY DISCRIMINATION ACT 1995

The Disability Discrimination Act 1995 has been merged into the Equality Act 2010. This requires employers to make reasonable adjustments to overcome physical barriers that might put disabled people at a substantial disadvantage compared to non-disabled people. Examples of physical features that may be barriers include:

- steps, stairways and kerbs
- floors and paving
- doors and gates
- toilets and washing facilities
- lighting and ventilation.

Reasonable adjustments to these barriers can be made by:

- removing the physical feature altogether
- changing it so it is no longer a barrier
- providing means of allowing disabled people to avoid using the physical feature.

Examples of overcoming physical barriers include:

- providing wider car parking spaces
- replacing steps with ramps
- fitting hand rails
- widening doorways
- using pictures alongside written signs
- providing clear passageways.

Different rules and requirements apply to listed buildings – often a retail business will exist in these buildings – and your local council can advise on these.

Overcoming physical barriers

WRITTEN HEALTH AND SAFETY POLICY

If you employ five or more employees, you must have a written statement of your policy on health and safety at work and the organisation and arrangements for carrying out the policy. The policy should include:

- a statement of general policy, which is signed and dated
- a risk assessment
- details of consultation with employee representatives
- details of responsibility for safe plant and equipment
- details of responsibility for COSHH assessments
- the location of the HASAWA poster
- details of relevant training
- details of responsibility for first aid and reporting of accidents
- details of responsibility for investigating accidents, sickness and safe working practice
- emergency procedures.

While the list of rules and regulations seems, on the face of it, to be endless, you're unlikely to have any problems as long as you have a policy of keeping the workplace and the people in it as safe as possible and carry out the policy thoroughly.

CASE STUDY 1

Dwayne Katt is opening a hardware shop and has organised shop fitting and delivery of the stock, and recruited staff. He is bringing in the staff during the week prior to opening the shop to carry out training. As part of their training, he will be stressing their responsibilities in respect of the HASAWA. He has carried out a risk assessment and realises that he will also need to cover COSHH and the Reporting of Injuries, Diseases and Dangerous Occurrences Regulations (RIDDOR) 1995.

Dwayne decides that he should walk the staff around the store, pointing out areas where hazards exist, explaining the types of stock that will be covered by COSHH and where they will be stored, and making sure that the staff understand the kind of situations that they need to report to him so that he can follow RIDDOR.

He also drafts a handbook that every member of staff will be given and will be required to sign for, so that he can show that they have received the information. Included in this booklet are:
- a policy statement
- the employees' responsibilities
- fire and emergency procedures
- first aid
- reporting accidents and incidents
- manual handling
- working at height
- working safely in a hardware environment
- display screen equipment.

He also arranges to display the HSE poster in the staff room.

EMPLOYMENT LAW

Employment legislation is the fastest changing area of legislation. It is essential that you know and understand both your rights and responsibilities as an employer and your employees' rights and responsibilities.

CONTRACT OF EMPLOYMENT

A contract of employment is an agreement between an employer and an employee setting out the employee's rights, responsibilities and duties. You should give each employee a written statement of the main employment terms within two months of starting work. This is known as the 'principal statement', and must include:

- the name of the employer and the employee
- the job title or job description
- the date employment begins
- the rate of pay and when it will be paid
- hours of work
- holiday entitlement
- place of work
- sick pay arrangements
- notice periods
- disciplinary and grievance procedures
- details of any **collective agreements**
- pension schemes
- the date employment will end if the job is not permanent.

This information may be included in the letter offering the job, in a separate written statement or in the form of a contract of employment.

EMPLOYMENT LEGISLATION

Equality Act 2010

This Act replaces almost all anti-discrimination legislation, including:

- the Equal Pay Act 1970
- the Sex Discrimination Act 1975
- the Race Relations Act 1976
- the Disability Discrimination Act 1995.

The Act makes it illegal to treat someone less favourably because of a 'protected characteristic'. The protected characteristics are:

- age
- disability
- gender reassignment
- marriage and civil partnership
- pregnancy and maternity
- race

- religion and belief
- sex
- sexual orientation.

Work and Families Act 2006

Under this Act, all working mothers are entitled to 52 weeks' statutory maternity leave, regardless of length of service. If mothers want to return to work before the end of the 52-week period, they must give their employer eight weeks' notice. Where this happens, fathers or partners with parental responsibilities can take up to 26 weeks' additional paid paternity leave.

The Act also extended the:
- periods of statutory maternity pay (SMP), maternity allowance and statutory adoption pay. SMP is paid by the employer, who then recoups all or most of the cost through reduced National Insurance and PAYE contributions for the employee
- right to request flexible working to those caring for adult relatives
- minimum annual holiday entitlement from 20 days to 28 days.

Working Time Regulations 1998

Under this legislation, workers aged 18 or over cannot be forced to work more than 48 hours a week on average over a 17-week period. The hours worked include:
- work-related training
- travel as part of a worker's duties
- working lunches.

The hours worked do not include:
- travel between home and work
- lunch breaks
- evening classes
- day-release courses.

There are exemptions for workers in some sectors and workers can choose to opt out of the 48-hour limit. Workers aged 16 and 17 cannot be forced to work more than 40 hours in a week or eight hours in a day. This is not averaged out and there is no opt-out available.

Workers aged 18 or over should take a minimum 20-minute break for every shift lasting more than six hours, and a minimum 11 hours' rest between each working day. They should not be forced to work more than six days in every seven or more than 12 days in every 14.

Workers aged 16 and 17 should take a minimum 30-minute break if they work more than four and a half hours, and a minimum 12 hours' rest between each working day. They should have two consecutive days off every week.

The Working Time (Amendment) Regulations 2007 increased annual holiday entitlement to 28 days (which includes public holidays) for full-time workers, pro-rata for part-timers.

While the Equality Act and the Working Time Regulations cover the basic rights and responsibilities of employers and employees, there is other employment legislation that you need to be aware of, including:

- the Employment Rights Act 1996
- the National Minimum Wage Act 1998
- the Employment Relations Act 1999
- the Human Rights Act 1998.

If you are employing part-time workers you will need to be aware of Part-time Workers (Prevention of Less Favourable Treatment) Regulations 2000, which ensure that part-timers are not treated less favourably than full-time workers. You also need to check that potential employees have the right to work in the UK, as recruiting an employee without the right to work is an offence under the Asylum and Immigration Act 1996.

FAIR OR UNFAIR DISMISSAL

As an employer, there will be times when you feel it necessary to dismiss an employee. Employment legislation limits the conditions under which dismissal is considered fair to the following:

- the employee's conduct is unsatisfactory
- the employee's performance is unsatisfactory
- the employee's work has become redundant
- the employee is unable to continue working without breaking the law, for instance a driver who loses his licence.

Outside of these conditions, there is what is called 'another substantial reason'. This might include imprisonment, unreasonably refusing a change of employment terms, relocation of the business or an unresolvable personality clash.

Dismissal for any other reason is unfair. Some reasons for dismissal, including the employee exercising his or her employment rights, are automatically unfair. Dismissing an employee for a fair reason without following the proper procedures is also unfair.

You need to be wary of constructive dismissal. This is where the employee resigns because of the unreasonable behaviour of the employer.

DATA PROTECTION ACT 1998

As an employer, you will hold information about your employees as well as about your customers. This information is subject to the Data Protection Act 1998. There are eight principles of good information handling outlined in the Act, which state that data must be:

- fairly and lawfully processed
- processed for limited purposes
- adequate, relevant and not excessive
- accurate
- not kept for longer than is necessary
- processed in line with your rights
- secure
- not transferred to other countries without adequate protection.

There are also new rules about being compliant – these have been brought about by updates to the Data Protection Act and apply to any retailers who take payment via electronic equipment – such as PDQs (see Chapter 7) or computers. You must be compliant or there are penalties and fines, and there are certain procedures to go through to become compliant.

If your records are held only for the purposes of staff administration, or for advertising, marketing and public relations, or for accounts and records, you do not have to notify the Information Commissioner's Office. If you process personal information for any other purpose, or are not sure whether you need to notify, go to www.ico.gov.uk to check.

CONSUMER LAW

? JARGON BUSTER

Implied terms are those that apply to every contract, whether they are written into it or not.

When a customer purchases goods and/or services they are entering into a legally binding contract with you. The contract includes **implied terms** laid down by law that cover quality, description and fitness for purpose. The contract will also contain **express terms** such as a specific delivery date. Failure to comply with the terms of the contract means you will have to offer a refund, repair or other form of compensation. A contract does not have to be written but, where there are key express terms, it is best to detail these in writing so there can be no dispute later on.

? JARGON BUSTER

Express terms are those that apply to a particular contract.

By displaying or advertising your goods in a shop or catalogue, you are stating to customers that the goods are available at the price indicated; this is legally referred to as 'giving an invitation to treat'. The customer will then request to buy the goods, referred to as 'making an offer', which you can refuse or accept. Once you accept the offer and the customer makes a payment or some other commitment to purchase, the contract is made. You always have the right to refuse an offer and to not sell an item to a customer.

The most common breach of contract by customers involves them changing their mind. While in the case of a retailer selling stock products to a customer, the stock can be resold to another customer, in many businesses, such as hotels and travel agencies, a lost sale often cannot be recovered. The cancelled hotel room will often remain empty, and the cancelled plane seat unfilled. In these cases the business is entitled to claim loss of profit and pursue the customer for any extra costs reasonably incurred. The usual remedy for this is for deposits to be considered non-refundable should a customer simply change his or her mind.

CONSUMER LEGISLATION

Sale of Goods Act 1979 (as amended)
This applies to the sale and supply of goods, including hire purchase, hire, part exchange and contracts for work and materials. The goods must:
- correspond with the description
- be of satisfactory quality
- be fit for the purpose.

Supply of Goods and Services Act 1982 (as amended)
This adds to the Sale of Goods Act 1979 by saying that any service provided must be carried out:
- with reasonable skill and care
- for a reasonable price (unless a price has been agreed)
- within a reasonable time (unless a date has been agreed at the time the contract was made).

Misrepresentation Act 1967
A misrepresentation is a false statement of fact, which is intended to persuade another party to enter into a contract. The party who has relied on the misrepresentation will be entitled to a remedy, ranging from the contract being cancelled to the payment of damages.

Unfair Contract Terms Act 1977
Under this legislation a trader cannot limit or exclude liability for death or personal injury arising from his or her negligence; attempts to exclude or restrict liability of other loss or damage must meet the test of reasonableness.

Unfair Terms in Consumer Contracts Regulations 1999
These Regulations say that a consumer is not bound by a standard term in a contract with a trader if that term is unfair.

Consumer Protection Act 1987 (Part 1 Product Liability)
This legislation gives people injured by defective products the right to sue for damages. All those in the supply chain, from retailer to manufacturer, may be affected.

Contracts (Rights of Third Parties) Act 1999

This legislation gives rights to anyone who was intended to benefit from a transaction. For example, if someone buys a gift for a friend and the gift proves to be faulty, the recipient or the buyer of the gift can take action for breach of contract as long as it was made clear that the goods were to be given as a gift to a third party.

Torts (Interference with Goods) Act 1977 Section 12

Occasionally customers fail to collect their goods after having them repaired or forget to pick up items such as dry cleaning. This legislation sets out what action you should take to get the goods collected and makes it clear what you can do if they are not. It's sufficient to display a notice, which is easily visible to customers, stating how long you will keep goods after repair and an intention to dispose of them after this date.

Consumer Protection from Unfair Trading Regulations 2008

These Regulations replace a lot of previous consumer protection legislation. Effectively they prohibit trading practices that are unfair to consumers. There are four different types of practices covered:

- 31 specific practices that are always considered to be unfair, such as false claims of membership of trade associations, pyramid schemes and aggressive sales
- misleading actions and omissions
- aggressive practices
- a general duty not to trade unfairly.

While all of the legislation above can lead to **civil liability** if you fail to comply with it, much of it can also lead to **criminal liability**. The major principle, however, is that if you treat your customers fairly and deal with any complaints reasonably, you are unlikely to have any problems.

JARGON BUSTER

Civil liability means that you can be sued in a civil court, where a judge will decide who is right, between you and the other party, and may award damages.

JARGON BUSTER

Criminal liability means that you can be prosecuted in a criminal court, where a judge will decide whether you have broken the law and will pass sentence.

CASE STUDY 2

Marcus Parkinson runs a tool hire company. A customer asks to hire a light-duty diamond driller kit for two days. Marcus quotes him £68.25 plus VAT and points out the availability of Damage Waiver for an additional 10 per cent, which will cover insurance against accidental damage to the kit, or Damage Waiver Plus for an additional 15 per cent, which will also cover loss or theft. The customer hires the equipment but says he is not interested in the Damage Waiver. Marcus takes payment by credit card and the customer leaves with the driller kit.

Continued

Two days later, the customer returns the driller kit and when Marcus inspects it he realises it is damaged. He points this out to the customer and says that they will have to get the kit repaired and will charge the cost of the repair to the customer's credit card. The customer says this is unreasonable as the equipment has clearly been hired out a number of times before and the shop has had more than the value of the kit in hire charges.

Marcus points out to the customer that the contract clearly states that the hirer is responsible for the cost of repairs to damaged equipment where Damage Waiver has not been taken out and that the customer chose not to take out this cover. The customer says this is against the Unfair Terms in Consumer Contracts Regulations and he will be visiting his solicitor. Marcus replies that the contract has been drawn up by his solicitor and he is confident that the terms are not unfair.

The customer's solicitor confirms Marcus's view and the customer has to pay the full cost of the repair.

INSURANCE

Insurance reduces your exposure to the effects of risk. Most businesses are obliged by law to carry Employers' Liability Insurance and some professions, such as law, accountancy and financial services, are also obliged to take out Professional Indemnity Insurance.

Almost all businesses will also insure against risks such as:
- compensation claims against the business
- damage to or loss of assets such as premises, stock or equipment
- business interruption.

When buying insurance you should get quotes from different insurers and compare the levels of cover. Other factors to take into account include the **level of excess** and whether legal advice and emergency helplines are provided.

? JARGON BUSTER

The **level of excess** is the amount of each claim that you will have to pay yourself.

TYPES OF INSURANCE

Employers' liability insurance
Employers' liability insurance enables businesses to meet the costs of damages and legal fees for employees who are injured or made ill at work through the fault of the employer. Employees injured due to an employer's negligence can seek compensation even if the business goes into liquidation or receivership.

The NHS can also claim from you the costs of hospital treatment, including ambulance costs, in cases where personal injury compensation is paid.

By law, an employer must be insured for at least £5 million. Your insurance must cover all your employees in England, Scotland, Wales and Northern Ireland unless the business is:

- not a limited company and the owner is the only employee or employs only close family members
- a limited company with only one employee, where that employee also owns 50 per cent or more of the issued share capital in the company.

You can be fined up to £2500 for each day that you do not have appropriate insurance. You can also be fined up to £1000 for not displaying the certificate of insurance in a place where it can be easily read by your employees (this can be done electronically).

Professional indemnity insurance

Professional indemnity insurance protects your business against claims for loss or damage made by a client if you make mistakes or are found to have been negligent in the services you provide. Professional indemnity insurance will also cover legal costs. Many professionals are required to have professional indemnity insurance cover as a regulatory requirement or as part of their professional authorisation. This includes solicitors, accountants, architects, mortgage intermediaries, insurance brokers and financial advisors. Many consultants, advertising and PR agencies and designers also choose to have this type of insurance.

One important aspect to bear in mind is that a policy will usually only cover claims that are made while it is live. If you plan to change insurers, you will either need to arrange run-off cover or get agreement from your new insurer to accept new claims for previous incidents.

Public liability insurance

If members of the public or customers come to your premises or you go to theirs (including if you work from home), you should think about taking out public liability insurance. This insurance covers any awards of damages given to a member of the public because of an injury or damage to their property caused by you or your business. It also covers any related:

- legal fees
- costs
- expenses
- hospital treatment, including ambulance costs, that the NHS may claim from you.

While public liability insurance is not compulsory, horse-riding businesses must have public liability cover.

Product liability insurance

Product liability insurance covers you against damages awarded as a result of damage to property or personal injury caused by your product. If damages are paid for personal injury, the NHS can claim to recover the costs of hospital treatment, including ambulance costs.

Products must be fit for purpose, and you are legally responsible for any damage or injury that a product you supply may cause. If you supply a faulty product, claimants may try to claim from you first, even if you did not manufacture it. You'll be liable for compensation claims if:

- your business name is on the product
- your business had repaired, refurbished or changed it
- you imported it from outside the European Union
- you cannot clearly identify the manufacturer
- the manufacturer has gone out of business.

Otherwise, the manufacturer is liable, or the processor, where the product involves parts from multiple manufacturers.

However, you must also:

- show that the products were faulty when they were supplied to you
- show that you gave consumers adequate safety instructions and warnings about misuse
- show that you included terms for return of faulty goods to the manufacturer or processor in any sales contract you gave to the consumer
- make sure that your supply contract with the manufacturer or processor covers product safety, quality control and product returns
- have good quality control and record keeping systems.

Business premises insurance

Most business premises insurance policies will insure your buildings against:

- fire and lightning
- explosion
- riot
- malicious damage
- storms
- floods
- damage caused by vehicles.

'All risk' insurance policies do not name the risks covered but list the risks excluded, so all unnamed risks are automatically included.

Property insurance policies do not cover:

- wear and tear
- electrical or mechanical breakdown
- gradual deterioration.

If your premises are left unoccupied, cover may be reduced to fire only and exclude malicious damage. If you are a tenant, you should check with your landlord, who is responsible for insuring the premises.

Contents insurance

Because property insurance covers only the buildings, you will need separate insurance cover for stock, machinery and contents. Contents will be covered against theft, if there has been forcible and violent entry to or exit from the premises. A business interruption policy insures against loss of profit or additional costs resulting from incidents such as damaged machinery. Public Utilities coverage insures against interruption of the supply of electricity, gas or water caused by loss or damage at the premises of the supplier.

Remember, it's not advisable to under-insure your business. Insurers will pay only a percentage of the value of the claim if they feel there is inadequate cover. For example, if premises valued at £500,000 are insured for only £250,000 and suffer £100,000 worth of damage, the insurer will pay only £50,000 towards the damage, as this reflects the level of cover paid for.

It is important, therefore, to check the level of insurance cover you have, as the value of the premises or contents may have increased.

BUSINESS-RELATED TAXES

It's important to remember that as soon as you start a business, you effectively become two people for tax purposes. You will still be liable, as an individual, to pay all the taxes you have always paid – Income Tax, VAT on purchases, Council Tax and so on. In addition you will be liable, as a business, to deal with business-related taxes.

TAXES RELATING TO BUSINESS

Value Added Tax (VAT)

VAT is a form of purchase tax. If the final user of a product or service is an individual, or a business that is not registered for VAT, they cannot recover the tax paid. Registered businesses can recover the VAT on products and services they buy. The total VAT at each stage of the supply chain is therefore a percentage of the value added to the product, and most of the cost of collecting the tax is borne by businesses rather than the government.

VAT rate	Examples of products and services
Exempt	Education, health and financial services
Zero	Most food, children's clothing, books, newspapers, passenger transport
Reduced (5 per cent)	Children's car seats, domestic fuel and power
Standard (20 per cent)	Everything not included in the exempt, zero or reduced categories

Current VAT rates

Obviously we have only been able to give a very few examples of products and services eligible for the different VAT rates. You should check www.hmrc.gov.uk for current information on every type of product or service.

You may wonder what the difference is between exempt and zero-rated products and services. The main difference seems to be that businesses that supply exempt products and services cannot reclaim the VAT they pay on their purchases, while those that supply zero-rated products and services can.

The current threshold for registering for VAT is a turnover of £73,000 a year. Businesses with a turnover below £230,000 can choose to pay a flat rate of VAT between 5 and 12 per cent of their turnover, but this should be discussed with your accountant or financial advisor. Thresholds and rates change from time to time (this is typically announced in the Budget). For up-to-date information, check the HMRC website: www.hmrc.gov.uk.

Further information on registering for VAT and the paperwork involved can be found in Chapter 7.

Corporation Tax
Corporation Tax is a tax on the taxable profits of limited companies and other organisations, including clubs and societies. It is currently set at two different rates:

- Small profits rate (20 per cent) for profits under £300,000.
- Main rate (24 per cent) – for profits over £1.5 million.

For businesses whose profits fall between £300,000 and £1.5 million there is a calculation used known as marginal relief. As with VAT, the rates may change, so for full up-to-date information you should check www.hmrc.gov.uk.

Further information on filing returns for Corporation Tax can be found in chapter 7.

Business rates

Business rates are a local tax paid by the occupiers of non-domestic property in England and Wales. They are used to help fund local services such as the police, fire and rescue services. The amount you pay will depend on:

- the rateable value of the property
- the business rate multiplier
- any rate relief schemes you are eligible for.

The rateable value of the property is set by the Valuation Office Agency (VOA) and is based on the rental value of the property, currently as at 1 April 2008. These rates will change, so for up-to-date information, visit www.voa.gov.uk.

The business rate multiplier is the number of pence you pay in business rates for every pound of rateable value. The current multipliers are shown below.

Region	Standard	Small business
England	43.3p	42.6p
City of London	43.7p	43.0p
Wales	42.8p	42.8p

Business rates multipliers

For example, a small business in England with a rateable value of £17,400 would pay 17,400 x 42.6p = £7,412.40 in business rates.

There are rate reliefs available to businesses with a rateable value of less than £18,000 in England or £25,500 in London. For details go to www.businesslink.gov.uk. Search for 'small business rate relief' and follow the links.

If you think your rateable value is unreasonable, you should contact the VOA and ask them to review it. The VOA can be contacted on the VOA Helpline, 03000 501 501, or the VOA Helpline – Wales, 03000 505 505.

Employee-related taxes

As an employer you are responsible for collecting taxes from your employees and paying them to HMRC. These taxes include:

- National Insurance Contributions (NICs) – These are deducted from the employee's pay based on rates provided by HMRC. Employers add their contributions to those of the employee before paying them over to HMRC.
- Pay As You Earn (PAYE) – This is the Income Tax that is deducted from the employee's pay and paid over to HMRC.

Detailed information on NICs and PAYE can be found at www.hmrc.gov.uk.

Not all income is subject to NICs and PAYE; for information on thresholds and rates go to www.hmrc.gov.uk.

HMRC provides a useful calculator for working out deductions from pay, which can be found at payecalculator.hmrc.gov.uk/paye0.aspx.

Information on registering as an employer and the forms you need to fill in can be found in Chapter 7.

STAKEHOLDER PENSIONS

If you employ more than five people, you may have to offer a stakeholder pension to your staff. You should:
- select a scheme from the Pension Regulator's list
- discuss the choice with your employees
- give contact details of the scheme to your employees
- give the scheme provider access to your employees
- deduct contributions from the payroll
- forward the contributions to the scheme provider.

To find out if this applies to your business you can follow a 'Stakeholder Decision Tree', which can be found at www.thepensionsregulator.gov.uk.

From 2012, changes to pensions law will affect all employers with at least one employee in the UK. For more information, go to www.thepensionsregulator.gov.uk.

Dealing with business-related taxes will seem daunting at first, but there is plenty of help and information available. As with all other areas of the business, consider whether it is more cost-effective to use professional help or to use your own time to deal with these issues.

WHERE TO GO FOR MORE INFORMATION

The following sources will help you get to grips with health and safety:
- The main HSE portal page is www.hse.gov.uk and you can find information and guides for managers on health, safety and welfare at work, thermal comfort and risk assessment as well as industry-specific information. It also has links to information on HASAWA.
- www.dwp.gov.uk – The Disability Discrimination Checklist gives hints and tips on complying with the Disability Discrimination Act 1995.

Further information on employment law can be found in the following places:

- www.human-resource-solutions.co.uk – Provides links to a free employment contract template, Business Link, the Advice, Conciliation and Arbitration Service (ACAS) and the Start Up Donut (a National Enterprise Network website).
- www.businesslink.gov.uk – This is the homepage of Business Link, which is a self-help portal for small and medium businesses. It gives information on a range of topics covering maternity, paternity and adoption.
- www.direct.gov.uk – Gives information on the Equality Act 2010, the Working Time Regulations 1998 and fair and unfair dismissal.
- www.ico.gov.uk – Gives information on your responsibilities and obligations to data protection. You can download a useful 'How to comply' checklist from this website.

For further information about consumer law:

- www.consumerlaw.co.uk – Gives information on consumer law.

The following sources will help you get to grips with insurance:

- www.hse.gov.uk – Gives information on Employer's Liability Insurance.
- www.businesslink.gov.uk – Gives information on a wide range of issues. Simply enter your area of enquiry into the search box.

Further information on business-related taxes can be found at:

- www.hmrc.gov.uk

CONCLUSION

This chapter has attempted to cover the rights and responsibilities of employers towards their employees as well as their customer. As you can imagine, this is a minefield of regulation and legislation, which has been introduced by successive governments over the past 200 or so years. The overall effect of this red tape may make the prospective employer wonder whether it is possible to employ staff and not contravene the regulations, but in practice businesses of all sizes manage to employ staff without too many problems. If you treat your staff fairly and consider their welfare, you should meet your responsibilities as an employer.

INDEX